ARSÈNE HOUSSAYE

Man About Paris

·

The
Confessions
of
Arsène Houssaye

Translated and Edited by
Henry Knepler

LONDON
VICTOR GOLLANCZ LTD
1972

The frontispiece photograph of Arsène Houssaye
is used by permission of Culver Pictures, Inc.

ISBN 0 575 01332 X

Printed in Great Britain by
Lowe & Brydone (Printers) Ltd., London

To John J. Seguier

Preface

•

Have you told everything? I know myself—I would tell all. That would
be awful. When I look at what goes on around me, I see myself as a
saint; when I recall what has gone on within me, I see myself as a
monster. Don't tell anyone.

Alexandre Dumas *fils* wrote this in a long letter dated October
25, 1890, to Arsène Houssaye. As the letter serves in place of a
preface for the last two volumes of Houssaye's *Confessions*, the
injunction not to tell was clearly not meant seriously; Houssaye is
discreet enough not to tell everything, though he does tell much in
these six volumes of memoirs, observations, and revelations.

Social historians of nineteenth-century France very generally
draw on the *Confessions*, yet they have not been reprinted in the
original since their appearance in 1885 (four volumes) and 1891
(two more). Only one section has ever been published in English, the one concerned with Houssaye's tenure as Director of the
Comédie Française. (*Behind the Scenes at the Comédie Française*,
London, 1887.)

The *Confessions* are long even for the age of the three-volume
novel and five-volume memoirs. Houssaye realized this himself and
said, perhaps somewhat sheepish at adding two more volumes to the
original four:

One day someone will remove from my *Confessions* those pages which are too personal and those that live only for a day, in order to preserve the chapters dedicated to the things I have seen and to the great men who have been my friends.

The contents of *Man About Paris* were selected from all six volumes and are, I hope, those pieces that will be most interesting to a reader of our time. Within the selections themselves cuts have rarely been made and materials have not been rearranged. The *Confessions* tempt an editor's appetite to tidy up his material, but the temptation was resisted except for leaving out an occasional digressive observation which would be meaningless to the reader without an extensive explanation, or a section which simply repeats what has already been said earlier. Houssaye was a voluminous and facile writer and dictated all his work once he could afford to have secretaries. He rarely seems to have troubled to rewrite or edit: some pieces have opening paragraphs of vague relevance, others proceed beyond their natural conclusion to add anticlimactic bits of story or observation. Such beginnings and endings were also omitted unless they seemed interesting in themselves. Three short poems were also omitted.

Houssaye's easygoing, facile prose is not difficult to render in rather straightforward English. For his witticisms and puns I have looked for English equivalents rather than accurate translations, though I tried to avoid the purely modern or temporary. A translation should read somewhat in the spirit as well as the letter of the original.

The *Confessions* are preceded by a biographical sketch of Houssaye, and followed by a bibliographical note on his work, and by a glossary explaining the more frequently mentioned persons and places in the book.

The University of Chicago Libraries, and in particular Mr. Stanley E. Gwynn, deserve my thanks for the many courtesies they extended. To Illinois Institute of Technology, and to my colleagues there, I am grateful for their interest as well as their forbearance. James Landis, my editor at Morrow, gave me considerably greater assistance than I had a right to expect. Mary Nowinski and Wendy Bulger were of great help in preparing the text.

My wife became quite interested in Houssaye, which pleased and helped me, but would have worried me considerably had it all happened a hundred years ago, in Paris.

CHICAGO, AUGUST 1969

Henry Knepler

Contents

·

Man About Paris

.

*THE
CONFESSIONS
OF
ARSÈNE HOUSSAYE*

Arsène Houssaye

•

When one looks at a portrait of Arsène Houssaye in his middle age
—patriarchal beard, long, curly, carefully combed hair, serious
mien—one sees a Victorian likeness and gets a Victorian impression
that is as deceptive as the age itself. Arsène Houssaye is not simply
a gentleman who sowed his wild oats as a young romantic and
revolutionary and then settled into respectability as Director of
the Comédie Française, editor of journals, critic, novelist, poet, art-
historian and Inspector General of Provincial Museums. He is much
more of one piece, and yet also an example of the basic contrasts of
his era.

Houssaye's family name was Housset; at some time he adopted
the other spelling, laying claim to an aristocratic lineage he did not
have. This was not uncommon in France in his time. He was born
in Bruyères, near Laon, in the Department of the Aisne; the date
usually given is March 28, 1815. If a story he told to the Emperor
Napoleon III is correct, the year must have been 1814—but then it
is not always easy to believe everything Houssaye tells. His father
was a simple, conventional landowner, a member of the local gentry
who played the violin and failed to understand his son. His maternal
grandfather Mailfer was a stonemason and part-time sculptor who

had been on friendly terms with *les Dames de France*, the two elderly daughters of King Louis XV, who lived at the nearby Château de Bove. They left their extensive library to Mailfer and from childhood on Arsène liked to spend many hours in that dark, wood-panelled room.

In 1824 his father took Arsène to Rheims, a few hours distant by coach, to witness the coronation of Charles X, the last Bourbon king of France. Sixty years later, in his *Confessions* Houssaye described the event, showing his talent for a quick, trenchant sketch which creates atmosphere through personal experience:

In our part of the world Napoleon dominated everything: so much had been told me of that great man that it hid the person of Charles X. I felt humiliated to see a mere king when I could have seen an emperor. In vain our teachers tried to deceive us about history by putting on airs: the simple engravings which could be found in any cottage told more than all the teachers. The gentleman-king who had been brought back to France like just another Frenchman inspired no one. So much had happened in a quarter of a century that people felt as if they were witnessing no more than a comedy; perhaps the king himself felt that way when he saw around him the last Marshals of the Empire, like Moncey, smiling at the thought that God protected France altogether too well, from the cathedral all the way to such small change.

The one thing that impressed me was the royal coach; but I was equally impressed by the words of an old republican lady who was in our party. She had long ago acted the Goddess of Reason at Laon; she remembered her role, saying: "Yes, a gilded coach! It's a good deal more elegant than the one he came back to France in, not to talk of the one in which he beat it out of the country."

That was said in the great square; everyone around us began to laugh except for my father whose imposing "Be quiet" subdued the zest of the Goddess of Reason. We had four seats for the ceremony and we were five people, but I managed to enter, hidden in the petticoats of the Goddess of Reason. She continued to make her biting remarks in the cathedral, but that did not prevent me from being moved by the ceremony.

In the spring of 1830 Arsène's great-uncle, the retired court-painter Fründt, took him for his first visit to Paris. As a former art-teacher of the Duchesse de Berry, mother of the heir to the throne, Fründt managed to obtain an invitation to a ball at the Palais-Royal, the residence of Louis Philippe, Duke of Orléans. King Charles X was there, and a galaxy of foreign and domestic royalty. It turned out to be the last great social occasion of the Bourbon monarchy. A few weeks later—Arsène was safely back in Bruyères by then—the king whose coronation he had witnessed was in exile and the Duke of Orléans was king.

The ball—on the edge of the volcano, as Houssaye did not fail to say—intoxicated him and strengthened his resolve that, "having entered the great world by the main gate," he would do his utmost to join it. Less than two years later, he had won out at home and was on his way to Paris. By the time he was twenty he had published two novels, *La Pécheresse* (*The Lovely Sinner*) and *La Couronne de bluets* (*The Cornflower Crown*) and was off on his lifelong pursuit of cultural and social life in Paris.

The Paris of the early 1830's was that of the new Citizen King, Louis Philippe. Instead of a Second Republic the people had accepted a new liberal monarchy which, at the time Houssaye came to Paris, was busily shedding the trappings of freedom that had brought it to power. Houssaye threw himself enthusiastically into the only proper pursuit of young artists and writers—revolution. His active participation was very brief, but his rebellion, first as a Bohemian, and later as a liberal, lasted through the whole July Monarchy until its overthrow in 1848. He participated in that revolution, though with considerably greater circumspection than in his little cat-and-mouse game with the police in 1832. He presided at a student banquet which crystallized much of the spirit of resistance to the monarchy and ran unsuccessfully for Deputy in the republican National Assembly from his home district of the Aisne.

In the years since coming to Paris, Houssaye had written voluminously, generally to keep himself in necessities, and at last the appearance of luxuries; poems, novels, art history, stories of various kinds. His *Histoire de la peinture flamande et hollandaise*

(1846) enhanced his reputation; he collaborated extensively with Jules Sandeau in a number of novels most of whose titles are, simply, the names of women. His *Maîtresses délaissées* (*Abandoned Mistresses*) (2 volumes, 1840) indicates his bent in its title, but he is at his best in these years perhaps in the *Histoire du quarante et unième fauteuil de l'Académie Française* (*History of the Forty-first Chair of the French Academy*) (1845), a charming collection of imaginary acceptance speeches at the French Academy, made by some of the most famous men of the eighteenth and nineteenth centuries who did not make it into the chair of one of the Forty Immortals.

As a man of letters, he is limited; his work indicates his talent: it lies in the occasional, the social, the witty, not the profound. He is an occasional poet, not a serious one; his novels, now or later, are largely *romans à clef*, novels on contemporary life and loves, to be read by the initiated for the spice they contain about real people, not for a portrayal of the human condition. He is at his best as a connoisseur: of art, of letters, of men and especially of women.

Houssaye was obviously a clever rather than a profoundly intelligent man, whose quick wit was paired with the kind of audacity that one needed to survive in the shark-infested waters of the Parisian social and cultural mainstream. He did survive, quite brilliantly in fact; he had relatively few important enemies, which bespeaks his judiciousness in selecting sides in battle, and in choosing and retaining friends. He was aided by the additional advantage that, though he enjoyed his success and reputation as a writer, he had no profound literary pretensions and was therefore no great danger to literary lions. He also did not take himself so seriously that he could not lightly forgive and forget. His great talents as an observer and participant in a society based on brilliant social intercourse and discourse came early and easily. Sainte-Beuve introduced him to Chateaubriand when he was in his early twenties; Sandeau introduced him to Balzac. Théophile Gautier, Alfred de Musset, Gérard de Nerval, Delacroix, Dumas became his close and clearly quite genuine friends.

In the 1850's, as Director of the Comédie Française, his range widened immensely, to include the great society of the Second Empire from its Emperor Napoleon III to its leading cocottes like Cora Pearl. He knew, lunched with, danced with, talked with simply everyone: the great actresses from Rachel to Bernhardt; the great artists from Ingres to Manet; the great writers from Balzac to Baudelaire; the great ladies from Madame Recamier to the Empress Eugénie; the political leaders from Talleyrand to Morny. His evident enjoyment lay in knowing everybody and about everybody. Of course, only everybody who was anybody. One would search in vain for anyone outside society, art or letters in his reminiscences, except for some *grisettes* in his youth or an occasional helper at the Comédie Française. The great ones, the "beautiful people," were his meat and drink.

Meat and drink are no idle terms for nineteenth-century Paris. To be part of that society, to observe it constantly in action, needed uncommon physical fortitude. Houssaye had it. He went from banquet to *bal masqué*, from salon to soirée, for fifty years or more, and he gave some great fêtes himself. There he shone; and there he saw, with that mixture of the man of the world at its very center and the man from Bruyères, never ceasing quite to be surprised to find himself lunching with the Emperor at Saint Cloud, or receiving M. Ingres in his office at the Théâtre Français. A refreshing, almost humble surprise breaks through his observations of the intimacies of the talented and powerful, even after decades in their company.

Houssaye was lucky. He did not really share Victor Hugo's republican sentiments which drove that poet into exile. After 1848 his liberalism went no further than some graceful duels with the Imperial censor. He was lucky because he spent the best years of his life under the government most congenial to him, the Empire. He settled into the Third Republic with ease and insight, but it was no longer quite the same. Through the 1850's, 1860's and 1870's, and into the 1880's he lived at a steady, frantic pace. He had his social life, he served the Emperor in various official capacities, he headed, briefly, the Théâtre Lyrique, he edited several journals,* and he wrote, voluminously, in an amazing number of genres: art history, including a book on Jacques Callot, eighteenth-century history and biography, including a book on Voltaire; novels like *Le Pantoufle de Cendrillon* (*Cinderella's Slipper*) (1852), *Mlle. Cléopâtre* (1864), *Lucie, histoire d'une fille perdue* (1873), *La Comédienne* (1884); collections of stories like *Les grandes dames* (4 vols., 1868), *Les Mille et une nuits parisiennes* (4 vols., 1876). There were volumes of poetry, articles in the *Revue des Deux Mondes*, the *Revue de Paris*, and *L'Artiste*, plays like *Les Caprices de la Marquise* (1884), and *Juliette et Roméo* (1873), volumes of essays and travel books.

If Houssaye kept a journal or diary, like the Goncourts or Delacroix, he did not publish it. That makes its existence unlikely. Fairly late in life, in his sixties, he began to write reminiscences and reminiscent observations, calling them *Les Confessions*, which by 1891 amounted to six sizable volumes, a total of about 2,400 pages, not counting the many pages of facsimile reproductions of letters to him from the people he talks about. The first four volumes have a vague chronological order. The last two, added later, have none. Mainly, of course, they look to the past: the life of the Parisian *bohème* in the 1830's; literary and artistic contacts; affairs with women; friendships with men; the years at the Comédie; the fringes of Imperial power; and of course, endlessly, the festivities, the balls, the cocottes, the actresses, the artists, the conversations, the whole excitement. But there is more: all kinds of observations on sex, on style, on human behavior, on art and letters, on politics; amazingly frank, dispassionate remarks on his private life, especially his affair with the singer Marie Garcia.

His own confessions were not the only ones he wrote:

> Through force of circumstance, if I may say so, my picture gallery in the Avenue Friedland and my office at the Théâtre Français became

---

* In which he was one of the first to publish the early works of such men as Flaubert and Baudelaire.

confessionals. Let me explain: a man of imagination whose books have caused much feminine curiosity is often assailed by romantic women who, at moments of crisis or despair, come to open their rebellious hearts to him, as if he had the duty to assuage them. On such occasions even the most mysterious women tell all, with complete abandon, cursing God, family and their own passion. The outcry of truth burns their lips. Quite unintentionally the confessor is at that moment initiated into all the most intimate secrets of an enticing woman, be she from Paris or from a foreign country.

Houssaye should be remembered for what he does best: observe, judge. He has a dry sense of humor, a piercing matter-of-factness which leads him to underplay the drama of events. At the same time he displays the hyperbole characteristic of the Romantics. He can be ruthlessly timeless or modern, deflating hypocrisy around him by showing his own; he can be very conventionally nineteenth-century, taking the moral axioms of his time at their face value. Above all, he is very French, cutting through the veils of social custom and habit with passionate feeling dispassionately observed.

The *Confessions* span his life which spanned most of the century. He was born when Napoleon I was still trying to hold on to France and died in 1896, when the case of Captain Dreyfus was about to be reopened. In all he emerges as a child of his time who could stand off from it to look, and yet never cease to marvel at it. A witty, audacious, even rude, vain, self-possessed, yet humble man, a schemer who could be a selfless friend, a diplomat who could sacrifice advantage to principle. But only on occasion.

Springtime in Paris

•

In the early 1830's, a citizen of Bruyères who wanted to go to Paris had to rise early and leave town by eight A.M. *in order to be in Laon by ten. There he would take the diligence (or stage-coach). He would have dinner in Soissons at four* P.M. *and then settle back for the weary, jolting night ride which finally brought him to Paris the following morning.*

In middle age, when he went home by train, Houssaye could make his journey in less than three hours instead of twenty-four, but nothing could ever equal the early April morning of 1832 when, free at last, he rode into the city to stay—or so he thought. Paris was in the depth of a cholera epidemic which claimed twenty-one thousand victims. The two-year-old Orléans monarchy was still trying to arrest the aftereffects of the revolution that had brought it to power. But Houssaye was seventeen, an unknown romantic poet, and Paris was everything he had ever wanted. He ran into a fellow countryman, a jeweller from Soissons, who took him where he wanted to go: to the Latin Quarter on the Left Bank, near the Sorbonne. He took a room at the Hôtel de Malte in the Place Cambrai where he was received with open arms: because of the epidemic the hotel had only one guest besides him, another intrepid young man from the provinces named Paul Van-del-Hell, now a native Parisian of several weeks' standing, who began to introduce the newcomer to the pitfalls of Parisian life and customs.

"Montre-moi les dieux," *he commanded Van-del-Hell. But his friend had not met the gods of young romantic poets; he was looking for them himself. Houssaye tried. At a theater he once stopped in front of Alexandre Dumas* père:

"*Would you allow an unknown to tell you how he admires your work?*"

"*Why, certainly—you are a friend in that case.*"

"*I know, sir, that you have ten thousand friends, but I dare to introduce myself because we are fellow countrymen.*"

"*Congratulations! La Fontaine, Racine . . .*"

"*And Alexandre Dumas.*"

"*I was about to say so myself. Do you intend to become famous?*"

"*No, but I'll sharpen my pen for better or worse.*"

Dumas shook Houssaye's hand and invited him to his house—where he could never be found.

In the meantime Houssaye had to live.

.

Songs to Order

.

Van-del-Hell knew that I had come to Paris to write novels, plays and poems; he himself was preparing for a career of writing melodramas, though at the moment he was giving Greek lessons to officer candidates. He suggested that we go fifty-fifty on everything we earned. He undertook at once to visit all bookstores to try and sell the *Contes fantastiques* which I had brought from Bruyères. He returned in the evening, quite disillusioned, but we nevertheless had a gay dinner planning for the next day.

"How about the poetry?" I asked him.

"You are crazy, prose is bad currency, but poetry is counterfeit currency. If you had the *Iliad* in your pocket you would not get twenty francs for it."

"You mean to say that Homer would have been a beggar in nineteenth-century Paris?"

"Yes, if he was unknown."

"How did other poets become famous?"

"Well, there are the evil ones, Lamartine and Hugo. They started out famous, but those who don't start out that way never get anywhere."

"And Béranger?"

"Another evil one who managed to make all of France sing his first song. By the way, do you want to write songs?"

"Good heavens, yes!"

"A street hawker asked me for some yesterday."

"On the level?"

"I think so. He offered me forty-eight francs for twenty-four songs; he started by offering me twenty-four francs for forty-eight songs. He retails them in bundles of twelve, or perhaps of six."

"Well then, tomorrow I'll write him his twenty-four songs."

"Tomorrow?"

"Songs are easy. I won't write them in the silence of my study, like Béranger. I'll do them in the streets, the cafés, everywhere."

At dinner the next day I gave Van-del-Hell a pretty manuscript of twenty-four songs on existing melodies and on nonexisting melodies, political songs and love songs.

"But really, to tell the truth," said Van-del-Hell, looking through them, "some of them are very good."

"It's as fast to write good ones as bad ones."

The street hawker paid us that very evening. We dined gaily in the Place de l'Odéon, which cost us six songs. Later we spent two more at the Café Voltaire.

The satisfied merchant came back three times for further batches of songs; Houssaye managed to place what he himself calls a bad novel, De Profundis, *and a bad play*, La Vierge des ruines, *with a publisher; Van-del-Hell received a commission to translate* Daphnis and Chloë. *All were done with the same speed and gay abandon, and the money went as fast and as easily as it came.*

.

Nini-Blue-Eyes, Nini-Black-Eyes

.

Would you believe me if I tell you that in the month of May, 1832, in order to inaugurate the new season delayed by the cholera epidemic, a madcap student wanted to introduce a new fashion: red hats, violet hats, blue hats, as if men would want to hoist hats of all colors, just like women. That was an incredible cacophony; it even included red-white-and-blue hats.

The students, almost all of them republicans, strutted about in red hats; the more timid ones contented themselves with violet hats, the soulful romantics dressed up in blue hats. In the Latin Quarter the hats cost a mere ten francs and we each took a chance with a ten-franc piece for a red hat. We wore them at a very rakish tilt and everybody turned to see the red hats go by. They brought us good luck.

One morning we were crossing the Luxembourg Gardens when we noticed two girls completely entranced to see us so marvellously hatted. They were two escapees from their families in search of adventure, strolling from the Law School to the Medical School, past the Medici Fountain: a real Fountain of Vaucluse for the Lauras in search of their Petrarch. One of them exclaimed:

"What handsome hats."

"And so handsomely worn!" I answered.

We had been two, now we were four. Unlike us, the ladies were not dressed according to the latest fashion. They wore their hair open, one hanging down long, the other bobbed; one was wearing slippers, the other brown shoes; both of them happily wore foulard dresses that were so light, they clearly outlined the promontories and bays of their feminine geographies. Here we had two bouquets of youth, two amorous promises, two barely ripe fruits. I had no trouble convincing the two girls that, as they had chanced to cross our paths, destiny wanted them to have lunch with us.

Right away, Van-del-Hell took the hand of the blue-eyed one to tell her fortune. He did not impair his reputation as a soothsayer in telling her that she would deceive one man with another. I wanted to be equally wise: I read clearly in the eyes of the other young lady that she would ride down the Champs Élysées in a carriage. The poor girl did not have the wherewithal for the bus, and was deeply touched by such a prediction. We walked up the great tree-lined promenade of the Luxembourg to have lunch in a small restaurant named To the Bravest located where those ladies of the Closerie des Lilas dance today.

"What's your name?" I asked the one who was destined to deceive all men.

"Nini."

"And you?" Van-del-Hell asked the one who, according to my prediction, would ride in a carriage.

"Nini."

"Really," I said. "You have to be careful not to mistake each other; and your lovers, too, will likely get all mixed up."

"So what," said Nini no. 1. "What's so terrible if one of us is taken for the other? Aren't we both pretty?"

To tell the truth, they were. They had above all that freshness of youth which characterizes Parisian girls, but which lasts no longer than five or six seasons. As long as they have it, all's well. When it disappears, they have little appeal left.

As we were orderly men, we rebaptized our friends with our first glasses of Chablis. It was resolved that one would be called Nini-Blue-Eyes, the other Nini-Black-Eyes. It was not exactly hard to reach that decision.

Why did Nini-Black-Eyes become my student rather than Nini-Blue-Eyes? One was as good as the other. That day I would not have given a penny bunch of violets to choose between them; but, soon after, I found that I had made a lucky choice.

The luncheon was very noisy and very gay. As always I had song on my lips, and improvised a poem on the two Ninis.

We went back by way of the Luxembourg. While we were looking at the statues, the girls disclosed that they had posed at the Bosio and Pradier studios, naturally as goddesses or demigoddesses on Olympus. Van-del-Hell waxed indignant:

"What! Such well-brought-up young girls! Are you not ashamed to undress before a bunch of prying men who wouldn't pretend to be artists except for the nude models?"

"What do you want us to do? We are so badly dressed."

"All right, then, come and pose for us."

"How much per session?"

A woman selling violets was passing by. I made bold to buy two penny bouquets.

"Yes, a penny per session," said Van-del-Hell.

The two Ninis considered that good wages. With light steps they were soon mounting our staircase at the Hôtel de Malte. But who was really tricked? We were, because they did not want to leave again, giving us the most implausible reasons, such as: one, that they loved us; two, that they would be beaten by their mothers.

We allowed ourselves to be convinced until the next day. Nini-Blue-Eyes, born to play the field, or rather the streets—beware of blue eyes!—flew off the next morning saying that she would be back; but Nini-Black-Eyes held true: she dissolved in tears when I talked to her about an eternal separation. I had my principles, I did not want to live so intimately with a mistress. I unbosomed myself to my landlady who, after a motherly sermon, rented me for Nini a room below mine, at half price because she still had no tenants after the ravages of the cholera. Van-del-Hell was sorry for me for being too much loved. I was sorry for him for not being loved enough. In truth, I was scared to have a woman on my hands when I myself did not have enough to live on. But at seventeen the morning light always seems rosy; moreover, we still had bread on the table because of *Daphnis and Chloë*.

Three or four days later a pale apprehension began to creep into my heart: one cannot imagine what these maidenly teeth devoured from morning to night, beginning with apples, ending with oranges. Van-del-Hell was protesting more and more, as Nini-Blue-Eyes no longer burdened our budget.* I made a heroic decision: when governments are without a penny, they make loans on their signatures. I wrote to the notary at Bruyères, which was not easy to do because I had no money to buy pens. I asked him to send me a thousand francs, less than nothing for a man like him. Fortunately he had a son who was also womanizing. Without much ad·· he himself brought me, eight days later, a thousand francs in beautiful five-franc pieces. In those days gold and bank notes did not go by mail. The five-franc piece was in its heyday.

The notary surprised me with Nini-Black-Eyes, who was watering the flowers in the window.

"Who is this young person?" he asked me like a heavy father.

"That's the landlady's daughter, that's why she is wearing house slippers."

The notary understood. He was knowledgeable in matters of love because he was about to ruin himself with a young lady whose history I have told in *Les Trois filles du cabaret*. He was just about to pick up the bag with the thousand francs; but, when all is said and done, he was a good fellow townsman.

"Here are the thousand francs," he said. "You need not die of misery, like Gilbert and Malfilâtre.† I am not like your father; youth must have its day; one does not discipline one's children by cutting off their food: if my son wants to act like you, I'll be the first one to hold his stirrup to let him ride Pegasus."

The notary recited some more references to the ancients for my benefit; then, to the great despair of Nini, he took me to lunch

* As Houssaye and Van-del-Hell had pooled their financial resources, Van-del-Hell was not pleased to pay a share of the expenses of Houssaye's Nini, especially as his own Nini had flown. Oranges, moreover, were an expensive delicacy.
† Nicolas Gilbert (1751–1780) and Jacques-Charles Louis de Malfilâtre (1732–1767) were poets who died young.

at the Hotel Emperor Joseph where he was awaited by his mistress, whom I knew well.

I thought innocently that these thousand francs would last for a long time. I appointed Nini-Black-Eyes as guardian of the treasury. She resisted my temptations heroically but did not do as well against her own. Her struggle was in vain: when one does not keep count, one soon sees the bottom of the bag. What could we do? All three of us were gluttons for life: with love on one side and friendship—for Van-del-Hell partook of the fat days as well as the lean—on the other. He told me one evening that my doll was too well-dressed. I had always loved beautiful art objects; well, the most beautiful art object is woman. Why not put her beauty in the best light possible?

One day, when I put my hand in the bag, I found one solitary five-franc piece. I turned pale with astonishment. I took the piece and looked at it sadly: "What a beautiful picture!" I exclaimed. "I want to keep it."

It was the effigy of Bonaparte as First Consul.

"Undoubtedly," said Van-del-Hell, "you are a born artist."

.

The June Insurrection

.

Houssaye's springtime in Paris came to an abrupt end. The government of Louis Philippe, King of the French, was beset by the supporters of a Bourbon monarchy on the right and the republicans on the left; demonstrations, strikes, clashes with the National Guard, attempted coups d'état kept Paris on edge. The funeral of a moderately liberal general, Jean Maximin de Lamarque, turned, more or less accidentally, into a riot which developed into a brief insurrection.

Houssaye was by inclination much more conservative than the students and workers who turned a political demonstration by moderate opposition forces into a revolt, but at seventeen, in the Paris of the 1830's and 1840's, it was hard not to be a radical.

We were still waiting for a better day when the events of the sixth and seventh of June [1832] cut us short.

We had joined the funeral cortège of General Lamarque more as a result of curiosity than political concern. The gunfire, when it began, inflamed us and we were quickly part of the insurrection without really knowing why. In a civil war ardent young men always want to take sides—against law and order. We refused to leave off, drunk with powder and smoke, because we believed that we were saving France from "her oppressors." The ruling forces which defend themselves are always the oppressor. We were moreover among those who believed that we had been deprived of the fruits of the July Revolution, and that it was essential to establish a republic to regain the lost paradise. We very gallantly took part in a gunfight on the barricades in the Rue Sainte-Avoie. That was a waste of effort because we had no bullets, so that we had to court death without a better defense than bayonets. I knew how to handle a gun because I used to hunt. Van-del-Hell, in true Parisian style, had no need of lessons in anything, but gun in hand he was as much of a hazard to his friends as to his enemies. Near the Cloister of Saint-Méry I made the acquaintance of Godefroy Cavaignac, a friendship that was to endure for our lives. He wished us the best of luck and I talked to him about a cousin of his, Mme. de Corancez, a friend of my mother's.

He answered with a smile: "We don't have to tell her that we've been involved in this."

We did not stay long: the army counterattacked, spreading death at random here and there. We were swept into the church of Saint-Méry, which within five minutes became a veritable death-trap because we persisted in defending ourselves with our bayonets. It should be said, however, that the soldiers of the King, once they reached the chancel, ceased their vengeful acts.

I have retained a clear memory of that first morning, which instilled a revolutionary fever in me, and of those troubled days in which we all believed in the promised land. Here is the story of how this almost-revolution started.

The official mourners followed the funeral cortège of General Lamarque with such deep religious meditation that they knocked off with their canes all those hats that were not lifted reverently quick enough.

Van-del-Hell and a student who had taken part in the 1830 revolution were with me. We allowed ourselves to be swept along, saying, "We'll have fun." A general was being buried. We shouted "Long Live the Republic"—all still for amusement's sake. When some domino players outside a café did not rise to salute Lamarque, we collared them and dragged them along in the procession. The owner of the café cursed us. We broke some of his glasses and I absconded with his lady cashier. Until that moment nothing really drastic had happened, but now there was a fearful tumult. What had been a prank suddenly became an uprising. We shouted as loud as we could that we were now the masters of Paris. A contingent of soldiers arrived, which we promptly disarmed. But that proved not to be enough so that some ran to the gun shops while others dashed off to the knife merchants. Within less than fifteen minutes all of us were armed. While we were doing all these things so appropriate to a funeral, we were still somehow following the cortège; unfortunately General Lamarque did not rise from his shroud to lead us. Here and there soldiers were making their appearance, some mounted, some on foot. Soon we were split up like a snake: but the revolution intended to die rather than surrender. We did not have any ammunition; we took to our bayonets. The funeral tears turned to blood. People began to kill each other without really knowing why. In the flow of the crowd we were swept up and, finally, ejected. The two domino players were still with us. Like us, they had shouted: "Long Live the Republic." A strange epidemic of republican fervor! We promised to form a powerful committee with them that evening, but first we wanted to display our power at the Tuileries.

The army got the better of the revolt; soon all were dispersed, like dust in a storm. We returned by various side streets, constantly risking arrest. Here and there people were putting up barricades, but when the National Guard appeared on the scene and asked: "What are you doing here?" The answer was: "We are taking down the barricades."

I am telling you the truth, they played like children, striking poses for future revolutions. Night had fallen; a few skirmishes, a few alarms, silence.

We slept under the open sky near the Porte Saint-Denis. The next morning we mustered our forces in the Rue Saint-Denis and Rue Saint-Martin because the revolt not only made use of the streets but of the houses with their six stories. Our decimated regiments no longer dared to march forward toward the enemy who fought all over the place, especially at the Cloister of Saint-Méry. The King had the fortitude to act like a king: he showed himself on horseback at the City Hall. The revolutionaries shouted: "Long Live the King!" That was the final word of the revolt, as well as the epitaph of the Republic of 1830.

Anyway, at the end of an hour the Prefect of Police and his adjutant came to make their arrests at the Cloister of Saint-Méry, at the same time letting go the women, the children and the bystanders who had happened to take refuge in there. Our friend the student disappeared miraculously, but Van-del-Hell and I were caught. Van-del-Hell said that he had fought like a lion not knowing why or for what; he was held prisoner.

Then it was my turn: "Oh, no, that isn't you, is it?"

I also recognized him.

"Yes, that's right," I said, trying to sound heroic.

"Monsieur," said Jennesson, winking his eye, "I shall keep you last." And turning to two policemen he added: "You will be responsible for that man."

I had recognized Jennesson, a friend of my father's, raised in Bruyères, where he still spent some time and where his house, built as a mineral water factory, still showed its handsome Louis XVI façade. I looked at him without understanding his intent and asked to be reunited with Van-del-Hell; but my friend had already gone off with his escort.

When order had been more or less restored in the church and the majority of prisoners marched off to Police Headquarters, Jennesson signaled to me to march in front of him. Soon he was marching by my side.

"I take it you have gone out of your mind," he said. "Oh, there is no justice in this world: you deserve to be shot. But I shall content myself to send you off in the direction of Bruyères tomorrow morning after you have spent the night at my house."

I wanted to bristle with my freshly born revolutionary mustache.

"For god's sake, boy, don't try to swagger. If you say one word, I leave you to the Military Tribunal."

I did say one word: "Give me the release of my friend Van-del-Hell, who was arrested by my side; he fired some shots but he is so clumsy that he killed only rebels."

"Well, I'll pardon him."

Jennesson ordered one of his men to take me to his house, Rue Boileau, if my memory serves me. Mme. Jennesson softened my revolutionary ideas with grace and charm. We waited until midnight for her husband to come home to supper; in vain, for Jennesson had to spend the night at Police Headquarters. I was given a campbed but I hardly slept; I was feverish. I kept hearing the echoes of gunfire even though Paris was quiet, like a playwright who is hissed by the audience during the evening's performance and then believes all night long that he can still hear these hisses. I thought about the risks of revolution: it would have taken little more to overthrow the government and to proclaim a republic, but what kind of republic would that have been? Would it be the shore after the storm, or the storm after the shore? Why had I, a man of the mind, tried to become a man of action? I reproached myself, I who had volunteered for the army in 1831, for having betrayed a soldier's duty and taken up arms against the army. I swore to myself only to engage in peaceful revolutions hereafter.

I was in despair at having been ordered home to Bruyères; Jennesson had flatly refused to reconsider my exile. What would now become of my literary labors with Van-del-Hell? Would I

see that first Parisian friend again? Would I really have to say
farewell to all my dreams of being a poet or an artist? My mother
would surely embrace me with tears of joy, but my father would
greet me with a scowl. What would I do there? He would probably make me finish my studies and either enter the civil service
or pick up the plough.

On the next morning I had to leave. M. Jennesson, who was
a kind man, almost consoled me with an unexpected event. When
we were having some cake soaked in Bruyères wine, a police officer brought in Van-del-Hell.

"Sir, you are free," said Jennesson to him.

I threw myself into my friend's arms. Then I had to leave; we
said farewell. I never saw him again.

I forget—I saw him half an hour later. I had gone back to the
Hôtel de Malte to collect my clothes; moreover, the diligence was
not to leave until evening. I found Van-del-Hell quite philosophically smoking his pipe. He had promised Jennesson to hide at his
father's house during the next troubled days, but he had quite care-
lessly come back to the Hôtel de Malte.

"I've come back for you," he told me. "I do hope that you
won't go back to your family as the fatted calf to be killed."

"Nor, I hope, will you."

"Heaven preserve me! I'd rather follow you to Bruyères than
to play Daphnis to some Chloë back in the provinces. By the way,
you know that the princess has a fever, she is as pale as a lovely
evening in autumn."

Van-del-Hell turned this last phrase into song, calling for Nini,
who was song personified at all hours; there were no known or
unknown airs that had not caressed her lips. I was no longer so
much in love but I could not live without the songs of that black-
eyed warbler. So it was with a real pleasure that I drew Nini to
my breast. She had shed many tears; after an absence of two nights
she believed me already a victim of tyranny; she began to cry
"Long Live the Republic!" But now that we were having lunch
together her cheeks again took on their lovely color; we had not

yet reached the dessert when she was already singing once more. I am pretty sure that she sang the *Marseillaise* that day, though not until she had first closed the window.

Shortly before evening I opened my heart to her. I told her that I was about to die of unhappiness, but that on pain of going before the Military Tribunal I was forced to submit to the authority of my family, that is, go to Bruyères.

"I'll never get over that," she said, in tears.

The next day Van-del-Hell wrote me that she was getting over it quite nicely. Thus is love in the Latin Quarter. As for me, I carried Nini-Black-Eyes in my heart—until the day after: man is more steadfast than woman.

Bohemian Life

·

In the year that Houssaye was forced to spend at home in Bruyères he evidently managed to convince his father of the hopelessness of trying to make a notary of his son. Houssaye managed to scandalize society with a large dose of Parisian behavior; he also found some friends who believed in his literary talent. De Profundis, the novel he had written the year before, appeared, mercifully under a pen name. One month later he was back in Paris, with a new work this time, La Couronne de bluets, to which he signed his own name.

Paris was full of poor, talented young men like him, but not many had his facility for making contacts, and his social ease. Godefroy Cavaignac, whom he had met at General Lamarque's funeral, introduced him to Armand Carrel, the influential editor of the National. A few articles, a few poems were accepted and published, and Houssaye was off on his lifelong pursuit of social and intellectual Paris.

His first home was the Paris that Houssaye's friend Henri Murger described in La Vie de Bohème, the book on which Puccini's opera is based. Less of a dandy than Gavarni, less talented than Théophile Gautier, much less eccentric than Gérard de Nerval, Houssaye was nevertheless one of the central figures of that group of romantic poets and artists, all in their twenties. *All of them were of middle-class origin, but were proud to see themselves as being outside established society—the intellectual, if not the political enemies of the bourgeois kingdom of Louis Philippe. In the 1840's, when he once talked to the king, Houssaye was surprised to find him intelligent, well-read and pleasant. But now, in 1833, the very thought of Louis Philippe and his* juste milieu *merely aroused amused contempt.*

·

Long-Haired Théo

·

I met both Théophile Gautier and Nestor Roqueplan at the 1833 Salon, in front of a picture of "Jean-Jacques * Passing the Ford." They did not know each other. One could see at once that they did not belong to the same world, neither in attitude nor in dress. Roqueplan, like Gavarni and Beauvoir, strictly followed the fashion of the day, if not of tomorrow. Théophile protested against bourgeois painting through his long hair and his heavily embroidered frock coat. In playing with this elaborately baroque style he wanted above all to hide his shyness. He talked ferociously about Philistines. Roqueplan, a born unbeliever who mocked everything except perhaps the pictures by Camille Roqueplan, looked at him askance, his lips seeming to say: "Where does that thing come from?" That thing, after all, might be a critic—because of his hair— or an amateur painter because of his coat. For that reason he also let pass a few irreverent paradoxes which that thing said about his brother's picture. Théo had the sweet temper of a dove, but Nestor Roqueplan had the prudence of a serpent, except when he bit like one.

I was with my friend Constant, a set designer at the Opéra and the Vaudeville, born in Bruyères like me, who had become a citizen of Paris before me.

"Look," he said to me, "over there, that's Roqueplan-Figaro,

* Rousseau.

and over that way is a painter who writes verses, Théophile Gautier."

"Théophile Gautier?" I cried. And I wanted to throw my arms around him though I had never met him, I loved his work so much.

"Be quiet," said Constant who was not an impulsive man. "Do you want to make a live scene among all these painted ones?"

He introduced me to Gautier and Roqueplan, which created a small bond between them. The ice was broken, we began to talk in a friendly way, but not in a simple way because Théo already had his very unlikely manner of expressing himself, and Roqueplan completed all his phrases with clever little conceits. They got along, however, in front of that "Jean-Jacques Passing the Ford" because the romantic Théo confessed that he found it one of the best pictures in the Salon.

"Moreover," said Roqueplan, proud of his brother, "it's a historical picture like the one my brother did of Jean-Jacques throwing cherries to the little girls."

That gave me a chance to enter the conversation. I knew my eighteenth century better than that.

"Oh, but look what you are doing to history," I said with a smile. "You know very well that Jean-Jacques did not write his *Confessions* until long after Beaudoin's death; * there is an engraving by Eisen, after a gouache by Beaudoin, which shows the same scene: a handsome peasant up in the cherry tree who throws cherries at two ladies out for a morning stroll."

I am not sure if it is not often wrong to be right. In accusing Rousseau of having written a chapter of his *Confessions*, not as a result of an experience of his youth, but of a picture, I also accused Camille Roqueplan of having taken his picture from one by Beaudoin. Nestor Roqueplan looked at me out of the corner of his eye.

* This cannot be denied. The *Confessions* were not written until 1775; Beaudoin's picture was in the Salon of 1765. [Houssaye's footnote.]

"After all," I continued, "Molière took his ideas from everywhere."

Nestor Roqueplan bowed and left, pleased to have found admirers of his brother. Constant had settled himself before Decamps' "In the Studio." I bowed to Gautier, after having said a few words about his poems, but he took my arm and said, to my great surprise, "Where are we off to?"

"Wherever you want."

And arm in arm we walked through the sections given to painting and sculpture. When we parted, Théo said, "I request your presence without fail tomorrow for lunch at the house of those who gave me life."

"Where's that?"

"At the misnamed monument called Gentlemen's Gate, for my father is its customs house officer."

"I'll be there."

The next day I found my friend in delightful disorder, making a watercolor of his young sister.

"Oh, there you are! You can see that I am painting Nini: isn't she charming?"

"Charming; but that portrait does not resemble her in the least."

"You don't understand—she poses for another one, that little innocent."

"And who is that?"

"That's Cydalise."

Cydalise was Théo's great passion.

His father entered. Mlle. Nini flew off like a songbird, delighted not to have to pose any more. Théo took his father's hand and led him solemnly to me: "May I present to you the honorable gentleman who is the author of my being."

"And that was well worth it," exclaimed the father who constantly tried to draw his son into using a more filial way of speaking. But Théo would not have sacrificed his curious phraseology for the fame of Voltaire. We sat down to lunch. Another one of

Théo's sisters sat at the head of the table, but it was his mother who did everything possible to make us comfortable, especially her son, whom she adored. She had dragged her husband from Tarbes to Paris to help the poet get a reputation as fast as possible. Father, mother and children all were handsome Basque types, blondish hair, tan complexion, Spanish eyes. Mme. Gautier looked askance at me because she did not like newcomers, but her son reassured her by saying, "That man is my friend."

Gérard de Nerval appeared, who in those days was still Gérard Labrunie or, simply, Gérard. He soon took over the conversation, amazing us with his theories of the theater. D'Aubignac had never spoken better.

After lunch Théo said to me, "You know, I don't really know you; tell me eight verses of yours, and I'll tell you who you are."

.

The Beehive

.

This is how we lived together, Camille Rogier, Gérard de Nerval, Théo and I. Théo rented a small flat in the Rue du Doyenné behind Camille Rogier's apartment, in which he could receive his friends because his family home at Gentlemen's Gate seemed to us the end of the earth, and because family life was difficult for a man who had burning friendships and would not rein in his passions. That little flat was not ruinously expensive; it cost two hundred and fifty francs a year. Théo did not spread himself in oriental luxury; he had no more than he needed to sleep and dream.

Luxury could be found in front, in the famous apartment of Camille Rogier, a well-known artist by that time, who had managed to get some painters to cover the gold-framed wall panels of his salon with their masterpieces. That salon became a legend because it was the meeting place of the first Bohemian literary circle.

Gérard who, for a young man of good family, was intent on a rather gaudy life, had taken over a corner of Rogier's apartment, promising to do marvels with it; he was a very easy tenant because he never slept at home. We hardly saw him except now and then in the middle of the day. In the evening he went to the theater and during the night he prowled about totally absorbed by the fever of inspiration. When these struggles had wearied him he lay down to sleep wherever he happened to be.

One day I came to spend an hour in that flamboyant company, amazed to see so much wit and intelligence being dispensed like ready money. One evening Rogier offered us tea in a lovely Japanese tea service; we drank so much and so well, descending from the heights of philosophy to the depths of voluptuousness, that we ignored the passing of time. When dawn began to show in the east, Ourliac, Beauvoir, and I, who did not live there, at last decided to leave.

"I have one guest room," said Rogier, "but I don't have three."

I was the laziest; I went and threw myself on the guest bed. I rose so late in the day that Rogier said with a smile, "It is hardly worthwhile for you to go home because we dine together in any case."

That evening the conversation repeated itself. When Théo coined a paradox, he would not stop halfway; when Ourliac improvised a comedy, one had to wait for the ending; when Beauvoir exploded one of his improvisations, no one thought of cutting him short.

In the afternoon of the second day, I sent to the Rue Vivienne for my campbed because I wanted to live in that delightful company. Théo and Gérard as well as Rogier had asked me repeatedly to stay. Rogier refused to accept payment but I promised to pay him back with some festivities at the Frères-Provençaux on the day I got my allowance, for my mother did not forget me.

No one ever saw a fresher and happier friendship; every day was a real feast for heart and mind. It was a gay harmony of men at work; Théo on *Mademoiselle de Maupin*, Gérard on *The Queen of Sheba*, Ourliac on *Suzanne*, and I on *La Pécheresse*. I don't even count the sonnets and songs which Rogier set to music without missing a stroke of his pencil, for he was drawing all day or painting watercolors illustrating Hoffmann and Byron side by side.*

There was room for everyone in the big salon. One was writing by the fireplace, the other sitting in a hammock; Théo, always caressing his cats, wrote his chapters lying on his belly; Gérard, always elusive, came and went with the vague unrest of someone who is looking for something without finding it. Beauvoir appeared now and then with his burning rhymes.

That was not all: Gavarni was at the time publishing I don't know which journal of fashion under the patronage of the Duchesse d'Abrantès. When he, so lacking in beauty himself, was not creating something beautiful, he often came to draw with Rogier. He stood in total contrast to Théo, for if Gavarni resembled a fashion plate, Théo resembled a shaggy-haired Basque just descended from forest and mountain. He did not always wear his legendary red vest but often had on a scarlet jumper.

Those who saw us from the outside would not have bet two pennies on us, but those who penetrated our circle could already see that something was going to happen. We seemed like dilettantes, more preoccupied with adventure than with the world of ideas; it seemed that, if we were trying to succeed with our poetry or our novels, it was merely to make our adventures all the more exciting. But, when all is said, we were diligent, obstinate and determined. All of us had one priceless virtue in our literary work: we did not want to write except as our imaginations told us. We were poor, but not one of us had given in to let himself be deviated by some hack labor. A man of talent always finds some remunerative writing task, but if he condemns himself to hack work he is lost. For the daily labor of the journals someone ought to invent a writing machine just as we now have a sewing machine.

Literary life in those days was a life of self-denial and misery. The important journals did not publish any novels. They were still dominated by the old style critics. Only Loëve Weimars and

---

* Rogier did the illustrations for the original edition of the *Tales of Hoffmann*.

Jules Janin were bringing the new spirit into play. Except for them, Voltairism in its second childhood dominated everything. It was fashionable to poke fun at Romanticism with envious laughter. There was therefore no point in knocking at the doors of the journals. That left the book publishers; but these gentlemen were autocrats who did not publish any books they themselves did not like.

In the evening we did not fall asleep at our books. We went all over Paris, the old Paris and the new. We were afraid of nothing and thumbed our noses at public opinion. Once a week a noisy band of us went to La Chaumière. The first time I risked going to that resort I was edified by the simplemindedness of the ladies of the place. When I wanted to have a good time with one of these little intellectuals, she took me by surprise saying, "You must understand, Monsieur, that I am very clever."

"I have no doubt, Mademoiselle; but since when?"

"Since always: I never take more than one lover."

To have only one lover seemed to her the height of sagacity.

We always streamed into La Chaumière like a hurricane, shouting: "Come on, you horizontals, you odalisques, you pigs-in-law, shake your virtues and your fleas!"

The fifth or sixth year medical students did not create any more commotion than we. Everybody wanted to dance in those days; for example, Ourliac and I had quite a remarkable quadrille in which we gravely portrayed Napoleon the Great in all the supreme moments of his life, from the siege of Toulon to the weeping willow of Saint Helena. Field glasses played a prominent role in the performance. In that time, too, it was the mark of a successful event to fire off pistols or to break chairs, and these noises provided happy accompaniments for our battles. At the proper moment in the dance we carried the day—and made off with the women.

Théophile Gautier did not dare to undertake any other dance than the *Galop*, as it was then called. For it he violently took hold of the first woman he found, even if he had to take her from a student. Everyone said, looking at his long hair: "He really should act the weeping willow of Saint Helena." Roger de Beauvoir, Albéric Second, Charles de Lafayette, Clément de Ris, and at times Gavarni came along for these adventures. Beauvoir, Albéric, Gavarni and I stood in contrast to the other romantics because we dressed carefully according to the fashion of the day, if not tomorrow. We fully approved of the others' clothes but we also thought that we could dress according to fashion and still be perfectly genuine Bohemians simply by wearing our hats at a jaunty angle. The properly dressed Bohemians made fun of us and called us dandies, but we soon learned that women resisted us less than them. Women always love fashion plates, and Gavarni, who actually created fashions, was their ideal. In the solitude of the Point-du-Jour, much later, one could hear him protest against fashions. That was the Gavarni who had left women aside and who wanted, in his final years, to be thought of as a mathematician and scientist. Man always wants to pass from the known to the unknown.

The most outstanding characteristic of our Bohemian existence was our open revolt against all prejudices, I might say against all laws. We lived as if entrenched in a fortress from which we made belligerent sallies ridiculing everything. Our lives seemed to pass in the serious service of art, and the light-hearted service of love. Beyond heart and intellect we refused to go. Did Gautier not say once: "I would give my French citizenship for a view of Julia Grisi emerging from her bath." Julia Grisi was the Venus of Milo—plus arms—of the age. A real muse she was, on account both of her beauty and her voice. One had to see and hear her, in society or on the stage, to get a feeling for the radiance of this woman who was three times female: through nature, through art, and through love.

We all shared Gautier's attitude toward politics. We neither defended nor attacked the law; we had simply placed ourselves outside legal bounds. Everyone knew that I had had my quarter-hour of revolutionary folly at the Cloister of Saint-Méry. I had got off easy, considering the circumstances. In the midst of the battle I had written some verses which gave off a bad odor of powder and blood: I burned them, looking upon them as a memory of some terrible prank. Now, when we picked up the newspapers it was only to look for the literary section. Whoever talked politics was loudly criticized in the most vivid manner. He was threatened with torture: he would be broken on the wheel of the Chariot of State riding on top of a volcano.

Time went fast because we were hardly ever idle. Théo said once: "I don't do any work, on the pretext of writing a poem; and I write a poem to have an excuse for not doing anything." I urge all apprentices in art and letters to be as idle as he was. We all got up in the early morning according to Diderot's precept. Inspiration is a goddess who keeps early hours. At seven or eight everyone was up, even after a wild night.

On the rare days when we were discouraged we tried everything, even the unknown or inaccessible reaches of opium and hashish; but, fortunately for us, cigars and cigarettes remained our only constant opiates.

Théo never took to the pen without first having tried to draw or paint, mostly to draw; he was too lazy to set up his palette, and preferred pastels. Most of the time he did the same figure over and over, with the likeness of the head taken from his youngest sister, or Cydalise, or some other beauty.

What has become of these pastels which he always gave, with such good grace, to the first friend he saw?

Then came lunch, a real artist's lunch except for Théo-Gargantua. Everyone worked to prepare it. One day I had come back from the hunt with some partridges and showed everyone how to spit and roast them. That is a feat which you won't find in your cookbook, and so I shall in passing give my recipe:

Light a good fire and hang a partridge from a string in front of it—a well-larded partridge—which will then start to turn of its own accord. Let the juice drip on a plate. Mix two eggs with the juice and serve hot. It is exquisite. One partridge per person is quite enough for dinner, especially if it is moistened with a bottle of Château-Lafitte or Château-Yquem.

We never dined at home. Like a flock of birds of prey we descended upon the Palais-Royal, or the cabarets in the Rue de Valois, or the various restaurants in the arcades, according to our whim. After that we went to the theater if Hugo or Dumas were being played. We haughtily passed up the musicals and all other kinds of plays. Gérard joined us at dinner on occasion with some tickets to a play opening, which he had received from Dumas or Bocage. In that way we gained entrance to some great social occasions. It was the era of flaming punch, the true dish for romantic suppers. Various parties took us to different places after these events—one here, the other somewhere else—so that we rarely came home together. We were always astonished to run into each other at home the next day, after having cut such a swath through Paris nightlife. Gérard especially had total lapses of memory at times. He would come back after two days and try to prove to us in his sweetest manner that he had left us the night before, not earlier. We could never find out where he had been. He did have an official father in the suburbs, M. Labrunie, a former army doctor, but he kept him at a distance, for two reasons: first, because he believed himself to be a son of Napoleon; and second because M. Labrunie had thrown his first verses into the fire with many angry words against all poets.

·

Venus Improvised

·

One early morning Gérard de Nerval came and woke me up.

"My dear Houssaye, you are going to Greece with me."

"Today?"

"In one hour."

"And why?"

"To raise once more the altar of the great gods, in order to recall them to Olympus. We are being stifled in this Catholic, Roman atmosphere here. We must have a great gust of fresh air to revitalize our souls."

I had raised myself to see Gérard more clearly. He looked completely well.

"My dear friend," I said, "do you have lots of money?"

"Victor Lecour and Paul de Lavigne have each given me one hundred francs."

"Well then, the thing to do is to make out a salary budget for Jupiter, Juno, Vulcan, and Venus. As far as I am concerned, the great gods are not going to return to Olympus unless they get a proper budget."

"Don't joke," said Gérard impatiently. "When we get there, we'll make a government loan."

"At what rate of interest? We'd have to start by removing the King of Greece from his throne."

"That's done in a moment, in one clean sweep."

"Of course. After all, what's a mere king in the land of the gods?"

"When we are masters of Athens, we'll be masters of the world. Just think that as soon as we turn over that sacred soil we are bound to find priceless treasures—statues, bas-reliefs, busts, all the great works of ancient Greece. If France won't lend us money for it, we'll make our fortune in England because they will allow us to excavate Pompeii and Herculaneum."

Gérard looked triumphant; I was beginning to be convinced.

"Moreover," he said, proudly raising his head, "who is going to stop us from coining money?"

Alas, he would have needed to coin money that day to buy an overcoat. Théo or I would gladly have given him ours, but he never accepted anything.

"Well then, Gérard, it's agreed: we'll coin money on Vulcan's forge with the likeness of Aphrodite on it."

"And you think that such coins would not be accepted in both worlds?"

"Quite the contrary, they will be medallions in the manner of antiquity whose price will be beyond compare."

"Yes, let us not waste any time now."

c

"Certainly not! I am ready to leave."

I had dressed in the meantime. I picked up my hat and cane.

"We'll start out by having breakfast at the Café d'Orsay," I said to Gérard. "After that we'll take the express train to Siren-land and Cytherea."

Even though Gérard, thinking only of his Olympian gods, was far from the affairs of this world, he consented to do something for his stomach.

"Moreover," he said, "we'll run into Chenavard there and persuade him to come with us."

Unfortunately Chenavard was not having breakfast at the Café d'Orsay, but another of our friends, Édouard l'Hôte, a poet who sang—and still sings—of gods and goddesses, was at our usual table. I quickly signaled to him to be careful because it was important not to cross Gérard when he was in a state of exaltation. Édouard l'Hôte promised to come along on our journey. Gérard and I regretted that we could not have a proper Greek breakfast, but I ordered an aphrodisiac omelet, more commonly referred to as an omelet with truffles, and a steak with olives and Corinthian raisins, promising Gérard some Cyprus wine thereafter.

First we got some Chablis. I had noticed on several occasions that one could get the better of Gérard's madness by making him slightly drunk because one could then jar him out of his obsession. It worked again this time.

Édouard l'Hôte, who had to be at the Ministry of Finance at a certain hour even though he was already in a rather high position, took us along to the Tuileries. Gérard, his mind still on coining money in Greece, asked l'Hôte how he could organize a ministry of finance, when a girl, her hair flying in the wind, came toward us. We stopped her in front of us.

She was extremely pretty, a lonely bird of passage, its plumage ruffled by the wind. She seemed to ask for nothing more than a grain of wheat in exchange for her time.

I said to Gérard: "Here is your Minister of Finance; we can

entrust all our treasures to her for she will use them to the best advantage of our governmental authority."

"Well then," said Gérard, "let us take her along."

We had no trouble in persuading our beauty to join us. I only asked Gérard to delay the journey long enough to let her get clothes fit for Olympus: "You understand, Gérard, if we present ourselves to the goddesses when they hold court in their salon, this lady here ought to have a very low-cut dress by the foremost dressmaker in Paris."

"Yes, yes," said Gérard who had become quite cheerful, "an indecent dress is absolutely necessary."

Édouard l'Hôte remembered his duty; he bid us good-by to go to the Ministry, promising to work on a budget for the gods.

Gérard had taken the young girl's arm. We turned to go to the Café des Tuileries.

That was our first station on the way to Greece. We had reached the Sirens' Island.

The girl succeeded in doing what neither l'Hôte nor I had been able to do: she managed to bring Gérard back to reason. With two poets he indulged in all the phantasies of his disordered imagination, but with a strange young girl with her head in the clouds he realized that he had to come back to earth. Fifteen minutes with her turned him once more into the sanest of men. He not only stopped talking about going to raise the gods of Olympus but thought only of spending the rest of his life with that little tramp who had happened to get up early in search of adventure. She reminded him of the Sylvia he had loved so ardently in his early youth. He enthused about every aspect of her beauty, her burnished hair shimmering with flecks of gold because the lady had once been blond, her big blue astonished-looking eyes—she had reason to be astonished—her sensual mouth, red lips and white teeth. Her hands were, it is true, nothing to rave about, clumsy hands which did not know how to move; but Gérard did not look beyond the outline of her shape.

He wanted his lovely bird to have lunch because the glass of port she had just had was surely not enough. He rose to order, discreetly, a rather summary meal: he had no more than one franc in his pocket and did not want to ask me for help.

I decided to play fairy godmother out of friendship. I gave several twenty-franc pieces to the girl, all that I had in life, and told her, "Be nice to him; when you run out of money, tell him to come and see me with you."

And so I left.

You may think that this young girl was a streetwalker. Good lord, no. She belonged to that most honorable guild of *grisettes* who live from day to day, getting a dinner here, an apple there. Those were janitors' daughters in rebellion, dressmakers' apprentices who had snapped their needles, chambermaids who had thrown their bonnets over the roof, governesses who had tasted too fully of the tree of knowledge, actresses without theater, romantics in search of Prince Charming, all of those, in short, who loved the steep banks of the river of life though they might tumble into the waves at the first gust of wind. Nowadays a new Ovid has transformed them into Ladies of Fashion. They have their elegant houses around the Parc Monceau and their coaches to circle the lake: soon they will be the Fifth Estate.

Gérard, it seems, was content to go to Montmartre with his love instead of Mount Olympus. When he was unable to travel, Montmartre was the Promised Land to him. In those days that mountain, so dear to Parisians, was very picturesque, with its windmills, its lopsided houses, impassable roads, and sweet-smelling gardens where various Eves descended each morning half-dressed to gather plums or apples. The natives went about in the most unlikely clothes. Montmartre was the last bastion of the romantic Bohemians of the pure sort.

A few days later I ran into Gérard on the Quai Voltaire.

"Oh, it's you! And where is the lovely lady from the Tuileries?"

"Oh, if you knew how happy we were to part!"

"I'm not surprised. On the same day?"

"No, the next day."

"A whole day of love! That's a century! Are you going to see her again?"

"She does not know where she'll live, just as I don't know where I'll live."

All this did not prevent Gérard from travelling to his magic Greek isle. The passion for travel always swept him up, this passion for the unexpected which opens up to us not only the gates of the visible world but of the invisible world as well. I always place greater trust in the philosopher who studies life in the universal book of nature than in the one who studies his own heart in the vastnesses of a library.

If Gérard had been able to choose his country and his century, he would have been born in Greece in Helena's time or in Syria in the time when the Queen of Sheba came, like the wife of the sun, to shine at the court of Solomon. Gleyre had a beautifully luminous sketch of the Queen of Sheba's entry into Jerusalem. When Gérard saw the sketch, he cried out, "Oh! I remember!" On February 24, 1848, we were in Ziem's studio shortly after his return from the Orient, looking at all that he had painted on his voyage; the revolution flowed along the streets outside and the noise drew us to the window. But Gérard stayed behind completely absorbed in his contemplation of lovely girls and majestic ruins.

·

Théo in Love

·

The way in which Houssaye tells the story of Théophile Gautier's love for Cydalise is quite revealing of the attitudes of his time. "Fallen" women may be loved sincerely, but they may at the same time be treated with a certain unconscious cruelty as if they were a little less than human. Male friendship takes precedence over any relations with women be they good or bad. Even the enlightened, liberal Bohemians who scoffed at bourgeois society would not question these basic rules or doubt the fact of male superiority.

Camille Rogier now and then entertained a very romantic young woman whom we knew only by the name of Cydalise. She had all the characteristics of the romantic: she was slender, pale, dark eyed, somehow resembling a weeping willow, and talked only in monosyllables. In Théo she inspired some of his most beautiful poetry.

There was something Japanese about her which made the poet say that at her breast one breathed

> Something sweet and gentle like the scent of tea

In those days we believed that the end of youth came at age twenty-five, not a minute later. I remember that, five years after those days, Jules Sandeau invited us to dinner in order to chant the *De Profundis* and the *Miserere* for his youth; he was thirty. That evening he assumed his most fatal and Byronic air as if he had returned from another world.

"All is over," he told us. "I have bidden farewell to all beautiful passions; I turn resolutely to the harsh tasks of life. Look at me: I do not have a single hair left on my head; henceforth, when I sup with my friends, I shall only play the role of elegiac poet."

The strangest aspect of the whole thing was that he was perfectly serious in this comedy; just as we were ourselves convinced that he had passed his zenith. Thus, in drinking to Sandeau, we, too, shed a tear in our cups. This perspective of youth made us look upon Camille Rogier, twenty-five years old like Sandeau, as a patriarch. In the same vein, Gautier, who was hiding his true age, used to say that he could not understand why the lovely Cydalise would stay with so old a man.

Where did Cydalise come from? Rogier had waltzed with her at a costume ball, perhaps the famous ball given by Alexandre Dumas. She fairly melted in his arms, so much so that he would have swept her up like a feather at the end of the ball—but she had fled. The next day, alone in his studio, he felt the need for that vision of loveliness; he went in search of her; he enlisted one of his friends in the search, a man who had nothing else to do and was a veritable ferret where women were concerned. But the friend was as unsuccessful as he. Three months later she suddenly dropped into his arms like a miracle. He did not recognize her because he had never seen her unmasked, but she recognized him.

It was in the middle of the Rue Richelieu: "Oh, it is you, darling!"

He sensed that he had found the object of his search and did not want to lose her once more. It was near the dinner hour, they had an intimate dinner, so much so that Cydalise was astonished the next morning to wake up in the Rue Doyenné. Rogier, a master charmer of women, arranged an adorable little nook for her, a hideaway where she could read all day long and where she made tea in the evening for the friends of the house. The tea was exquisite, especially in the opinion of Théophile Gautier, who fell in love with Cydalise for her scent of tea as one might fall in love with a woman for her perfume. I can point to many of Théo's poems which date from that love; while he produced them under the spell of her eyes, she, too, learned to make songs of love. ·

A whole novel could be written about the love of Théo and Cydalise, a Desdemona completely suffused with romanticism.

The spectacle amused me greatly. It was a tragi-comedy. Camille Rogier laughed up his sleeve at seeing Théophile Gautier metamorphosed into the fatal lover. I stirred up the flames or poured water on them, depending on whether the lady's passion was fading or reanimating itself.

One evening everybody was in my room, Rogier and the lady, Théo and Ourliac. We chatted about this and that. Suddenly I began to praise the idea of *mariage à trois* as it is practiced in Italy, by means of an extra gentleman. I knew what I was saying.

"You must try to see," I exclaimed, "the advantage to the husband and the advantage to the lover, not to speak of the advantage to the lady! The husband has exercised his wife so much that he is not unhappy to send her to exercise with a lover. Every marriage needs intermissions, even a marriage gone askew. The play can only improve after a little pause. Finders are still keepers!"

Camille Rogier smiled but Théo was not at all amused. He wanted Cydalise for himself alone; he had only one thought: to kill Rogier.

Ourliac, who played the role of fool in our circle, was actually the wisest among us. He now poured water on the flames. I continued to develop my clever line without paying any attention to the discomfort of the lady who obviously wanted to change the subject. Rogier, delighted, did not interrupt me except to agree.

"As far as I am concerned," he said, "I only look for the day when a kind friend will take my mistress off my hands, at least to some extent. After all, there are only two ways in the end to be rid of one's mistress: to marry her or to use a friend."

And, having uttered his loud laugh which displayed all his teeth, he added: "For example, I'll bequeath the lovely party in question to those who want her, if there are any, because I'm leaving tomorrow for the south. In fact, I'll leave you right now to get ready."

"And you don't take Cydalise with you?"

"And what about my theories in that case?"

Cydalise now spoke up: "Go ahead, I know you well enough. You play the skeptic, but you are more jealous than Othello."

Another loud laugh from Rogier: "I'll never kill my Desdemona!"

Whereupon he left with Ourliac. I said to Théo: "Well then, are you happy now?"

"No," answered Cydalise, "Théo is not really in love except when Rogier is around."

That love was the cause of Théo's despair. He was violently in love with Cydalise, but she was dying of consumption and, moreover, she was the mistress of Camille Rogier! Yet she was also too kind a creature not to have given her heart to Théo as well. In that way I became the confidant both of Tragedy and Comedy; Tragedy was called Théophile Gautier; Comedy, Camille Rogier.

FIRST SCENE: THÉO'S BEDROOM.

TRAGEDY: I'll kill him.

CONFIDANT: Good God! Whom?

TRAGEDY: That horrible Rogier. Yes, I shall deliver Cydalise from that monster.

CONFIDANT: Master Théo, restrain your jealousy. It is enough to betray one's friendship without taking up a dagger.

TRAGEDY: You may imagine that I am not serious, but I swear to you, if I can lay my hands on him, I'll go through with it.

CONFIDANT: Go on! You must remember that Rogier is not only a gentleman but a true friend.

TRAGEDY: I hate him. Cydalise must belong to me alone.

CONFIDANT: And then you won't love her any more.

TRAGEDY: You know nothing about real passion. How can I stand being so much in love with her and know that she is in another's arms!

CONFIDANT: Good heavens, really, if she were not in Rogier's arms, she'd simply be in the arms of someone else!

Tragedy exits consigning me to the devil. I go to Rogier who welcomes me gaily. He never searched behind the scenes but lived philosophically above the battle; he was singing, improvising some music on lines by Alfred de Musset. Here is our dialogue:

COMEDY: What news have you? The world has not become less foolish since yesterday, I take it?

CONFIDANT: No, the *Constitutionnel* has been published like every day.

COMEDY: Have you seen Théo? Is he still scheming how to snatch Cydalise from me?

CONFIDANT: Yes, you need to hold on tight; I believe his horse is saddled up.

COMEDY: Every morning when I get up I believe that it has happened; but unfortunately my rival does not have

C*

the will power. I surprised them in the act—why don't
they draw the consequences?

CONFIDANT: Because they are afraid that they will cause
you grief.

COMEDY: I am saint enough to tell them freely: give me
pleasure and take each other; but they are not in love any
more.

CONFIDANT: I have told them that.

COMEDY: The ingrates! Every day I serve them the forbidden fruit on a silver platter. They munch at it and then
they aren't even grateful!

CONFIDANT: They are savages who insist on climbing the
tree themselves in order to pluck the fruit.

COMEDY: Civilized men and women are really the worst
savages.

Gérard de Nerval, Édouard Ourliac and I amused ourselves
greatly with that tragi-comedy. Théo, placid and humorous by
nature, had abandoned himself totally to his passion. When I saw
him deathly pale one day, coming on him unawares, engrossed with
his lady love, I began to be afraid that all would really end badly.
He had thrown aside his pen, he had abandoned his palette, he
neither wanted to write nor to paint. No, I am wrong, he still wrote
poems for Cydalise and illustrated them with likenesses of his pale
and deathly ill mistress.

One day she went to bed, never to rise again. Théo became
less attentive, but Rogier behaved admirably. No deathbed had
ever been brightened more with flowers and songs, for though Cydalise loved Théo's verses, she loved Rogier's songs as much. He
was at work on his illustrations of Hoffmann at the time. He drew
his sketches at the side of her sickbed, all the time telling her the
stories by the German novelist that went with them. Théo, himself
ill, was confined to his room but now wanted to continue to live
for the sake of his poetry. He passed his darkened hours reworking
La Comédie de la mort, that beautiful poem which he read out loud
to me in order to hear himself read.

Finally Cydalise died. Death bestowed on that young body some peculiar air of chastity and sweetness that touched me to the point of tears; but the real tears were shed by her two lovers. They had not spoken to each other in a long time; that day they held out their arms and embraced each other. Now Cydalise no longer belonged to either of them.

Cydalise's grave was covered with white lilac, an extremely rare luxury in those days, but no one followed the coffin except Gérard, Ourliac, Beauvoir and me. Neither Rogier nor Théo.

"People would say that I am the husband," said Rogier.

"People would say that I am the lover," said Théo.

To us, she was simply a poor girl who was now with God.

She had not led a godly life. She was one of those girls who come from who knows where, who serve as a mistress to who knows whom, who pass from one man to another, who are on the direct road to the sickroom of the poorhouse but who, one fine day, meet a gentleman who arrests their fall midway. That atmosphere of art and poetry had metamorphosed Cydalise.

She had learned art and poetry. She made drawings, she wrote verses. I recall some rough-hewn stanzas a few days before her death, in which she told how Rogier had spirited her away from a carnival ball in order to throw her into the dance of death. Romantic verses if I ever saw them. She was rather soon forgotten; the heart is like a graveyard in which weeds grow back ever more thickly.

·

Love and Honor

·

After a few weeks Théo became his old self again, as cheerful and spirited as ever: he had fallen in love with a young girl of good family, who in turn had lost her heart to his poetry. She was as lovely and as virtuous as they come, but he played the role of Captain Fracasse,* whose first adventures he was just then be-

* *Le Capitaine Fracasse*, a novel by Gautier, tells the story of an impoverished nobleman who turns himself into a swashbuckling play actor to pursue a ladylove.

ginning to set down on paper. After he had torn her from her family and given her a son, he effaced those pages of his life. That son was the only consolation for the woman he had harmed so much, but she forgave Théo because, in the blindness of her love, she resigned herself to everything.

She had a brother, however, who did not resign himself.

One fine day Théo was disquieted by the visit of two gentlemen completely dressed in black. He immediately said to me: "Those are obviously creditors."

That was no more than a figure of speech because he did not have any debts or, rather, because they were creditors in a debt of the heart. Our servant, like them impeccably dressed in black, silently indicated the poet stretched out on a rug, smoking his pipe like an oriental. The somber visitors turned away, taking him in his unlikely costume to be a displaced Turk.

"Would you please take us to M. Théophile Gautier?"

"Why?"

"That is none of your business."

"Perhaps it is my business because I am the aforementioned Théophile Gautier. Please be seated, gentlemen."

The two visitors looked haughtily at the rug. "We are not accustomed to sitting on the floor."

"You are quite wrong to be so fussy: it is much more comfortable to be seated than to stand up, and it is better to lie down than to sit: it is, after all, the proper position in the grave."

"Exactly, sir," said one of the visitors impatiently. "We have not come to hear your maxims, we have come for very serious reasons which may well put someone in his grave."

It was, in other words, the eternal scene of retribution. The young girl's brother had sent two friends to confront Théo with two choices:

"Either M. Théophile Gautier marries Mlle. X. or he fights a duel with me. I represent the offended family, and I choose swords."

One of the seconds, M. Blanc, a charming man about town

whom I got to know later, read out the proposition in a firm voice.

Théo answered simply: "Of two evils I choose the lesser. I'd rather fight than marry."

He called me over.

"It seems that we have a duel on our hands," he told me. "Piot and you will be my seconds."

Piot was the historian of antiquity with whom Théo later traveled to Spain.

"Well, my dear friend, we are up to our necks in a romantic novel. We could get a good story about a duel here, and from nature, too, because until now we have not had the good fortune of getting our throats cut; your duel in the studio was no more than a carnival adventure."

With the eloquence of a Demosthenes M. Blanc attempted to convince Théo that a gentleman always righted the wrongs he had done.

"My wrongs?—I have not done any wrongs. Since when is it a hanging matter to make off with a girl so long as she is beautiful?"

"It has always been a crime, sir. And there is an aggravating circumstance in this case because the lady is a mother as of yesterday."

M. Blanc was indignant by now.

"At least, sir, if you do not wish to marry the lady, you will not refuse to give the child your name; that is our second proposition."

"Give the child my name! The child of a poet! Do you mean to say that he should be consecrated to all the fiends in hell? And besides, I have a very fixed opinion in such matters."

"Would you care to explain, sir?"

"Well," continued Théo, "here it is: one has to be the lowest type of Philistine still to believe today—after all the scientific discoveries—that men have anything to do with the creation of children. Women tell us that for no other reason than to please us, but the truth is that they become mothers whenever it pleases them, by sheer force of will. Don't you know thousands of girls who bring children into the world only in order to compromise men who have done no more than doff their hats to them in passing —or not even that? I appeal to Arsène Houssaye who himself is the victim of many of these ladies. He is a sceptic who'll never go to the altar. And I won't go either."

I knew the whole story. I had strong feelings of sympathy for the young mother, a girl of good family, beautiful, pensive and sweet, a real muse for Théo. It would have been the very best thing for him to marry her.

"It may be your good right," I told him, "not to go to the altar, but what you are saying is a lot of nonsense. Your theories are very original: yesterday you proved to me that the sun circles the earth, and tomorrow you will prove that Jupiter is still on Mount Olympus; but here we are dealing with a very precise proposition. These gentlemen here know very well that you are the cleverest man in the world, but today they merely want a yes or a no as an answer; if you were to say yes you would perhaps show yourself at your very cleverest."

"No! No! No!" Théo thundered like Jupiter.

That eloquent response ended the conversation. We all rose and bid each other a glacial farewell. It was as if the first cut of the sword had already been made.

When the tribunal was set up, the decision was made to fight with swords on Montmartre in the gardens of Saint-Ouen, at dawn the next day.

In preparation for that meeting on the field of honor, Théo decapitated some flowers and played a few passes with me. He almost laid me out, he was so infuriated. I advised him to hold on to himself until the next day.

The following morning ushered in one of those dark winter days which make one doubt the existence of the sun. Piot and I managed to make Théo say that it was an excellent day for a duel, but he managed to make us say that it was a disgraceful day for journeying to the other world. But he was ready for anything.

Though he was hardly a born fighter, he was too conscious of his dignity not to face death bravely. The furor of the previous day returned when he saw his adversary. And why? The brother trying to avenge the outrage done to his sister was a brave man devoted to the best of causes. What Théo refused to forgive was the man's desire to kill him "for something that everybody will continue to do until the stars fall down."

They took their positions. Théo attacked and touched his opponent's arm, but so lightly that the blood hardly flowed. M. Blanc made a peace proposal:

"M. Théophile Gautier, one last appeal to your heart. This duel will prove no one right, neither you nor your adversary: do you still refuse to give the child your name?"

"You still don't understand," shouted Théo. "Yes, I'll recognize him after the duel, but only on condition that he'll not recognize me."

"Well then," I said, "there is no reason for continuing the duel. Please realize that, if you are killed, you can no longer give your name to your child."

Théo, who had lowered his sword, put himself on guard again. His opponent, pale, intent, silent, seemed to want to make an end of him, when M. Blanc at last assuaged Gautier's fury by saying:

"If you kill your opponent who was once your friend, you will have committed two wrongs."

Even though we were Théo's devoted friends, Piot and I had the strongest sympathy for his mistress' brother; we were vividly aware that we were not acting in a good cause, that neither law nor honor were on our side. We helped M. Blanc to disarm our Captain Fracasse.

Those were the origins of Théophile Gautier, the second of his name. He became more of a scientist than poet. Politics captivated him when he left school. The fall of the Empire shattered his career but destiny has not yet spoken its last word on him. He is a noble spirit and a brave heart: he has done honor to his name.

It is the misfortune of most artists that some wild, breathless creature will cross their path and sweep them up in some gilded whirlwind. It was Théo's misfortune, too: a lovely dark-haired girl with purple mouth and devilish eyes crossed his path and destroyed with jealous hands the loveliest page of a destiny that had seemed fully determined. She was called La Victorine, and she took hold of Théo with the claws of a lioness. She was one of those creatures who lived on other people's money no matter what it did to them. Théo drew on all the prodigious resources of his genius, turning out articles and books. To house Victorine elegantly he housed himself elegantly. He played the gentleman of means, giving great dinners and renting carriages. That macabre dance lasted until the day when he was overwhelmed by seeing Carlotta Grisi dance Giselle, for the great poet never went to the theater except for the ballet. With Grisi he reverted to his earlier mode of life; she was another Cydalise who inspired thousands of poems in him. Poets are like birds which sing when they are in love; passion and lust do not sing; moreover, Victorine could not have converted verses into diamond earrings.

The Muse of the Dance loved elsewhere and gave the poet her sister Ernestine. It was all in the family, but love does not take well to consolation prizes. Ernestine was such a good and kind person, however, that Théo became attached to her as if she were his wife. She gave him two daughters whom the fairies endowed with beauty and poetry. It was a treat for all eyes to see them be so lovely in their childhood, even lovelier in their youth, these two joys of the home whom Théo rebaptized, as he used to do with everybody, with strange and curious names: *The Great Shabrack* and *The Green Monster*.

The Great Theater of the World

•

The word salon *has several meanings. It is the drawing room in which one converses before or after dinner. As "the Salon" it describes the annual exposition of new painting and sculpture. In the way in which Houssaye uses it most often it refers to one of the great vehicles of social intercourse in Paris. On certain days of the week, at certain hours, a lady—rarely a man—would be "at home" to all suitable callers. These included friends who came regularly, famous men who wanted to see certain others, or be seen; and those who were not famous but intrepid enough to brave the wit, the social chill and other pitfalls of the occasion. Houssaye, in his twenties, was clearly still in the last category when he entered the salons of Mme. Recamier or Mme. Vigée-Lebrun.*

In referring to salons in the next selection, Houssaye speaks of "combat help." The salon was an arena in which men and women met, on an equal footing, to match their finely honed wits and conversational prowess. Conversation—witty, cool, often cruel conversation—is central to French social culture. The English speaking world never had anything to equal its intensity, or to compare to the zest with which French society participated in this sport.

The salon was particularly appropriate for a society which circumscribed the role of the woman but at the same time did not deny or mask her power. For the most part only women had salons, and their influence, wit, and manipulative skill were measured by the brilliance of the event. Money was needed, though great wealth was not a necessary requirement, just as beauty in the hostess was an asset but not a necessity. The drive needed to achieve and maintain a great salon was the important asset, and competition was keen even before the nineteenth century, the age of competition.

The great salons after the French Revolution, Mme. de Staël's and Mme. Recamier's, were political in keeping with the time. When the Bourbon Monarchy was restored in 1814 a series of salons headed by noble ladies of the ancien régime opened up, together with those of Mme. Recamier and Mme. Sophie Gay. They disappeared abruptly with the July Revolution of 1830 when the House of Orléans and limited democracy replaced the House of Bourbon and rule by the old nobility. Democracy turned out to be increasingly limited, but by then great salons were no longer so concerned with politics. The salon of Mme. de Girardin, wife of a powerful publisher and daughter of Mme. Sophie Gay, became a center during the Orléans Monarchy and the Second Empire.

·

Salons

·

The old salons closed with great suddenness because they lacked the necessary combat help. What could Mme. de Montcalm, the Marquise de Castries, the Duchesse de Broglie, the Princess Bagration do in the face of the upheaval of 1830 which allowed all kinds of views to flourish?

Unfortunately, the new society which took the place of the old was hardly to the manner born. For some time the parvenu reigned. Though men do not change, women fortunately adapt themselves quickly to good manners. By 1832 one could no longer recognize those women of 1830 at the opera, the theater, or at the great receptions, at least the young ones; once a woman has passed her second youth she is no longer able to shed her bourgeois trappings.

If it was Lamartine who fashioned the women under Charles X, one can say that it was Balzac who fashioned those after 1830. Poetry gave place to fiction, but Balzac at least had the poet's stamp on him. George Sand, in overbidding the role of the sentimental woman, gave her a more exalted station. Woman soon exercised her power by means of her passionateness. Until that time the ladies of the bourgeoisie had been rather withdrawn. Now they emancipated themselves like the ladies of society; moreover, they gained entrance into the aristocracy through marriage. They knew the force of money, and they used it to the hilt. Eugène Sue proved that, if the theater is the school for morals, then fiction is the school for social conduct. I am astonished that no one has yet asked the Academy of Moral and Political Science: "Does fiction determine morality or does morality determine fiction?" The former is definitely the case.

In novels we find those heroines who become examples of conduct: heroines who go hunting, carry arms, play the stock-market, ride horses intrepidly and swim without fear. They light your cigar; they let you smoke only because they smoke themselves. One has to see them making fun of women as they used to be: obedient, servile, in the shadows. Those days are over; yesterday they ruled the home, today they rule the government. We are far from the century in which the Duke of Wurttemberg told his wife, when she dared to speak of affairs of state, "Madam, I took you to have children, not give advice."

Mme. Roland, Mme. de Staël, Mme. Tallien, Mme. Recamier, Mme. de Girardin changed all that.

·

Waning Moon

·

Every salon ought to be a theater, which means that it needs actors of great talent; whatever the setting, the play at least ought to be good, but if there is a flow of great men there is also a flow of mediocrities. During the Restoration we had the battles of wit and intelligence presided over by the Duchesse de Duras and carried out by Chateaubriand, de Maistre, Bonald, Lamartine, Hugo, Lamennais, Laplace, Cuvier, Vigny—illustrious names at any rate, though not always witty. Baron Gérard and Mme. Sophie Gay competed with each other for the great actors of the salons. Mme. Lebrun, old as she was, had the ability to bring the most opposite personalities together with the excuse that she had painted the most diverse women as long as they were beautiful. One was completely taken aback seeing her still vibrantly alive and coquettish. She spoke of her third spring of life like an ingenue speaking of her debut.

Mme. Sophie Gay always stoked the flames, tying, untying and retying the passions as in the times of her youth. I studied from close by both of these superannuated Célimènes,* but how far removed from me were these figures! And I saw quite a lot of these marvellous figures who for an instant made us the contemporaries of six or seven generations.

It was in 1836 that I ventured into the salon of that lady, almost one century old, who had found friends once more. It would have taken little persuasion to have her do my portrait. At least she made a drawing of me.

That centenarian who was already famous in 1775 and will still be famous in 1975, and ever after, was Mme. Vigée-Lebrun, the incomparable portrait painter who cast such an extraordinary spell on all the persons she painted, from queens to shepherdesses.

* In Molière's comedy *Le Misanthrope*, Célimène is a coquettish woman endowed with a sharp tongue.

Accident made her a character in one of my novels; she spoke to me with that pretty romantic smile of women who loved under Louis XVI. I had thought her dead long before. "I got used to living even after I lived no more," she said softly to me.

If she had not bundled herself up in the fashion of 1836, if instead of that silly bonnet, which then framed all faces so badly, she had gaily worn one of those old Rembrandt-type hats with ostrich plumes, one could still have recognized in her a denizen of Trianon.

In the end she did not find even herself any more. Where, in effect, were all the famous men of her day? She consoled herself by continuing to paint and by writing her memoirs.

"What," Janin said to her, "you still paint those magnificent portraits that are the joy of my eyes?"

"No," she said sadly, "people don't want to pose for me any more, they are afraid that I'll age them."

Janin offered to pose for her as an angel. "No," she replied, "I am satisfied painting landscapes. Nature does not create any problems when I pick up my brush. And moreover, haven't I painted all the poses of the human figure? Do you know that I have done six hundred and sixty-two portraits, a whole world, in all the capitals of Europe? There is not one great family that does not have one of my portraits, I have singled out character and race everywhere. I am a historian."

The old artist said these words with fierce pride. She spoke true; I would prefer the six hundred and sixty-two portraits of Mme. Vigée-Lebrun in a library to all the histories written in the last seventy-five years.

Every one of us naturally swung his censer piously to her. She told us, however, that nature, no matter how good and how beautiful, did not satisfy her.

"When I painted my portraits," she explained, "I painted for people who flattered me and covered me with gold, while nature neither flatters me nor pays me."

Mme. Vigée-Lebrun was at work on her two hundredth landscape, which nobody seemed to want even though her eye and her hand still spoke true. The newcomers, Rousseau, Dupré, Marilhat, had made all the old French landscape painters unfashionable.

Pradier was among us. Mme. Vigée-Lebrun asked him abruptly if masterpieces could be made in the caverns of the Academy.

"I never go there," answered Pradier.

"You are perfectly right; I don't forgive that old nuthouse, even older than I, not to have elected me in my day, because I belong to all the other academies in the world."

"You did not get that as a reward for your lovely eyes," answered Pradier.

"Ah! Ah! Ah! In the reign of Louis XVI you would have pursued me along the quais with gusts of wind, O maker of goddesses!"

She spoke with great perception of the past and understood nothing of the ways of 1836. I can still hear her telling us with some poetic fervor of her return to France; we knew that during the Revolution she had travelled across the world. Listen to her speak, if I remember correctly:

"After all my pilgrimages I returned to France, but I did not find my native country again. What can you say—the country of the artist and the woman is youth; and it had begun to snow on my forehead. The sweet reign of hope was past: the severe duties of life had already carved their furrows on my figure, my beauty had faded like an autumn evening, winter had heralded itself, and I no longer found once more the friends who recreate spring for us with their memories.

"And so I found myself alone with my recollections; no matter how I stretched out my arms to these shadows of the past, they reappeared only in a shroud. O my youth! I had the consolation at least to have laid you to rest in a grave, white and pure like a lily.

"And now that I have counted the rosary of memory, now that I have no hope except in God, I shed a final tear for my first twenty years, thanking heaven to have consoled me through the joys of art for never having experienced the joys of love."

She lowered her head in sorrow. I said to her:

"God is not prodigal with his gifts to his most favored children. Those who have one thing don't have another, but all taste of the bitter cup. If one loves one's transitory stay on earth too much, one does not think of heaven. That is the native country to which everyone returns."

·

Chateaubriand

·

Houssaye often gives character to his association with a great man by setting the description in some specific context. In the case of Chateaubriand the context is the French Academy, the Forty Immortals whom Houssaye saw largely as a group of elderly nonentities. (This did not prevent him from wanting to join them at one time, unsuccessfully.) The faded Abbaye-aux-Bois where Chateaubriand and Mme. Recamier held court in her salon, the out-of-dateness of the whole experience is thereby given its framework.

This is how I met Chateaubriand. Sainte-Beuve found in my poetry I don't know what spirit of abandonment and rustic grace; he saw my muse as a genuine peasant woman running through the wheatfields to gather cornflowers and poppies. I had captured his friendship with two little poems: "Le Foin" (Hay) and "Le Blé" (Wheat). He introduced me to his mother who invited me to dinner that same day; it seems that I spoke to her heart so well that she often asked me to return to her table. They were scant dinners if they were any at all, but Sainte-Beuve always felt comfortable there because his complicated love life had never turned him from that holy threshold. I have not forgotten, I shall never forget that house where the son rested in his mother's love from aspirations and criticism, where that mother nourished her last years with the fame of her son. She proudly planted one foot on

Olympus, that good woman who had hardly thought of aiming so high when she conceived Sainte-Beuve.

At that time he was beginning to cultivate a solemn bluestocking called the Academy.

"One ought to be one of the Forty," he told me one day, "and do you know why? Because once one has his chair one is sheltered against all literary battles, one can defy all opinions. The Academy gives you complete peace. Look: all men of kingdom come, I meant to say, of the old kingdom, who are in the Academy, not only believe that they are immortal but that the world has not taken one step since the time of their elevation. Ask M. Jay, M. Jouy, M. Baour-Lormian and the other illustrious occupants under the cupola. That's why I am going to see Mme. Recamier this evening. Would you like me to introduce you to Chateaubriand?"

That frightened me: Chateaubriand was the grand old man of the time, as Victor Hugo is the grand old man of today. What should I do, a complete unknown, in that legendary salon where all the reputations of the young century had passed in review?

A few days later I met Sainte-Beuve at Alfred de Musset's door, in front of the drowsy fountain by Bouchardon, and told him that I would be very happy to pay my respects to Chateaubriand. He happened to be on his way to the Abbaye-aux-Bois; he looked me over to see if my clothes had too romantic a cut; he found me presentable, offered me his arm and took me along. I did not express my feelings as I was ascending the stairs: all men of letters, all artists had gone through these palpitations here. We entered underneath the penetrating stare of Mme. de Staël painted by Gérard; the two illustrious personages were half asleep even though Ballanche was in the Salon. But then Ballanche was a figment rather than a man.

Sainte-Beuve gave my name to Mme. Recamier, whose look seemed to say: "Why should I care." Chateaubriand, on the other hand, deigned to wake up a little, undoubtedly not as a result of my compliments: he was weary of bearing his glory as if the laurels overburdened his forehead like those Italian sopranos who suffocate underneath their bouquets.

The author of *René* pretended that he had heard of my novels. Pure politeness on the part of a great man who had no need to do this. He told me that, for him, his only regret was to have been engaged in writing. Phrases used by Lord Byron! He also told me that, if he were to live his life over again, he would not do anything that he had done, save his actions as a Christian, because Jesus alone does not deceive. To live forgotten, that was his final word. That's because he knew himself to be unforgettable.

Sainte-Beuve, who had conversed with Mme. Recamier and had proved to her that one should always live under the Directoire or the Consulate, came up to Chateaubriand and told him eloquently that, had he lived unknown, the modern spirit would never have made its appearance: "We owe all to Chateaubriand, that Christian Homer."

The audience was not long, however, because M. von Humboldt arrived escorted by two ambassadors, soon followed by Mme. de Boigne.

When we had descended the staircase, I stopped admiringly to look at a beautiful but poorly dressed girl who was walking toward a nearby well, an earthenware pot in her hand. Sainte-Beuve, whose mind was still in the salon of the Abbaye-aux-Bois, said to me that it was beautiful to see the shining reflection of these two personages who had been the whole spirit and the whole beauty of an age that was already far away. But, completely taken with the beauty who had just dazzled me and who was now turning around, I said to Sainte-Beuve: "These twenty years who just passed by us, aren't they beautiful?"

But let us talk some more about the god and the goddess, for I saw them again at the Abbaye-aux-Bois. Mass was said every day. God was called Chateaubriand, the Holy Virgin Mme. Recamier. A virgin unquestionably, but not at all holy. There was an altar, with artificial flowers, priests, priestesses, and choir boys. Among the choir boys were all those who saw themselves as destined for the Academy, for there are people who feel themselves destined for immortality just as there are those who feel themselves destined for the hardware business. Both kinds, when they are dead, get the same epitaph. In that church there was much scattering of incense. The God only breathed well in the fragrant smoke of duchesses; because only women know really well how to stitch together a compliment. When Zeus Chateaubriand was satisfied with his world, he deigned to declaim a page of his memoirs—memoirs from Beyond *—because one wondered, when one looked at him, if he had not been dead for a long time. One day I heard him read pages from his youth. One hoped to see his well-beloved sister appear, but the makers of memories do not tell what they want to lose sight of. M. de Chateaubriand spoke of his role as soldier. That was not worth much for he had not been at Jemappes or at Austerlitz. Mme. de Boigne, a lady of intelligence, said of him: "Do you want to know why Chateaubriand is greater than Jean-Jacques [Rousseau]? Because, even in his youth, he already knew that one day he would write his memoirs. He marched through life with that mental reservation. That was his conscience. That's why all his actions are worthy of being recorded and that's why Jean-Jacques who did not have that conscience lived like a footman." I did not comment.

At the Abbaye-aux-Bois one could find some of the furniture which seemed old-fashioned by 1824, but which I liked because of its lofty character. A whole nation of heroes had sat in these armchairs and taken tea at these tables from which the caryatids and bas-reliefs had been looking on with boredom since 1815. That is why the ladies, even those who make Academicians, don't enjoy themselves in their setting sun.

Chateaubriand, always bitter, told me during my third and final visit: "My dear sir, I have read your article 'Aurores Littéraires' (New Dawn in Literature), a pretty title, a pretty subject, a pretty article. You say in it that you prefer those who are

---

* *Mémoires d'outre tombe* was the title of Chateaubriand's autobiography.

coming to those who are leaving. I am one of those who are leaving, sir."

I did not know what to answer, especially as Mme. Recamier looked at me glacially. I tried this: "Men like you, M. de Chateaubriand, never leave or always come back."

The ice melted. M. Ballanche deigned to smile, but M. de Chateaubriand, still in the same tone, replied: "I assure you that I would be very happy to leave and not come back."

A new arrival interrupted us. I went up to Mme. Recamier to talk a little about the Directoire in order to restore an air of youth to that morose figure. "It is sad, isn't it," she said to me, "not to able to resign oneself. M. de Chateaubriand is desolate to be alive, but he will also be desolate to die. All day long he says that he is bored and that he bores everyone. I assure you that he is always stimulated by what he sees, and that he stimulates us with his great thoughts."

"The great thoughts come to him from your heart."

Nothing was more untrue, and nothing could give greater pleasure to Mme. Recamier.

·

An Interview with Talleyrand

·

I mentioned before that I have memories of the eighteenth century as if I had lived in it. The reason is mainly that in 1832 many personalities of the reign of Louis XVI and of the First Republic still paraded through the salons in the white-and-red reflection of that *fin de siècle*. It was as if a historical society had been created in which almost all the public figures, old and new, congregated. There I met Barrère and Jullien de Paris in company with Michelet and David d'Angers. Jullien de Paris with his long hair looked an absolute fright. He believed he had labored well for his country; while Barrère, quite the jovial old gentleman, seemed to say that the past which does not get the better of the future is nothing but a vanished dream. I was anxious to study these ancient figures as one would study them today at the museum of Versailles; they seemed to me portraits rather than living beings.

In my ardent curiosity, I wrote without any ado to M. de Talleyrand asking him to grant me an audience. I explained that I was a very young historian who wanted to consecrate to him a few pages in a history of the principles of contemporary thought. Principles! Wasn't he the man who had juggled with all the contradictions and all the opposites of his time? I hardly expected to be received, when one of the Prince's secretaries came to look at me to assure himself that I was really a writer and not just an idler. He arrived at the judgment that I was worthy of an audience of five minutes.

On the following morning that same secretary conducted me in silence to the bedchamber of the Prince of Diplomats. Stretched out in his bed he seemed to sleep, so much so that I felt face to face with a mummy with the parchment-like pallor of a corpse three thousand years old. I bowed—I almost felt like crossing myself.

"Ah, Monsieur," he said, "you are a historian! Write fiction, for history is nothing but fiction. Those who know most about it never put any trust in it. As for me, if I were to write the history of my life, where would I ever find once more the guiding truths for all the chapters? I often write pages for my memoirs. I try to fashion them with all the honesty of which I am capable, but no matter how I try to assume a universal view, I plainly see that all too often they take on a purely personal perspective. And yet the personal view has its dignity, for it bears the mark of man."

I hardly recall all that M. de Talleyrand said. Yet I remember clearly that this thought sprang from his lips:

"Look, diplomacy is a fencing academy where one gets hurt in sport. All words are swords, and one must know how to hit home. I knew my work well, but I did not always hit home. Thus, in 1815, I made an error; I could have been Napoleon's best soldier when I was in Vienna during the Hundred Days. A nation like France needs prestige. Louis XVIII did not have any. As all of France acclaimed Napoleon it would have been best to prevent the war. Well—I fanned the flames. I created the war when I could have prevented it. But, when all is said, the diplomats themselves are no more than the humble servants of destiny. No one is master of his actions or even his words."

We exchanged some thoughts. After a fit of coughing the Prince said, "If you paint my picture, you will pass judgment that I have often been wrong, but you will also see that I have more often been right."

"Your grace," I replied—I really owed him that title—"I judge that you have always had too much wit to commit a foolish deed."

Upon which the audience was concluded.

·

The Social Side of George Sand

·

Houssaye's views notwithstanding, George Sand had a salon, though it was not one in the conventional sense. She was not a conventional woman; she wore men's clothes and pursued an intellectual existence in a manner which a man like Houssaye would reserve for men only. She was not merely a hostess, even a clever, talented and witty hostess like Mme. Recamier in her youth, or Mme. de Girardin. She was an intellectual moving among her peers, and her salon was a gathering place, not of the brilliant necessarily, or the famous, but of the men whose ideas drew them to her: Leroux, a philosopher with radical and socialist views; the Abbé Felicité de Lamennais, a priest condemned by his superiors and his Church for the reforms he advocated; Michel de Bourges, a militant republican. Yet she was not herself involved in their plans, merely drawn to them for the intellectual stimulus they provided. In addition, several of the persons mentioned in the selection below—Michel de Bourges, Musset, Didier, Mérimée, Chopin among them—had been her lovers. Liszt was not, but he was a friend whose mistress, Comtesse Marie d'Argoult, served often as Sand's fellow hostess. Houssaye probably first visited George Sand in 1835 or 1836.

Mme. Sand never had a salon. In Paris she had no more than a smoking room, here and there a dining room, but above all everywhere a work room where the philosophers and musicians rubbed elbows. Men of letters were less frequent; she saw Musset, Heine, Balzac, Malefille.

Two painters met there, Eugène Delacroix and Paul Huet, but they came as intellectuals more than artists. Whether they wanted to or not, they had to immerse themselves in socializing with Pierre Leroux, Michel de Bourges, Lamennais, Anselme Petetin, or Charles Didier. The most startling fact was, however, that George Sand did not at all like political discussions, in which she would become the center of attention; but at the point at which her guests no longer agreed with each other, a point that always came rather soon, she signaled to Liszt, to Chopin or Pauline Garcia who then went to torture or to caress the piano. After that came a frugal supper; that was the custom of the era.

The determined romantics, male or female, did not know the art of eating well. They talked a great deal about their great orgies, but they drank plain water.

Likewise, those who dazzled the eyes of their readers with their radiant descriptions of princely interiors, lived quite obliviously in apartments which the ordinary man of today would refuse to inhabit. Mérimée, Sainte-Beuve, the Academicians did, like all outsiders, not know how to live in style—even Lamartine was in that class. I am not sure that Victor Hugo, Janin, Beauvoir, or Karr did not belong among them, too, though they understood about luxurious fabrics and furniture. As for me, I had elegant Gobelins even before I came into money. I preferred to dine simply but surrounded by *objets d'art* rather than have excellent food in a poor setting.

At Nohant George Sand finally managed to have a bedroom of some distinction, even though one could observe good picture frames enclosing a mish-mash of engravings. Why this one? Why that one? Why "The Woman Taken in Adultery" by Rembrandt? Little by little the bourgeois character was submerged by the character of the artist. George Sand put an ivory Christ on the mantelpiece, she had Gothic chairs, she could see herself in a Venetian looking-glass; but the thing that gave the room its glory was the bed in which her grandfather had died, a majestic piece surmounted by four gilt ornamented posters. Then there were daggers here and there, and pipes lying about in a provocative manner. For George Sand's pipes were not merely something to be smoked; they provided voluptuous dreams. But that volcano was not actually in need of stimulation; George Sand had to do no more than to take her pen in hand to feel herself on a pedestal, to be a pythoness or a demon. Inspiration flogged her images into being. All the characters who came to live in her novels loomed up around her like a witches' Sabbath, and her pen could not move fast enough to capture all those whirlwinds of eloquence, great thoughts hurled forward at full speed, the heart broken on its battlements. But then George Sand calms her heart with gentle hands, like calming a child with caresses; she puts down her pen and falls into a sleep-like trance. But, behold, the night is a time for labor: she flings aside the hair which fell into her eyes; destiny instructs her: "Spin your tale!"—until the rosy fingered dawn opens the gates to the sun. Then her own expiring dawn bids her good day and goes to rest on a masterpiece.

And when she awakes it is art once more that rules her: she acts the role which she must act for her friends. Her real salon is a theater: Nohant.

·

Lunch with M. de Balzac

·

Houssaye must have met M. de Balzac (the "de" was self-conferred) in 1836 or early 1837, for the Chronique de Paris *mentioned below failed rather quickly, like many other ventures which Balzac undertook. By 1830, when fame first began to come to him, he had already lost heavily in three business enterprises and was deep in debt, which did not prevent him from having servants,*

horses and such whenever he could, and even when he could not,
afford them. He liked to move in aristocratic circles and once ran
unsuccessfully for the Chamber of Deputies as a Royalist candidate.

He worked almost exclusively during the night when visitors,
printers and creditors would not disturb him; dressed in his robe,
he wrote for hours on end, with cups of strong coffee to sustain
him.

Jules Sandeau had been sent, by Balzac, as ambassador to Théophile
Gautier to ask him to write for the *Chronique de Paris*. That was
a journal without subscribers which the great novelist insisted on
publishing every Sunday. So, one day, we found Jules Sandeau
entering our studio, which was the meeting place of the Bohemian
world. There he found us, Camille Rogier painting a gouache,
Gérard de Nerval rereading *Faust*, myself rhyming a sonnet,
Théophile Gautier playing with his cats and dandling Cydalise
who was sleeping in the hammock. Cydalise, a light woman, was
more than light enough to dandle.

Jules Sandeau was rather insistent in also asking Gérard,
Ourliac and me to write for Balzac's journal. I thanked Sandeau,
who was already one of my favorite novelists. I thought that he
had mentioned my name out of mere politeness, but he had read
La Couronne de bluets. That man really searched for the new
dawn, even in the fog. He invited me to dine with Risbeck who
then owned the golden mansion of the Latin Quarter in the Place
d'Odéon.

That was an unequaled stroke of luck for me because our
friendship, I might say our blood brotherhood, dated from that
occasion. There was no more fascinating intellect and spirited
heart than Jules Sandeau's.

As we were taking a walk before dinner we met up with
M. de Balzac at the Luxembourg gate. "Do you like your horse?"
the author of *Eugénie Grandet* asked of Sandeau. "Excellently! I
have just come from the Bois de Boulogne which I rode through
in five minutes."

In his constant stream of illusions Balzac, who had promised a horse to Sandeau, imagined that his friend was already mounting that horse even though he had not yet given it to him.

I looked first at Balzac, whom I had not met, and then at Sandeau, whom I thought I knew.

"He did not take the bit between his teeth?" asked Balzac.

"No, because he knows who I am."

It was really admirable how Sandeau entered into Balzac's illusions. As Balzac looked at me out of the corner of his eye, Sandeau said to him: "I would like to present to you the author of *La Couronne de bluets*."

"Yes, yes, a beautiful novel, if I had put my hand to it," he answered.

I bowed, Balzac bowed imperceptively: "Monsieur, if you would like to come to lunch one of these days, I shall tell you how to write a novel."

With which he left us after giving us both a charming smile.

"Don't worry," said Sandeau to me. "He will not tell you how to write a novel because he does not know anything about it, his genius leads him on without knowing the way. If you go to lunch with him you run a considerable risk of not lunching at all, but you won't be wasting your time."

I could not get over seeing M. de Balzac decked out in so bourgeois a way. There was nothing of the artist about him except for his eyes, searching eyes with the look of truth, and shining like the sun. Rather, he looked like a bustling lawyer. Especially to me, living as I did entirely among the unrepentant romantics, it seemed strange that Balzac did not seem strange.

Though Sandeau had told me that I would lunch badly at M. de Balzac's, I lost no time in going to the Rue Cassini and knocking at his door: a mysterious-looking house where he wanted to make believe that he was hiding from his women while he was really hiding from his creditors. I had to ring three times. Finally a servant looking like a churchman opened and asked me why I was ringing.

D

"I have come to lunch with M. de Balzac."

"Are you sure, sir?"

"Now really! I am quite sure, unless M. de Balzac does not take lunch."

The good man seemed very cross: I was going to inconvenience him and I was going to inconvenience his master. He made me go into the dining room, not, to be sure, because I had come for lunch but because the living room, like the living room of some ladies of the *demi-monde*, was still waiting for the marvels of the paperhanger. Nothing on the walls, nothing at the windows, but Balzac had himself written on the wall panels: "There a Raphael, here a Titian." All of them were covered with imaginary masterpieces which Balzac discussed with a sturdy faith as if he were seeing them all the time.

Here was also the chaos of his books and journals, with the materials of the *Comédie humaine* strewn everywhere. Balzac was content with this lumber room as his study.

After a few minutes the great novelist appeared in his famous monk's robe, his hair dishevelled, wearing Chinese slippers singed by the fire.

"Ah, I am delighted to see you. We'll have lunch; but I must warn you that I lunch like a monk."

"I shall take whatever you take; lunch is not an affair of state for me; it's happened more than once that I've had no lunch at all."

"You are right not to linger at the table at noon; whoever takes lunch seriously in Paris never gets anywhere. A man of genius hardly lunches. Napoleon stayed ten minutes at the table if he did not lunch standing up."

Alas, I was as hungry as a wolf that day. All that Balzac was saying merely whetted my appetite. His pale servant arrived bearing on a large china platter six raisins and four penny rolls.

"That's excellent," I said to Balzac; "you love beautiful porcelain, that's already a feast."

"Isn't it? Unfortunately my servants break everything. Look here, they are serving us chipped plates."

The servant had put some plates on the buffet. They were domestic ware of about 1830, when French industry did not have an iota of art in its work.

In the meantime I said to myself: "That's the dessert, but the lunch?"

Well, the dessert turned out to be lunch. Balzac signaled to me to sit down at the table; he placed himself opposite me in a stately manner, telling me in the kindest way possible: "If you are a glutton, speak up! I am going to send for a chicken or a partridge for you."

I was about to say yes to the partridge when Balzac cut off my appetite: "A poet like you should live on nothing but fresh air. Look carefully at these beautiful Venetian glasses which the Duchesse de Duras gave me; you will drink the best wine of Cyprus from them."

Saying this, Balzac poured me some water after which he passed me the raisins. "Only one raisin? You have the right to three raisins, my dear guest." He emptied the platter on my plate and kept only the three smallest raisins for himself.

So here we were, having a great time at this sumptuous meal.

"My Cyprus wine is good, isn't it? It was given to me by a great-grandson of the Doge, a Contarini. You will see—when you are famous your readers will send you the best wines; as for me, I have some Johannisberg, some Champagne, some Malaga, I have all vintages except ordinary table wine. Very simply, I get all these great wines and don't have the money to buy ordinary ones."

"Monsieur de Balzac, I don't doubt that your Cyprus wine is magnificent, but have we drunk it already?"

"You see how absent-minded I am," Balzac answered as he himself went to the sideboard. "For the last ten minutes I have been convinced that we were drinking Cyprus wine."

Such were Balzac's illusions that he truly believed we were

drinking the wine of Cyprus while he poured us water from the Seine.

He did not find any wine from Cyprus, but he did find a long-necked bottle containing four glasses of Rhine wine which we drank ceremoniously.

Meanwhile I was picking my third raisin. Balzac, seeing me break my second penny roll, said: "Wait, we are not finished, we have tea and coffee."

I told him that I was not used to eating bread with tea, let alone with coffee. "Yes, but I lace my tea and coffee with a drop of milk. And what milk! You will be delighted with it! A great lady who has a château in Normandy sends me, every morning, a bottle sealed with her own coat of arms, a bottle which encloses all the perfumes of the meadows. The cow never gave more flavorful milk."

"That's only to be expected. Aren't you a demi-god on Olympus?"

"Yes, a god of fables; but I have turned my back on all the vainglories of the pen. Look, my young friend, down here all that counts is money. In spite of all my genius I do not cut a wide swath in the world; but when I'm very rich, I'll finally get the better of all these idiots."

"And why not," I said, "as you have already got the better of the intelligent people?"

"Don't you find it irritating not to have a penny? For instance, yesterday I was invited to dinner at Mme. de Girardin's, and I spent my last ten-franc piece on my way to take a carriage and to buy some gloves; I ran into a friend and into a poor man, so much so that by midnight, on my way home, I did not have the penny needed for the Pont des Arts. I was challenged: 'Stop!' I seriously asked myself, raising my clenched fist to the stars, if I would not do better to throw myself into the Seine than to turn around and go home via the Pont-Neuf."

Tea and coffee were brought in: Balzac served me coffee and passed me the famous milk sealed with the arms of that great lady. That gave me the opportunity to eat my second roll. The great writer did not only put milk into his coffee, he put tea in it as well. I ended up doing the same—anything to help appease my hunger.

But Balzac wanted to nourish my mind. He taught me the art of being a great novelist by telling me the following: "Look, my dear friend, you must start by having an independent income of twenty-four thousand francs (that was quite a sum in those days); move in good society; keep a saddle horse; devote yourself, in order to play the game of love, to the passions as divided between two women: to die for one while the other is in despair over you. You must become a seeker after gold, with the driving force of a miser, but throw money out the window with the prodigality of a playboy; you must rummage through Paris with disreputable people; have the best seat and the best spyglass in the theatre; not forget the backstage during intermission; see death from up close, be it in war, be it in duel. And besides you must never speak in vain, but always put questions; to speak is to waste time, to listen is to study; there is not a single fool who does not teach you something. Every man shows you man, if you know how to look."

That is how Balzac spoke to me. I looked at him somewhat sceptically while at the same time admiring the lesson.

"That's very well," I answered, "but if I do all you tell me to do, I won't have any time left to write. And moreover, your theory is surely not within everybody's reach. I don't doubt that an intelligent man can become a great novelist in following you to the letter, but, if he has an independent income of twenty-four thousand francs, he won't write, he will be satisfied with his stories in living them, and he will most likely be right, for those are the best stories."

Balzac smiled bitterly. "I believe," I continued, "that there is no point in a school for novelists, even your school; I imagine you don't have an independent income of twenty-four thousand francs; you have not had all the adventures you recommend. Look, my dear great novelist, only trades can be learned, but art cannot.

You are right to study man, that is the duty of everyone who takes up the pen. And especially when one is called M. de Balzac, one studies the whole universe and the infinite in one's heart; every man of genius is a copy of God's book—that's all!"

"Well then," cried Balzac, "let us drink a toast to God, the foremost novelist of the world."

And we bid each other farewell with light hearts as well as stomachs.

In the Demi-Monde

•

The theory of morality in the July Monarchy and the Second Empire was age-old and unchanging: there were good women and bad women; the good ones remained maidens until marriage and confined their attentions to their husbands thereafter; all the rest were bad. The practice was infinitely more complex; otherwise a term such as demi-monde would not have been needed. The demi-monde lay between good society (le monde) and the professionals of street and brothel. Even that is an over-simplification; Houssaye and his contemporaries in society knew somehow who was accepted where, and how far the different moral-social classes could mingle, but it was a matter of instinct, not of explicit rules. When Houssaye tried to flout some of these rules later in life, with Marie Garcia, he came to grief.

The rules for men were entirely different from those for women, and the double standard was as axiomatic as the official basic standard of good and bad. A husband who could prove his wife's adultery had legal recourse; he could have her thrown into prison, as did the husband of one of Victor Hugo's mistresses. She came out of jail ruined socially and financially, and Hugo had to find work for her as a hack writer. Men, on the other hand, sinned with impunity.

The great courtesans were above all objects of conspicuous consumption: that, rather than physical attraction, is the only way to explain the phenomenon of Marie Duplessis (The Lady of the Camellias) or Cora Pearl, great ladies who were hotly competed for and on whom hundreds of thousands of francs were spent in one stroke. They were, by the time of the Emperor Napoleon III, no longer really demi-monde. *They were as much Society as any others. Below them came the great* cocodettes, *lovely, vivacious, witty women who could not only adorn beds, but also great dinners: they often had to be booked far in advance but were considered adornments because the element of display was at least as important as sex.*

Below them came the lorettes, *named after Notre-Dame-des-Lorettes, the church of the district where many of them originally lived. They were separated women, women of lower origins who had risen to middle-class style, still above the ordinary prostitutes of street and brothel.*

To confuse the matter further, there were the grisettes *whose outlook and social position differed from those of the* lorettes. *They were working girls—seamstresses, shop-attendants, laundresses—whose prime object was not money. A* grisette *generally had three men at a time: the mature lover for weekdays who provided for the necessities like rent, food, clothes; her wages were never enough to keep her from severe poverty. Then she had a young lover, perhaps a student or an artist, with whom she spent Sundays picknicking in the country, or dancing at the Bal de la Chaumière. And, waiting in the wings, there was the man of her own class who would eventually marry her and provide her with the meager amenities of a working-class existence.*

Origins of the Demi-Monde

The registration of compliant women was not well planned under the Citizen King, who made a constant display of high morals at the Tuileries. Louis-Philippe was more a family man than a King of France, because he was king for no more than a quarter of the time while he was a family man all the time. The courtesans generally did not dare to show themselves in broad daylight; unlike today, they did not have legal status and their place in the sun. They were seen neither at the Opéra nor at the Comédie Française. They hid in the more secluded boxes of the smaller theaters; they did not use the main drives in the Bois de Boulogne where, in fact, they were hardly ever seen. When the woman referred to only as the Lady in Brown offered Ponsard a seat in her carriage-and-four with its two footmen, it created a scandal. Ponsard himself was shocked, but the lovely Mathilda did not in the least mean to infringe on the virtue of the author of *Lucrèce;* she merely wanted, she said, to de-provincialize Ponsard. She died much later in a state of grace with the blessings of the Archbishop of Lyon, at about the same time as Ponsard passed away with the blessings of Jules Janin, whose guest he was at Passy.

Further, there was the girl called La Gioconda, and Esther Guimond, Carmen, The Dove, Mogador, Russian Salad, and all that more or less mixed lot of light actresses like Alice Ozi: the theater provided the baptism which saved them from original sin. Moreover, all these girls wanted to be actresses. But their circle was a very small world, one of which Malte-Brun would have disdained to make a map—because there were no provinces to it: the ladies barely emigrated beyond Notre-Dame-des-Lorettes. The *demi-monde* was not yet in existence, because the fallen women who belonged to the aristocracy still kept these other women at a distance. Slowly, because they sought amusement or because they shared a lover, the miracle of fusion took place. One or the other took a step forward and they ended up by giving each other a Judas kiss.

This confusion of professionals and of women of good family, of marquises and actresses, made for a much more serious revolution in morals than one would expect: the rise of the *demi-monde* really marked the end of good society.

The dowagers and the duchesses, the old-fashioned ladies and the virtuous ladies of fashion had need of a call to arms, for their salons were emptying rapidly. Only future academicians and diplomats-to-be still lingered in them because the comedy of that high society in which an air of boredom was proper behavior was really getting boring.

The ladies of society and the *demi-monde* began to rub elbows at the charity balls and at the races. At first glance they were the same women dressed by the same dressmakers, with the only distinction that the *demi-monde* seemed a little more chic. The term chic goes back to that time, at least among women; among artists it had been current earlier than that.

Yesterday, at a dinner at Mlle. Phryne's, Prince Radziwill reminded me of the occasion at the races when we first saw those ladies. At one of the great events, a Jockey-Club affair, the ladies of good society nearly choked when they saw these women boldly entering the reserved grandstand and blithely taking the arms offered them by gentlemen; it was the downfall of morality; the feminine riffraff established its General Assembly.

The great ladies of society sent their masters of ceremonies to point out to these women that they had no right to the Council Chamber. Esther Guimond replied that she was there with the consent of the gentlemen involved and that she would leave only at the point of a bayonet.

The word carried because she spoke to the lover of a "very chaste lady." Attempts were made to calm Esther Guimond who was talking very loudly; but she was afraid of nothing. "I may not belong to the world of these ladies, but I belong to the world of these gentlemen here."

On the return trip from the races, she gave her coachman a twenty-franc piece to make him drive side by side with the coach of the Comtesse de Courval. In the Comtesse's landau were three more very chaste ladies, among them the Comtesse Le Hon who had been unable to find either her own coach or her servants.

Esther Guimond was not enthroned in a landau; she had a smart little victoria in which she could make a provocative display of her petticoats, in the company of two great strumpets, one called

La Madonna and the other La Gioconda. Théophile Gautier once wrote a charming sonnet about these two lovely jades. Of course, if Esther Guimond wanted to accompany the Comtesse de Courval, it was not in order to throw her a bouquet: during the entire journey she improvised a song of thirty-six stanzas, sung to the melody of *La Rifla,* a real masterpiece of impertinences and risqué rhymes.

All of Paris was singing it the next day, and that song spread both among all the men as well as all the ladies, at least those ladies. Everybody added his grain of salt and dash of pepper—garlic salt and cayenne pepper. "And so," Esther Guimond said gaily, "I made my debut in society."

All this came to pass during the reign of a virtuous and family-minded king, and in an age in which romanticism, with all its beautiful sentiments, was in flower. The black sheep called Paris put that strumpet under its protection. That woman who had neither beauty nor any charm or grace became the strumpet-of-honor to the gilded youth simply because she was strong and loud. She climbed as high as diplomatic dinners, and even became the bellwether of backstairs politics because she had access to all statesmen.

When Louis XIV was embarking on a new policy, he used to ask: "What does Ninon * think of it?" The austere Guizot more than once asked Esther Guimond what she thought of this or that policy, but more often asked her opinion of men in power or men aspiring to it. Often she needed only one distinctive point to paint a character. If her memoirs were to be published one would find much gossip and drivel in them, but also a few pages which shed light on the intimate history of the nineteenth century. Above all, her correspondence should be published—if it could be found. At the hour of her death she was stripped of all interesting letters addressed to her. On her deathbed she had two pillows, one to

* Ninon de Lenclos (1616–1705) had a brilliant and gay salon in the reign of Louis XIV.

sleep on and one to dream: the pillow to dream was completely filled with letters from her friends. One day she had said to Roque-plan and to me: "Would you believe that I have eight hundred letters from Girardin and he refuses to buy them back!" It is well known that she was in the habit of directly selling these auto-graphs. She was a good schoolmistress: how many women are there now who exchange, for banknotes, the notes written to them in an hour of passion? "Darling, do you want to buy back your letters?" is a well-known phrase today.

Lola Montez showed the strumpet's way to success.

That theatrical heroine, armed with her legendary riding crop, went on, via a thousand and one beds, to conquer the King of Bavaria. Once enthroned, she even grew in favor: The dethroned queen displayed her friendship. She conferred the order of Saint Theresa on Lola, she called her "my dear countess," she drew her into the circle of her intimate friends. The ladies of the Court as well felt they needed the favors of the favorite, who thus found the whole world at her feet. But that amazing story has its final page. The King of Bavaria awoke from his dreams. Lola returned to us, a countess bedecked with truly royal diamonds—his crown diamonds.

It is reported that she intended to have a riding crop em-blazoned on her coat of arms, because she had made most of her conquests and reached her heights at the point of that whip which was a scepter in her hands.

Lola built a small palace at Beaujon. She asked me if she could call it Palais Royal.

"Madame, you should rather call it the Palace of the Thousand and one Nights."

"Very well, Monsieur, I offer you the one thousand and second night free."

Lola Montez continued to play at being Diana Vernon and the Duchesse de Polignac, cultivating a love of the dance and the dance of love, sinking from theater to theater. But that was fated to be. After many other escapades she finally came to die of

starvation in New York, in the tenement of a despicable woman
who beat her with a riding crop—her own riding crop—when she
refused to "work."

The beautiful Marie Duplessis also has her legend. She already
has her poets and novelists. One nicknamed her the Lady of the
Camellias, not because she wore them, like Lantour-Mézéray or
Gilbert de Voisins, but because one of her platonic lovers imprisoned her in a castle of camellias. Every morning armfuls of
them were thrown into the windows of her mezzanine apartment in
the Boulevard des Capucines. She was a lovely creature who was
not beautiful; a great actress of adventure who was a poor stage
actress; a clever woman who talked nothing but nonsense; but in
spite of all that, or because of all that, she came by her great
reputation by means of her charm. When one was with her, one
had no wish to leave, and besides that she had the talent of choosing her setting. "Tell me the names of your lovers, and I will tell
you who you are." Ask, rather, Alexandre Dumas, second of his
name! Does he know that his Lady of the Camellias was a little
Norman peasant girl whom her family had sold to some strolling
players? That was the college where she found her first teachers.

The Lady of the Camellias had her own salon when her likes
had no more than a dressing room. That is not all; Alexandre
Dumas twice made her a saint in the calendar of strumpets. When
that lovely girl passed to a better world, the angels could hardly
contain themselves!

The Lady of the Camellias was surely not the most beautiful
nor the most devilish, nor the most romantic courtesan of her
time. How many of these captivating women have we known who
accentuated their magic with the spice of cruelty and betrayal—
the true weapons of woman! Like Marie Duplessis, many of them
died of that insane life, barely sped on by a short silent prayer,
followed on their last journey by a handful of professional colleagues in perfunctory mourning who, in order to keep in practice,
made eyes when a likely gentleman passed by.

I am not speaking here of the scrapings of the slums, the

ordinary streetwalkers, the diseased derelicts whom Parisians of the Decadence metamorphosed into ladies of pleasure, but of those handsome creatures of reasonably good families whom a first misstep threw into a life of evil, there to die after tasting it—in full harness, as it were, for the sake of thirty cents a day in front of a tapestry or a painting.

How many harvests of love were reaped before their time by cruel fate! How many roses faded on the grave of my early youth! How many joyful songs which I sing no more except to the *De Profundis!*

I saw it all pass: the gods, the kings, the beautiful people, the whole menagerie. I saw the fatted calf pass—it will not come back. I saw the descent from the Courtille pass by: here lies the Carnival. I saw the crowd at Longchamps pass by: *Requiescat in pace!* The only one which has not yet passed by is the Carnival of Liberty.

After all is said, I liked best the gaiety of the wine harvest in Burgundy. We danced on the tables and we rolled under them. But all this is gone; all gone! The Comte Germain whom all the girls called their cousin-German. Gilbert de Voisins who never knew if he had really married Taglioni; d'Alton-Shee who danced the Carmagnole; Roqueplan who harangued crowds disguised as Figaro; Prince Belgiojoso who had a different princess every day; Romieu who buzzed like a cockchafer. I have seen myself pass by and ask myself if I am dreaming beyond the grave, saying with the psalmist: may my sins be upon my head.

.

Gilded Youth

.

Paris deprovincialized me quickly, the more so as I was a Parisian by nature and soon found it, I don't know how, to be my second native city. I learned at once the art of accepting its atmosphere of paradox and fantasy. I learned, too, the geography of love in the Parisian manner, which is completely different from the geography of love in the provinces. Provincial virtue lowers its drawbridge only after a siege according to rule; if not after several weeks then at least after several days.

One March evening in 1837 the brother of Champfleury, that great archeologist, took me to a flowershop in the Rue Marie Stuart where he obviously studied the history of prehistoric races. One of the young florists, Mlle. Athénaïs—remember her name well—asked me if I wanted to learn the art of making lilies and roses. She was very attractive. I threw myself upon her, asking what evening she would go to supper with me. I thought that she would put me off for a week, but she replied, "This evening, at my place, Rue Marie Stuart, at the stroke of midnight."

She gave me her key, and I understood that I was no longer in Laon or Soissons. That stroke of midnight proved to me that in Paris suppers were not put off to the next day.

At the end of a few days, when I had fallen stupendously in love with her, I noticed that she did not put things off to the next day with other lovers as well. A lover in hand is worth two in the bush. This put me on guard against these angels of chance. I did not love them any less; but I set my faith in them at a bargain price and did not trap myself into the saintly foolishness of the Romeos who chant their despair under Juliet's balcony.

I was moreover soon attached to bad company which never crossed the Bridge of Sighs and lived by the motto: "A gentleman ought to have several women in his cards and must not content himself with the Queen of Hearts." He should also have the Queen of Spades, the Queen of Clubs and the Queen of Diamonds.

Who has not gone through the intoxication of the wine houses? Well before Eugène Sue played Rodolphe in the *Mysteries of Paris,* where he ventured to take the grave reader of the *Journal des Débats* to Red Lantern Street, he disguised himself as a go-between to pander for the pretty hussies who made bold at the Courtille at Carnival time. Many other friends converted themselves in the same way into friends of these ladies.

I saw the craziest scenes at our favorite wine house, at Carnival time. We ate badly but in very gay company: Théo, Beauvoir,

Lafayette, d'Alton-Shee, Belgiojoso, Gavarni, Rogier, Malitourne, Roqueplan, lots of others. A scion of good family made his debut in society there; I am not so sure that his family tutor did not wait for him at the door. He was dressed like a perfect fashion plate.

"That's not the present fashion," Roqueplan told him. "You can clearly see that we are all dressed like Lord Crapulous."

The scion, already worthy of his upbringing, was confounded to find himself too well dressed. Clément de Ris advised him to throw some Burgundy on his white waistcoat to liven up the company. He obeyed happily by pouring a whole champagne cup full of red wine on his chest. That was the baptism for a stormy life according to the style of the time.

Romieu was the most cynical as well as the most sentimental beast in these gatherings. He would say suddenly: "Long Live the Working Girl! * All those nice girls who give us a workout and look so fetching with their dresses appropriately torn, but what good are they really?"

"You are quite right," said Prince Belgiojoso, "these girls have no heart: when you tell them to jump out of the window to give us pleasure not one of them will do it."

Malitourne spoke up, playing the Greek philosopher. "Look here, there is nothing more beautiful than a little working girl who has a lover like me and is content with her lot."

"Oh, well, that's easy to find," I told him. He bristled.

"Ah! You think a man cannot be loved for himself by a simple flower girl who thinks of nothing but her flowers and her love?"

Malitourne, half drunk, wiped away a tear. I asked if there wasn't a doctor in the house but he continued with heartfelt emotion: "You can't imagine how happy I have been for the last three months since I met Athénaïs—her name is Athénaïs like that of Mme. de Montespan—but she is worth more than the mistress of

---

* Romieu refers to *grisettes* who are working girls but with a lively sex life and additional income. They are not streetwalkers, yet they are also not just milliners or flowershop attendants. The pun Romieu makes on *grisettes* is difficult to reproduce.

Louis XIV. I have taken two pretty rooms for her in the Rue Marie Stuart, up under the roof, and there she sings like a bird. She has already bought natural flowers for the coming spring. . . ."

"Which she will water with her tears," said Roqueplan.

"While she waits," added Prince Belgiojoso, "she will, I am sure, water some pretty artificial flowers."

"Don't make fun of it," answered Malitourne. "You would give anything to be in my place, for Athénaïs is as pure as the driven snow."

We all burst out laughing.

"Why not?" said one of our ladies of the dinner hour. "There are days when I am as pure as the driven snow because I melt in someone's arms."

Malitourne rapped for silence: "I tell you that my mistress is the eighth marvel of the world because she is happy without money."

"I absolutely believe you, O Malitourne!"

"And I don't give her a penny so as to make her love her work! You should see her hands speed along—like a fairy!"

"Why don't you marry her?"

"Marriage would kill my love."

"I move, gentlemen," said the Prince, "that we go and inspect that eighth marvel of the world."

"Very well!" said Malitourne in an imperial tone. "You will find her chastely asleep on a white bed, like a virgin."

"Yes—the sleep of innocence. Let's go, gentlemen!"

Malitourne now seemed hesitant: he wanted and yet did not want to show off the girl whom he had more or less accidentally conquered at a working-class dance. As he had just returned from a mission to Spain he led the naïve girl to believe that he had been ambassador to darkest Africa.

"Look at Malitourne having second thoughts," said Roqueplan. "His Athénaïs is just an invention."

At that taunt Malitourne rose and invited the three of us, with him making the fourth, to enter the Prince's carriage.

Fifteen minutes later we were in the Rue Marie Stuart. We observed the silence of that old house which seemed completely asleep. The concierge readily admitted us for a tip of one franc.

She put on her skirt and lit a candle.

"I believe, sir, that Mlle. Athénaïs is out."

"What, at four in the morning?"

Malitourne said that that was pure calumny. He took the candle from the hand of the concierge and showed us a key, with the air of a man who had no doubts whatever. We entered. Athénaïs had flown, but she had left a note on the mantelpiece. I recognized the curious handwriting and advanced orthography:

My dear freind, if you come bye you won't find me hear I have took a boocay to the lawier. Come thursday in day tomorrow I expec the cosen of the prefec.

I said to Malitourne: "No less than three! Not counting myself who once had the honor of untying the shoes of the lady in question."

He was pale and shocked like a man who had been hit on the head by a flowerpot.

"Why three?" he asked me.

I counted on my fingers: "One: the one whom she has gone to a dance with—or to his house. Two: the one who is supposed to wake her up in the morning. Three: the prefect's cousin who is expected during the day."

What was funniest in the whole business was to see Malitourne, in turn, count on his fingers, not knowing whether he was coming or going. Fortunately the philosopher superseded the lover:

"Well, my friends," he said when the laughter had died down, "all women are the same as La Rochefoucauld said; or rather, you can go to the School for Wives all that you like, you'll never get to know them."

To tell the truth, the Carnival amused me in those days with the various Athénaïs. Perhaps it did because I was twenty-one.

•

Art and Life in London

•

In 1836 Félix Bonnaire, the editor of the Revue de Paris, *sent Houssaye to London to report on an exposition at the Royal Academy. He went across the channel in the company of a young Scots painter named George Arisson (which is presumably Houssaye's way of pronouncing Harrison). Below is the beginning of his first review, which characterizes the differences, as Houssaye saw them, between the French and the English attitude toward artists. The much longer selection which follows explains why Houssaye sent his reviews almost too late to have them printed and paid for.*

(A letter to the *Revue de Paris*, May 1836)

The intractable pride of lords and ladies seems so strange to me here: artists are no more than laborers in the eyes of high society. They do not enter mansions and palaces; only the iron will of a Brummel or a d'Orsay can brave that nonsense because they rule fashion. And even when a painter like Landseer has access to great houses, the mistress of the mansion forces him to paint religiously her Amazon's robe, her gloves, her dogs and her riding crop—and all that with such condescending disdain that one wonders why Landseer does not take that riding crop to whip her as she whips her dogs. The biggest press of the curious at last year's exposition at the Royal Academy was around some family portraits in which Mr. So-and-so had himself painted with his two grooms, his four horses and his fifty dogs. I saw that legendary work: is it an act of defiance of aristocracy, of art or of reason? Everyone in that painted crowd, including Lord So-and-so, had a number which informed the world of name and genealogy of each of these admirable beasts.

That is not all; the painters themselves are separated from each other by the same sense of pride. The paintbrush indicates the distinctions. One artist plays the lord by reason of his fame. Another, a portrait painter, disdains the painter of animals. There is a whole palette of social distinctions, a whole comedy of social reverberations. That is why there are no artistic friendships, no groups, no schools in England.

Perdita

(London, May 1836)

All I remember of the whole exposition is one adorable portrait by Leslie inspired by Shakespeare's *Winter's Tale*. It was of a very lovely girl with a crown of marjoram and daisies, a Perdita casting about handfuls of flowers. Leslie had managed to illustrate the poet's world through the charm of his portrayal.

While I was admiring that Perdita I thought only of Shakespeare's and Leslie's creation. But then, on the following day, my Scottish friend George Arisson told me that nothing would be simpler than to see the original, if I wanted to. That evening between ten and eleven, on the pretext of wanting to sup on ham and pale ale, he took me to a foul-smelling den. I recognized the lovely girl at once across clouds of tobacco smoke. She seemed lost, not in a poetic reverie, but in a hazy intoxication which that tavern induced even in those who did not drink. After all, what do you expect her to do there, that poor abandoned girl? Such is London: when one is not an impeccable lady of society or a family matron, one simply drifts wherever the wind carries. Perdita—Leslie had given her that name and she had forgotten her own—had come to London from Ireland in a small group who had gone in search of luck: she came from one of those huge families we have heard of, who find their house too small and who simply disperse like birds flying the nest.

Perdita had that ineffable beauty of Northern girls: dark hair and blue eyes. Her pale skin sweetly shading into pink, her uncertain smile, her maladroit grace—so much more appealing than studied grace—an animal grace sweeter than all the tricks of a clever mind; a slave girl if there ever was one: sweet if one treated her sweetly; wicked if one treated her wickedly; addicted to beer if one gave her beer.

Unfortunately, Perdita, in spite of her seventeen years, had already drunk so much beer that she had condemned herself to perpetual intoxication. One had to knock three times at her door —I mean to say, call her three times by her name—to recall her to reality.

My traveling companion went up to her and asked her if she modeled still.

"I am thirsty," she replied.

We seated ourselves at her table. As I abhor beer, I ordered champagne.

"Yes," she finally said and gave me her loveliest smile. It seemed as if this had awakened her spirit; it also seemed like a proposition: for she threw herself into my arms like a frightened bird; the hat which had been perched on her head fell to the ground —an unfashionable hat which a duchess' chambermaid had given her.

She seemed even more beautiful to me with her tousled hair undone. I did not speak English well enough to express my admiration to her, though all I really needed of her language were the words of love; my traveling companion was an excellent interpreter who mistranslated everything, but that did not matter; the following day I found myself besotted with her. The painters who had used her as a model had been satisfied to clothe her in color; with her badly fastened dress and her flimsy shawl, she might as well have passed nude through the world. If Perdita retained any fastidiousness at all, it was only for her natural beauty. A sadder frame had never been set about a more charming picture. Beauty obliges those who love it to enhance it. I went to a French dress shop where, for two hundred francs, Perdita was transformed into a duchess, at least in the morning twilight. It made her lose some of her natural grace but at least I could now show myself with her in London. She believed that she had put her hand on a prodigal son who was immediately going to take her to Golconda or to some other country filled with golden marvels. She knew as much French as I did English, just enough to answer me in French when I spoke to her in English. I could not have found a woman more easy to live with, for she had early lost all will power except the will to drink. Nothing could keep her from fondling a glass of bock with her lively, ever-smiling lips. My Scots painter —whom she told twenty times a day that he should meet her sister in Dublin—had himself a Perdita of his own, less lovely than mine but also less drunk. That one was interested only in singing. She sang all day in the English manner; I preferred the silence of my Perdita.

For a few days Perdita shook off her perpetual intoxication. It seemed as if the sunlight of intelligence dried up the clouds and dispersed them. The blue sky appeared, she spoke of Shakespeare and asked me to take her to *Hamlet*. She took a vivid delight in the performance and showed that she could understand the greatness of that poetry. On the following day we took in both the Museum and the Exposition. Though she judged the pictures superficially, she had an occasionally remarkable understanding of color and artistic reality. Leslie's keepsake to her had been a taste for beauty. But all that was no more than a ray of light, a glimmer. That evening she supped for four; I could not tear her away from the tavern; she fell asleep singing and could not be aroused for two hours.

George Arisson's mistress told me that my Perdita once happened to play Sleeping Beauty, that is, she once remained asleep, or half asleep, for a whole week—which, however, did not prevent her from consuming her dinners and suppers.

Though I was not interested in her past, I asked who watched over her during her nocturnal days. Her friend told me that she was a favorite of aristocratic tavern crawlers who did not haggle about money, so that her neighbors took care of her tenderly. I was present at a little scene which showed me that the sporting gentlemen were very fond of Perdita. One evening, after supper, as the four of us were having our cigarettes, two young lords came to seat themselves at the next table, intent on attracting Perdita—to her duty. As their glances did not succeed, one of them imagined that there was a reason behind that virtue and threw some gold pieces before her, which was at the same time an invitation to a boxing match addressed to me and to Arisson. I was acutely aware that I was not on my home grounds though I had already, by force of circumstance, had a lesson in fisticuffs in one bout: one learns to box by boxing. But my Scotsman did not let himself be asked twice. The pub brawler now looked ridiculous because he neither wanted to pick up his money nor withdraw.

Perdita was more charming than ever that evening. She was happy to have shown me that money meant nothing to her.

We threw ourselves into our innocent adventures with all the ardor of youth, and found many pleasures: our breakfasts of minced ham and eggs, our dinners of roast beef and fried potatoes were as gay as songs. So it came to pass that I sent my article to the *Revue de Paris* too late. On my return Bonnaire sent it back to me saying that I had been preceded by other travelers who had not studied the Exposition in taverns. I replied that, if I had been able to send him Perdita, he would not have left her unprinted. That reply made him publish my piece.

Did I mention that I was so bewitched by Perdita's beauty, seeing her weep on the evening before my departure for Paris, that I decided to carry her with me to France while making her swear that she would not drink any more beer? At Dover she told me that she needed to have one more half bottle of pale ale to bid farewell to England; on the boat she proved to me that she would not be seasick if she continued to drink. The Channel was rough and I felt sufficiently unstable on my legs to show an iron will. Perdita continued to drink until she passed out. So we arrived at Calais.

"Captain, what will you charge me if I ask you to repatriate this lovely girl? She wants to see France, but I would like Calais to be the end point of her journey."

"You know very well, sir, what the passage costs."

"Yes, but the stay in Calais?"

"There won't be any stay in Calais, we will simply transfer her; she won't really wake up for three or four days."

I shook the Captain's hand. When we were about to debark I went up to Perdita. She seemed in a dead faint, she was so pale and sweet.

"Isn't she lovely?" I said to the Captain, who looked at her philosophically but perhaps also with some hidden motives.

"Yes," he replied, "there are thousands of them in London who live and die of drink because they are too beautiful to do anything else."

I bent over Perdita to kiss her hair.

"I commend her to you, Captain, she is one of the best creatures I know."

"Rely on me, she comes from the tavern, I'll put her back in the tavern."

A little later I woke up Perdita to finish the journey with her. I loved her beauty, I was not far from loving her herself, I was on the point of tears.

"Adieu, lovely vision," I said sadly. And I left without turning around. In love, he who turns is lost.

When I returned to London almost exactly twenty years later, it was with a much less serious purpose. I had told a lady of society three or four times that I was in love with her. She ended up by telling me that, for the sake of her good name—she was not referring to her husband from whom she was separated—she would not forfeit her honor except in the mists of England, though she had very highly placed friends there. I made the trip with her, a lady friend of hers, Admiral Gudin and two of his fellow officers. It was a very gay journey which made me see London from its other side, the aristocratic, through trips to some of the great houses. I did not have a single evening to look through the taverns. I had some small reputation as a novelist and historian of the eighteenth century; many doors closed to others opened graciously to me. Fortunately I had a cast iron stomach and could defy the devil over glasses of champagne.

In the end I got surfeited with the great world and wanted to catch my breath. I had a friend in London then, thanks to the various revolutions: Alphonse Esquiros. I had gone earlier to say hello to him in his little cottage. Now I took the time to stay with him. We had a lot to tell each other, he about London, I about Paris, for we were the kind of friends who live a little with each other in their minds because we are intellectually of the same family.

He initiated me once more into London nightlife, like a determined explorer who has made himself the historian of that great city without sun and without poetry. I encountered a few of those Parisians whom one nods to from afar on the boulevards and with whom one shakes hands when one is far from Paris. My last evenings were spent in nocturnal wanderings in Byron's, Hogarth's and Shakespeare's country, so much so that I always returned too late for the tea which my lovely traveling companion prepared nightly with her white hands. The next morning, at breakfast, I then told a thousand stories to prove that I had not been myself the evening before. That managed to deceive the lady once or twice, but the third time she told me that she would serve tea no more. I managed to recoup my position, but then told her impertinently that I loved English women in London as much as French women in Paris, which created a gulf between us.

O magic of memory! In all my nightly walks in which I retraced the London of 1835 in the London of 1857, I always searched for Perdita, that is for that vision which had been both so poetic and so banal. What wouldn't I have given to find her once more, even for one hour, sitting in her cloud of smoke, with her halo of youth and beauty all disheveled by drink. One of my friends asked Leslie about her; he barely remembered.

"Don't you know what became of her?"

"I am told she threw herself into the Thames."

"Because of a broken heart?"

"No, because of a raging toothache."

"And she had such lovely teeth!"

·

A Doctrine of Love

·

A curious lady wrote me once: "I want to believe, monsieur, that your memoirs are not confessions from beyond the grave; * we don't want the solemnities of Chateaubriand or Lamartine. They assume too godlike a tone. Fortunately you are not a god, or even a demigod, you write the confessions of a man. But, once you are on stage, don't hide everything behind the curtain. I am perfectly willing to pay my twenty francs for a seat, but I want value for my money: for example, I want to see you seized by passions, even by bad passions. This is said without intending to give offense; you are, after all, the same as other men."

Oh, certainly, madame, I am no better than others. God has cast us from the same mold. The proud ones have made themselves over in marble or terra cotta or bronze. As for me, I cast myself in snow; the snow has melted, but the man of nature has remained, a humble servant of opportunity without need of a pedestal; that's why I make no pretenses in telling you the fortunes of the former Arsène Houssaye.

The world used to say of me—I don't know why—that I was a quasi-Don Juan who loved all women because I never really loved any; that I never bothered with the preliminaries, never took the long way round, and therefore made a massacre of virtue in my time. One referred to one lady, one referred to another, a whole litany. Of course you must discount many stories when it comes to matters of seduction; but when all is said it still seems that more than one beauty was downed on the field of battle. Yes, I was neither an Antinous nor an Apollo; rather, I was a faun both thoughtful and amusing who could bite with a glance as well as with his teeth. Sentimental women said that I had a great heart, cynical women that I had great wit. Pure calumny. I had above all the great ability to show women that love bestows no prize for

---

* Referring to Chateaubriand's *Mémoires d'outre tombe*.

virtue and that virtuous maidens never become saints. As I saw it, God's work was love's work; I never talked about fusions or effusions or transfusions with poetic fervor; I showed the power of the senses in action.

To live, I said, is to love; not to love is contrary to the will of God who is love. That doctrine, which is as good as any, at least at the right moment, took in many fascinating hearts, the more so as I had eloquent eyes and never waited for the next day to prove that my doctrine was the best.

·

The Peach-Colored Shoe

·

Madame, you would like another story; here it is. I am sure you know the lady involved.

It's that young blonde, tall and supple as a reed; her face intelligent, her eyes blue but veiled and deceptive, hiding a soul full of the artful candor of innocence; profile of a virgin with an amorous mouth, teeth that smile well because they are white but also mock well because they are sharp; a finely formed chin that is perhaps a shade too prominent, sloping shoulders that show to advantage the grace and pliancy of the neck. Isn't it true that she spreads a strange air of charm around her? The hair is well set and smiles in its golden disorder; it glides hither and yonder, undulating; it waves without seeming rebellious; it does not resist kisses. The bosom is somewhat hard to discern, but that fine leg with its little arched foot is a stunning piece of sculpture. There is no slender woman who does not also have her promontories. Arms and hands are well fleshed. And what transparently white skin! The pallor of a blonde, the savor of rare fruit. Here is the texture of peaches and of strawberries. Her hair pours out a scent of freshly cut hay and pressed violets.

Where does she come from? What does it matter! She is in Paris; she is furiously Parisian. She will live on love in Paris; in Paris she will also die of love.

I will not tell you more than her first name; her last name is that of a famous family. But what difference does that make? She only loves her first name—Diana.

We met one evening at a ball. She waltzed, and we took a turn at it. We felt that we were cut from the same cloth, in body and in spirit. Here was a real man; here was a real woman. Moreover, in less than five minutes we knew each other—or, rather, we recognized each other—for there are people whom one has always known, be it in this world, be it in another.

Diana was not a prude, she was much too spirited to evade the impudences of certain conversations. There is a German word I wish I could translate, a word which means approximately, a mouth of fire—which is to say that the woman is already corrupted by way of her lips. Words caress them sensuously in passing through; chastity is violated in the act of uttering them. Diana was such a woman.

Aren't all Parisian women like that? Which one is there, even among the purest, who does not get some gratification from strange words which put spirit and senses in heat? We can call it stabbing with grammar.

Diana always collected men around her at salons. Her company was never boring; no one expected to defeat her virtue, but the skirmishes were amusing. She countered attacks with so much sparkle and surprising tartness that all men were enchanted to cross swords with her.

I told her very quickly that she was captivating and that I was going to fall in love with her.

"You will be thoroughly trapped," she said laughingly. "Love is an old-fashioned little gent whom you don't see any more nowadays except in plays, and who never visits me."

"Perhaps; but if you would like to come and meet him at my house, you will find that he is not nearly as old-fashioned as his reputation."

"I do believe you are quite impertinent. Do you really imagine that I am looking for domestic adventures?"

"I don't imagine anything at all; only, as you are virtue personified, you won't be afraid of having a lapse on the way. What is virtue, anyway, if one does not take risks?"

Diana had heard about me from others. She had been told that I was one of the thousand men about Paris who were worth looking at more closely.

After a pause, "What does one do at your house?" she suddenly asked, in an offhand manner.

"Oh, I am a primitive man—no, rather, a mythological man: I wait for Diana."

"And if Diana does not come?"

"I lay a bet that you will not dare to come tomorrow at four on your way to the Bois, because you pass under my windows every day."

"Who knows? You need not make me a challenge."

"I do challenge you."

"What conceit! You perhaps imagine that when I am at your place, under your eyes—"

"Under my lips . . ."

"I will not be able to resist you? That's childish!"

"Well then, come tomorrow, as you clearly don't run any risk."

"You may wait for me forever!"

On the next day I had not the least expectation of Diana. So it was not without some surprise that I saw her enter my small salon unannounced. My manservant had simply let her go upstairs by herself; the rule of the house was, in fact, not to announce women.

Diana wore the heaviest veils—the shield of a fighter. The daring of her glance pierced the veils.

"Well, here I am," she said. "You can see that I am brave. Good-by."

"Good-by? You are not Caesar: You have come, but you have not conquered." I had seized her hand. "One does not come here only to leave again."

Overexcited, nervous and apprehensive, she asked me what would happen.

"I shall tell you."

And I drew her to a sofa on the pretext that one really could not talk anywhere except there.

"I know all your litany beforehand. I know your paradoxes: you are going to prove to me that virtue is not an inborn quality, but something to be conquered or rather to be reconquered. That those who have not battled for it do not have any right to wear its laurels. And other advanced opinions."

Diana refused to sit down. Her eyes were wandering about the room with that ardent curiosity which even the least curious women display.

Suddenly she made a quick, surprised move on seeing a small peach-colored shoe, placed on a side table with the artistry and the coquettishness deserving of an art object.

"What's that slipper doing there?"

"It awaits your foot."

"Do you think, perhaps, that I would not be able to wear it?"

"I would not insult you in such a way. Your foot is quite able to enter anything, even that shoe."

And I quickly lifted up the hem of Diana's dress.

"A divine foot! The foot of Venus striding on her virtue!"

"Don't be so poetic. That little shoe has, I am sure, got a story of its own. Tell it to me."

"Gladly; but as you would fall asleep standing up if I told you that story, you must resolve to sit down."

I made the chaste Diana seat herself on the sofa.

"In a few words, here is that story. I am very fond of small feet. I adored the one which adorned that shoe: a love which had lasted well for six weeks, six weeks which should have lasted six centuries. The tiny foot left never to return. Of all that lost happiness nothing remains except that shoe. Don't doubt that I have kissed it a thousand times. I swore that I would not love again until I found a woman who could wear it."

Diana had risen and picked up the shoe: "And no woman has dared to try that adventure? A camel will easily pass through the eye of a needle, if you don't put it to the test."

"So far, no one. But I am convinced that your little foot is getting impatient."

Diana measured the shoe, front ways and sideways, with her glance.

It was an adorable little shoe which bore all the marks of coquetry, elegance and roguery; it looked provocative, perched on its high heel; its tiny tongue undulated like a serpent.

The temptation became so great that Diana reached down and raised her foot off the ground. It took her two seconds to remove her shoe. "Would you like me to be your waiting woman?" I asked.

"Quiet! Close your eyes, or I won't do it!"

But the little shoe was still on her knee, defying her. It was harder to put on that shoe than to put on the other. For me it was a charming sight—I did not look at it in any other way—Diana forcing her little foot, dressed in a red, finely striped silk stocking, into the little peach-colored shoe.

Among the intimate acts of women, that one—putting on a shoe—is one of the most beautiful. If the eighteenth-century sculptors, libertines like Allegrain, did not sanctify it in marble, it is because marble does not come alive except in nudity.

"Well, here it is," said Diana, suddenly holding her foot heroically—and impertinently—under my nose. She had managed to put the shoe on her foot.

"You are my prisoner!"

"Why?"

"Because this shoe, like Cinderella's slipper, is full of curses. Your foot now belongs to the slipper, and the slipper belongs to me: You understand?"

She refused to understand. I had invested a full quarter of an hour in fruitless eloquence. All was lost—except honor—if I did not carry the day by direct assault.

Diana was a "very true lady" like the ladies of Brantôme, but, like Ninon,* she insisted on being taken by violence.

That was why, an hour later, Théophile, who also entered my salon unannounced, came indiscreetly upon Diana dressed in one brown- and one peach-colored shoe.

When that Parisian beauty took off that shoe toward evening, Parisian love had been all it could be. Three hours of oblivion! Why make eternity of a passing ray of light, of a perfume that evaporates, and of a little shoe that smiles? In the hurricane of life the rainbow shows itself only for an instant.

When we met again, we were delighted to see each other, but we turned our ways again without any more regret. One cannot always put on the same shoe. Diana and I had found other shoes to wear.

---

* The Seigneur de Brantôme (1540–1614), clergyman, soldier and courtier, left a set of courtly memoirs which describe the men and women he knew. Ninon de Lenclos (1615–1705) was for many years the center of Parisian society and amassed a distinguished collection of lovers.

How I Got Married

•

In 1840 Houssaye married Fannie Bourgeois de la Vallette, daughter of an adjutant of Napoleon's youngest brother, King Jerome of Westphalia. He describes the web in which he was caught, at the age of twenty-five, and the subtle or not-so-subtle maneuvers of the chaperons of two young ladies. His and Fannie's first child, a daughter named Edmée, died at the age of three. Houssaye clearly loved the child as he had never loved anyone, and was agonized by her death.

•

Fannie

•

In these sketchy stories, these portraits that evaporate like dreams, I have not put my heart on stage because my heart was not involved to any extent. How happy are they whom love carries to the shore one fine day after many perilous crossings! Some wise man of antiquity once said that once we are in Love's company we can never be sure where he will lead; we sing beautiful operatic duets with him, until the day when the scene changes and we sing tragic dirges not from the lips but from the heart, until our voice breaks.

So it was that, without watching, through the force of love, through the charm exerted by virtuousness, I was gently led to the altar.

It was a complete change. After boisterous festivities, is it not delightful to go to the country, to breathe fresh mountain air, to dream at the edge of quiet pools, and to enjoy, together, the solitudes of the forest? For those who have tasted too much of the life of Paris, that rustic serenity is marriage. In changing the climate the whole attitude toward life is changed. Those who are always bored continue to be bored, but those who are seeking for the new find unexpected pleasures. A dullard can spend a quarter century next to a woman without ever getting to know and understand her, like a miser who cannot enjoy his fortune. A dullard keeps his woman in the kitchen, not knowing how to use his mind, his heart, his soul, his passion in love; a dilettante, on the other hand, if he lights upon a real woman, opens up a rare book which he rereads with pleasure a thousand times. I had the good fortune of being a dilettante.

In the evening I often went to the Luxembourg Gardens to refresh my mind after its labors. One evening, walking with Édouard l'Hôte, I saw a fleeting figure whom I took for a shadow, for she seemed so light and slender in her long black dress; she was as lovely as can be with her fine supple dark hair and her eyes as blue as the sky. She seemed the ideal of femininity, as if Prud'hon had drawn her.

"Look," I said to l'Hôte, "there goes the picture of my life."

"A woman in mourning!" he exclaimed.

"Yes," I answered. "I sense some invisible and fatal bond between that figure and myself."

I would have pursued that young woman, or rather, young girl, for that she really was, but she seemed like one whom one does not pursue. I felt that I did not have the right to follow the same road and kept my distance, so great was my sense of respect. Moreover, she was accompanied by her grandmother. A feeling of chastity enveloped her that I would have profaned, I felt, had I followed after them.

"And yet," I said to my friend, "I have a real sense of sorrow to have seen her and to think that I will never see her again."

We continued to talk of these half-amorous encounters in which two souls are united for a moment with one glance.

That very evening I went for tea to the house of a lady of fashion in the Faubourg Saint-Germain, to whom my cousin O'Connor had presented me. She was the daughter of a former director of the Opéra and the Comédie Française, who had been married at an early age to some naval person who became mayor of the Tenth District after his retirement. You can imagine my surprise when I saw that young lady enter accompanied by her great-uncle, the famous botanist Dr. Fée.

I was strongly moved. I rose and bowed to her, and refused to continue a story I had been telling. But after a few moments the lady of the house told me that she would not let me pass on to another subject.

"Very well! I'll continue," I said.

But instead of continuing the story, some adventure I had traveling with Gérard de Nerval, I at once began to improvise a novel whose opening chapter was my encounter in the Luxembourg Gardens with the girl in black. Of course I took care not to include myself in it.

The girl, who had vaguely recognized me, was somewhat surprised. I developed a theory about the predestination of souls, of loves begun in a previous existence which must continue in the present in order to reach some seventh heaven. To support my theory, I told of some friend of mine who had been on the point of marrying a great beauty who loved him, and whom he thought he loved. That friend had met in the Tuileries Gardens, at the very hour when he had gone there to dream about his fiancée, a girl he had never seen before but who he nevertheless felt he knew much better than the other—even though he had been in the company of that other one every evening for many months. The lady of the house interrupted me to say that my friend had hallucinations. If he thought he loved his fiancée, then he loved her, but if one glance from a stranger had sufficed to carry him to the seventh heaven, then he surely was not worthy of happiness like an ordinary mortal.

The girl spoke up, "I am not romantic, I am a fatalist: what shall be shall be. If it is written on high that his fiancée shall not become his wife no one can change it, neither the notary with his marriage contract nor the mayor with his sash."

"Now really," Dr. Fée said laughingly, "you might think that my niece can read the stars."

"Not quite," she said gaily. "I am satisfied with palmistry; whatever is written on high is also written in the palm of your hand."

I took a chance, saying, "Would you give me your hand, mademoiselle?"

"Yes and no," she said with cheerful openness. She held out her hand, asking her uncle, "Will you allow me to have my fortune told?"

"Certainly," he answered. "But I would not allow it if I thought that you would be told one single truth."

"Why?"

"Because life must be lived without knowing the future."

"But, uncle, that's as if you told me we must walk without knowing our way."

"Who knows the way when he starts out?"

Nevertheless, I took the girl's hand, a sweet little hand; I took it in at one glance, following its manifold lines with an indiscreet eye. I lost myself so completely in the geography of that unexplored world that I said nothing as if I wanted to keep my discoveries to myself.

"Well," said the lady of the house, "what do you see in that hand?"

I had paled at seeing all too many broken lines.

"There are here," I said, to hide my emotion, "marriage and children like in a fairy tale, but all of life is a fairy tale after all."

"No," said my cousin O'Connor, "life is a novel."

"No," said Dr. Fée gravely, "life is a history."

While that was being said I continued to decipher aloud the meaning of the lovely hand so gracefully held out.

When I had finished, one attractive lady said that I sounded like a charlatan who translated from the Hebrew without knowing any of it—which, however, did not prevent her from giving me her hand in order to know if she would have a second youth. When I told her not only of a second but a third youth with a complete renewal of summer, she said firmly that she believed in the art of fortunetelling. I had confirmed her faith.

"By heaven," she said, "it seems clear that that young lady is the only one here who does not believe in it."

And, after a moment of silence: "I forbid you to give it another minute's thought."

Dr. Fée had asked for his carriage. I gently picked up once more the girl's hand as a sign of farewell. I made a detour on my way home in order to pass through the Luxembourg Gardens as if to see my vision once more through the fence.

"It was no more than a vision," I told myself sadly.

·

Yvonne

·

Jules Janin and I often went to a delightful and hospitable house in the Rue du Four-Saint-Germain. It was a patriarchal establishment, from the ancient hosts to the ancient appearance of pictures and furnishings. Nothing was modern. The master and mistress of the house shared more than a century and a half between them, but they loved youth and received a whole collection of young women and girls each week, who seemed more or less part of the family. The dinners were festive, we danced, had theatricals and enjoyed ourselves to the fullest; even Janin dared to take a turn at the waltz. How can one avoid falling in love in such a setting? In love I was, to the point of madness—the madness of marriage; and everybody around me said that that madness was wisdom. I had fallen for the loveliest pair of eyes in the world, great dark eyes, veiled and deep, belonging to a figure like that of a Roman Madonna, the kind who lives and dies for love. There was nothing French about her character, no Parisian unreserve. Given completely over to dreams and to love, such women are closed off like a fortress and no sense of curiosity ever makes them open the window.

To some extent it was Lully who held us captive. I still played the violin at the time, and she played the piano like Chopin. Ten years before Gounod, we led each other astray in the lost world of old French music. In a word, because of Lully, or because of the duets of violin and piano, or because of her twenty years and my twenty-five, we adored each other. It reached the point where we could no longer live—she without hearing me, I without seeing her. I amused her spirit, she was the joy of my eye and soul.

We passed almost the entire winter in that way. Our love, so mysterious to us, was well known to everyone else. Everyone asked, "When are you getting married?"

We were so happy in that iridescent atmosphere that we were afraid of touching reality. I ought to add that, in spite of the paradisical feeling engendered by that house, I continued my Bohemian existence as unrestrainedly as if there were two men within me; that sort of thing was quite common in Paris at the time.

All that could not last long. The grandparents of the girl, Mlle. Yvonne H———, asked me into the small drawing room one day and told me that they were terribly upset by what was going on. They had never wanted that delightful child to marry an artist, they had intended her for a high official or a diplomat, in a word, for a serious match. But as she had the misfortune to be in love with me, they were willing to sacrifice their dreams and to give me her hand in marriage.

That tiny white hand—I had never asked for it, but now I answered with a simple: "With all my heart."

And from here on decision followed decision. The wedding was to be during Easter week. That would give me time to see my parents, to find an apartment to make our nest, in a word, to prepare myself for the rigors of marriage. At that point Mlle. H——— was called in, who was too straightforward and too dignified to listen behind the keyhole. When she understood what was happening, two lovely tears came into her eyes, she bent over to kiss her grandmother, but I took her into my arms and drank her tears. Her grandfather wanted to say something, but she put her hand on his lips. "No," she said, "I understand, all is said, I am happy, but let us talk about something else. Have you read the evening papers?"

It seemed to that lovely girl, as it did to me, that all the blue-birds would fly away if we came too close to reality. We ended the evening with Lully, Mozart and Gluck, discreet friends who would not brutally violate our hearts and drive away our dreams; with *Armide, Le Nozze di Figaro, Orpheus* we would continue to dream.

Not long after that, we had the engagement dinner followed by a ball. Though it was intended to be a family affair, some of my artist friends were invited. A rather serious dinner therefore turned quite gay in the end. I noticed nevertheless that the brow of my lovely fiancée was clouded. She looked at me with some curious sense of sadness even though she attempted to smile. No matter how I tried to talk to her with my eyes, she seemed upset: she had forebodings that did not deceive her.

After we had risen from the table and I had conducted her grandmother to the salon, I went over to her, took her hand and said softly, "Don't we love each other any more?"

She replied with an adorable glance which seemed like a sun-beam chasing the clouds. She served coffee with her accustomed grace, oblivious to all the admiration directed at her. There was something divine about Yvonne; she did not seem to touch the ground. Her golden voice was music, her smile spread youth all around her, and everyone said of me, "How fortunate he is!"

I thought myself fortunate, too, for having met up with beauty, charm, and wealth, without having done anything myself to elicit that good fortune.

·

The Ball

·

One by one the guests began to arrive for the ball; a waltz started the dancing. The waltz had begun to charm everyone then, those who took a turn at it and those who watched. It was the age of the amorous but chaste waltz: a lady did not abandon herself orgiastically to it and did not rest voluptuously against her partner. Mlle. Yvonne had not waltzed before, and I carried her off into the whirlwind, somewhat frightened by it, but more delightful than ever. Then came a quadrille which at once became quite brilliant and joyful. Janin set the pace; he danced with Yvonne, opposite me, while I had one of her friends as my partner.

During the second quadrille something momentous occurred. Destiny showed its hand. At the first note an extremely lovely girl was seen to enter, accompanied by a lady of fashion: Mme. de Sainte-Preuve. My fiancée, delighted to see these ladies at her ball, even though she hardly knew them, came to tell me that I must immediately ask Mlle. Fannie to dance. I went straight to her. Imagine my surprise when I recognized, in that girl in white, the girl in black whom I had seen in the Luxembourg Gardens. You may remember that I had exclaimed: "There goes my destiny!" I remembered these words now; I stopped in front of her and remained silent. She did not seem to understand but at last I regained my voice and asked her to dance. She accepted gaily and we took off. I had seen Mme. de Sainte-Preuve a few times; she is the Baronesse Molitor now. She was the point of departure of our conversation. Women sense everything; Mlle. Fannie said at once, "Are you the one, Monsieur, who is going to marry Mlle. H———?"

"Do you believe it?" I answered in a distraught and skeptical tone.

"Where could you find a more beautiful woman?"

"And you?"

Silence. I was thunderstruck, I could hardly breathe, my heart was pounding.

At that moment, as we were passing along the line of ladies, I was recalled to my senses by Mlle. Yvonne.

"Take care," I said to myself, "this is not a romantic novel."

How did it happen that I found myself seated between Yvonne and Fannie at the midnight supper?

"Do you know," Mlle. H——— said to me, "that you have eyes only for your neighbor?"

"Don't you know that I have you in my heart, and that other women are only birds of passage?"

"Oh, I am not jealous, for if it is written on high that you won't marry me, there is nothing I can do to keep you. But tell me the truth: isn't Mlle. Fannie more beautiful than I?"

"You know very well that you are more beautiful than the most beautiful because I love you."

But I turned back to the other side, from gallantry or from attraction. I had hardly turned to Mlle. H——— when I wanted to talk to Fannie once more.

At the end of the ball Mlle. Fannie had just left after shaking hands with Mlle. Yvonne.

"Until tomorrow!" I said to my fiancée.

Her grandmother murmured with a smile, "You may kiss her."

Yvonne bent her head, my lips merely touched her forehead with a distraught kiss which did not come from the heart and did not go to it. It was like a break.

·

Always, Never!

·

Mme. de Sainte-Preuve had reproached me that evening for never coming to see her. The next day, when I was leaving a jeweller's shop in the Palais-Royal, my mind occupied with wedding presents, I saw her carriage in the Place du Carrousel. She stopped and called me over with a nod of the head.

"What does that mean?" she said. "Here you go and massacre all hearts; do you know that my niece is mad about you?"

"I don't believe a word!"

"It's true, all morning long she has spoken of no one but you. Hurry up and marry Mlle. H——— or I won't answer for anything."

Her words troubled me more than I care to say: I was both overjoyed and devastated.

"Your niece," I replied, "is a lovely cynic who will never love anyone but herself; moreover she is far too successful in society to be bowled over by the first man who comes along."

"Not exactly the first man; and besides, every woman obeys her destiny."

"Destiny again!" I exclaimed. "Do you really believe in that nonsense?"

"And how! Look here, it is your destiny and mine to meet today; why? I don't know, but you can be sure that our two destinies are mingling now only to deceive each other right after. Whatever it is, hurry up and get married."

With those words Mme. de Sainte-Preuve held out her hand and signed to her coachman to drive home. As for me, I immediately went to Yvonne's house. Though that lovely creature had forbidden me to make diamonds part of my wedding gift, I wanted to show her a pair of diamond and pearl earrings. I had hardly entered when her grandmother said, "Do you know that Yvonne is still in her room?"

"Why?"

"Why? I don't know. All I know is that she's been weeping a lot and is still weeping."

"Allow me to go and see her with you."

"No, but I shall ask her to get up, even if only for a moment."

Yvonne refused to rise. I asked her grandmother to bring to her, together with the earrings, a simple line: "I want to see you today, tomorrow, always." She answered with a single word: "Never."

I showed that word to her grandmother who said, "That's childishness, I'll go and get her to come here."

Yvonne actually did come soon after, very pale and faltering. I wanted to kiss her as before, but she turned away and held out her hand. I was about to kiss it when I felt the earrings drop into my hand.

"I have come," she said, "to bring you these jewels. You know that I do not want them."

No doubt my own evident sadness reopened her heart: she had at first intended to return to her room but now she sat down by the fireplace.

"That's better," said the grandmother. "Be happy, because you really are."

She left the room to leave us alone together: a sad meeting. In vain we tried to recapture the paradise of our love: the door had closed on it. I finally left, telling her that I would be back for tea that evening.

We had not mentioned Mlle. Fannie but her memory had darkened our meeting for both of us. Strange illusions of love: no matter how I tried, I could no longer convince myself of Mlle. Yvonne's sovereign beauty, so strongly had her rival cast her shadow.

That evening I had promised to go to a ball where Victor Hugo's two sons were expected, at the house of a president of the Chamber of Deputies, Rue de la Cerisaie. I had earlier decided not to go, but destiny itself handed me my white tie. And I had hardly arrived at the ball when I saw Mlle. Fannie enter in the full glory of her loveliness, the full triumph of admiration. All the young men threw themselves upon her to obtain a waltz or a quadrille. I alone pretended not to see her, so strong was my fear of her. I could not look at her without seeing Mlle. H——— before my eyes. But, passing near me, she said, "You know that I have reserved the first waltz for you."

A few more minutes and I would have been gone, but how can one take flight from so much grace and so much charm? I was caught in the golden net, I danced with her.

When the hour came to go to tea, I had forgotten Mlle. H_____. When I remembered, it was too late. I left nevertheless but could not find a hackney cab. It was pouring rain. I went back in again, saying to myself, "The die is cast."

I never spoke to Mlle. H_____ again.

Yvonne refused to receive me the next morning. Her grandmother, who also knew that I had spent the night at a ball where Mlle. Fannie had been, told me that I was behaving abominably. I was quite unable to convince her that all had been the work of chance and that I was still keeping my word. She replied that it was better for her beloved granddaughter to be unhappy for a day than for her whole life.

I left half out of my mind, seeing myself at the end of all my good fortune.

That evening a friend of the family came to see me to talk about Mlle. H_____'s desperate unhappiness; he said, though, that she had too much fortitude not to conquer her heart. He brought me the earrings in an envelope which also contained some verses I had written for her.

"You are losing a proud heart," he told me, "but as you are intent on marriage I advise you to marry Mlle. Fannie."

"Marriage is absolutely not our intention."

"Obviously. I am not accusing you of anything, by the way, because you are giving up a full-size dowry for a rather small one."

"Oh, I swear to you, if I ever marry I shall not count the money because the only value received in marriage, as far as I am concerned, is the lady in question."

"You are right. The thing that consoles me in your case is that Mlle. Fannie will be a real wife just like Mlle. Yvonne."

I wandered distractedly about the quais all evening like a soul in purgatory: I had left home to go to the theater but now I only wanted to be alone. What should I do? Re-enter Mlle. H_____'s house by force, to convince her that my heart and life belonged to her? Or abandon myself to the flow of events and break my will so as not to break my heart?

When midnight sounded from the tower of the Institute I was crossing the Pont des Arts for the twentieth time, still unresolved, longing in turn for those two pictures who had taken hold of my soul. No matter how I tried to tell myself that one simply cannot love two women at one time, I felt taken, retaken and held first by one, then the other.

I could not sleep. When morning came, the ambassador of the previous evening rang my bell. He told me that he had been to see the other party, that all was not ended yet, that I should go once more to see the grandmother.

Should I have gone? At noon I received a note from Mme. de Sainte-Preuve asking me to come.

At that moment I realized at last that my love for Mlle. Fannie was the stronger. It was with a joyous heart, in fact, that I ran to Mme. de Sainte-Preuve. She did not beat about the bush.

"Do you want to marry my niece?"

I answered yes because I could not possibly bring myself to say no.

"But what about your planned marriage?"

"The door there has been closed to me since yesterday."

"Then I am picking up a shipwrecked man?"

"You are disposing of your niece's heart—do you know if she even wants to marry?"

"Yes—if it is you."

"You astound me!"

"What do you think your astonishment is compared to mine? For the last six months she has refused every single suitor, every one of whom is worth more than you—rich men, wise men, saints. And now she says she will be very happy to give you her hand!"

And Mme. de Sainte-Preuve continued smilingly, "My niece is consoled by the thought that Mlle. H——— would have been very unhappy with you—in other words, she is saved from a bad match."

Mme. de Sainte-Preuve had hardly finished when I, as if in a dream, saw Mlle. Fannie appear, more delightful than ever in day-time clothes.

"Mademoiselle," I said to her, "I feel as if I were reading a fairy tale. I have not yet done the three heroic deeds that would make me worthy of marrying a princess."

"Perhaps not, but is it not a heroic deed to marry me?"

·

The Portrait

·

I had reckoned without my father. A few days later I arrived in Bruyères full of sweet hope. But my father furrowed his brow at the first suggestion of marriage.

"You are no more born to marry than I to become a cardinal. I'll never give my consent to that stupidity."

"But, father, you yourself did marry, for which I am grateful."

"I was sure that I could provide for my wife."

"Rest assured, mine won't die of hunger: I've got great fortitude."

"Is she rich?"

"No, but she is beautiful. Didn't you, a rich man yourself, marry a woman who had nothing? And you were completely right. I have always been moved by that kindness of yours."

My father remained completely unmoved.

"I am delighted," he said, "that you have one good thing to say about me."

"My dear father, for heaven's sake, don't joke! I am deeply in love with a girl and want to marry her."

"All right then. I forbid you to marry a girl without dowry. If you are that intent on marriage, I have a number of women on hand. And why, in that case, did you refuse last year to marry the niece of a cabinet minister who would have brought you a sub-prefect's job as dowry?"

"Because I did not love that man's niece!"

"So much the worse for you, and, perhaps, so much the better for that girl you want to marry."

"For goodness' sake, father, let me either be happy or unhappy on my own."

"No, I refuse to give my consent."

The word consent was meant to say: "I refuse to give you an income."

I turned to my mother and implored her to break that iron will, but she did not really support me because she saw some madness in this, too. In vain I told her that a dowry was of no concern to me; she knew well enough that life in Paris was financially beyond a simple pen-pusher like me. I was in despair. To hide my tears I went up to my chamber and gave myself over to my grief. I saw the shipwreck of my youth, the waste of my life. I considered marriage without my father's consent, but Fannie's family would not have agreed to that.

After a terrible depression I recovered my will power, because I was never the kind of man who let himself be defeated by circumstance. I wrote to Émile Wattier to paint me a watercolor of Mlle. Fannie as quickly as he could.

He produced a small masterpiece: her beauty reflected all the goodness of her soul. I placed the picture before my father's eyes without saying a word:

"What's that?" he asked me later during the day.

"You know what it is," I answered.

He replied with two words: "Marry her."

Houssaye returned to Paris, still conscience-stricken about the abandonment of Yvonne, no matter how he took fate as his excuse. "In America," he writes, "where young people flirt with incredible abandon, my action would have seemed completely natural; in France, where flirting had not yet spread in the social world, I was accused of playing with the pangs of love."

But all was not over. When he rushed to Mme. de Sainte-Preuve's side, she calmly told him: "Stop. We are no longer talk-

ing about marriage." A rival had appeared on the scene while they were waiting for Houssaye Senior to make up his mind, a handsome colonel, a friend of the Duc de Nemours, and Mme. de Sainte-Preuve, sensing the possibility of a more advantageous match, was rather cold to Houssaye. Houssaye was ready to strangle her; first she tore him from Yvonne, and then she denied him Fannie.

All ended well, however, and we never heard what became of the colonel.

·

The Wedding

·

Three weeks later I entered St. Thomas Aquinas Church, with a happy heart, Mme. de Sainte-Preuve on my arm, following my father who was leading Mlle. Fannie. Would you believe it? The first person who struck my eyes was Mlle. Yvonne, who had regained her sovereign beauty, though the pallor of her cheeks was still evident. I was struck to the heart. Mme. de Sainte-Preuve had just given me the wedding ring, telling me that there had not been time enough to have it engraved. I was so shocked that I let the ring drop. I vainly tried to find it on the floor. Great consternation. Several friends got down to search. I asked one of them, Gérard de Nerval, to run to the nearest jeweller to buy another one just before Mlle. Yvonne, who had found the lost ring, handed it to Mme. de Sainte-Preuve. So it came to pass that, when Gérard returned with the ring he had bought, I now had two for the ceremony. Because of that, my wife said more than once, in those rare moments of disagreement between us: "You made a mistake about the ring."

·

Edmée

·

God had given us a daughter. When I say that God had given her to us, my heart feels a revulsion; for that daughter, who was a delight, died in her dawn. However fully man submits to the decrees of providence, he will never comprehend such a bitter joke: children who come to us like grace from heaven, and whom death carries off in their first flower! Are we confronted with any more than blind fate? If God breaks our hearts, does He do it to create the wellsprings of tears in us? Yet, whatever the horrible pain of losing the light of the home, one would still want to suffer a thousand deaths to pay for the joys of parenthood. And even our desolation carries consolation within itself: to weep for those we love is to love them still. There is a sense of harmony in old griefs.

For three years, we had a continuous holiday not only in Paris but at my father's house in Bruyères because of that child, endowed with all the graces.

A sweet lark at sunrise, a warbler in the morning, a bouquet of roses at midday, a vision of the future cavorting in house or garden, little hands one wants to hold like a treasure, unexpected questions which draw us back to childhood, golden hair glittering in the sun, blue eyes whose every glance drives away a cloud, all these joys lost in a day because God willed it or because a doctor did not know how to combat death. I recall this only for those who had children and who lost them; others would not understand my pain.

However great the pain of seeing one's father or mother die— we resign ourselves because that is the law of fate; but to have a child torn from us who is not intended to die before us—that is heartbreak and desolation. There are some near-mortal wounds that slowly close; but that one bleeds every day.

Mme. Houssaye had lost her grandmother. The next day, when I came home, I saw my little girl all dressed in black: that was the first blow. I wanted her to wear a different dress, but the following day, the day of the funeral, she again came to me in her black dress and she seemed more pale than usual. After the funeral I found her asleep. For the second time I had her dressed in white because I wanted to go for a walk with her on the Quai d'Orsay.

"Isn't grandma dead any more?" she asked.

"No, she'll visit you."

"Tell her not to come, she scares me."

I tried to play with Edmée. She had her hoop with her, but she did not have the strength to play with it. She loved stories, and I told her one: she interrupted me to tell me that the lady in it should not die.

No matter how I tried to tell a funny story, she did not enjoy it. We were sitting on a bench opposite the Council Chamber; suddenly I noticed that she had fallen asleep; her head had rolled backwards. I carried her home. We lived on the Quai Malaquais then, and my wife was at home weeping for her grandmother. I did not tell her anything, but I had the presentiment that she should save her tears. Alas! Tears are inexhaustible. Edmée wanted to go to bed and I rushed to my cousin Bouillard, but that great physician was wrapped up in politics. He had just been made a Deputy and he talked only about the Chamber. First chapter of fatal events. When he came toward eight in the evening, he was too preoccupied with his speech to pay much attention to my child. He looked at her, murmured the "that's nothing" of the doctor who does not know what to diagnose. He left without giving any orders. The next day he came on his way to the Chamber. The child was asleep. I wanted to wake her up; he said no—the politician in him was in a hurry. He came back that evening and, no matter what I did, he would not talk about anything except Guizot and Thiers, "those political marionettes," because he was a proper republican, one of those who aspired to the Senate under the Empire. He later contented himself with the Academy of Science. During that visit my little girl said to me, looking at a picture of her grandmother's, "A Girl Picking Grapes": "We must growl at her, she does not want to give me her grapes."

"That's her fever," said Dr. Bouillard. "If she wants grapes, give them to her, but please be assured, she is teething, and that'll be the end of it."

It was the end of it, all right.

As soon as the doctor had left, I hastened to Chevet's to buy a box of grapes. The poor child smiled and picked out a few; her mother put some grapes to her lips but she did not want to part her teeth. I rushed to a famous pediatrician and brought him back with me, not without difficulty. He said that Dr. Bouillard was correct, there was no danger, and we should wait. I tried to talk to him about brain fever but he refused to listen. He ordered a bath for her and left mumbling that if anything needed to be done he would do it the next day.

When the child was in the bath, I saw her head fall forward and her eyes cloud over. Her mother went out weeping to call one of her friends who waited in the drawing room, Mme. Jules Le Fèvre, the wife of the poet. While I was alone with Edmée, holding up her head in the bath, Théophile Gautier came in. Théo knew medicine as clearly as he knew poetry.

He looked intently at Edmée.

"It is plain murder," he said, "to put that little girl into a bath."

I was frightened by Edmée's eyes because she looked at me without seeing me. She was no longer able to see me, or her mother!

I went to get a third doctor. Théo said, "A third ignoramus."

What did that third physician do? Nothing. He asked what had been done, and naturally he approved of everything.

"The child wants to sleep," he said, "she should be allowed to. Tomorrow morning I'll be back and consult with my two colleagues."

Théo shouted indignantly, "Doctor, you are an ass! The one who ordered the bath is an ass, the one who could not predict meningitis is an ass: don't you see that that poor little child is dying!"

The great doctor picked up his hat and never came back.

I am unable to portray all the despair. Mme. Jules Sandeau had come; my wife and her two friends watched over Edmée like three mothers, but they were three saints watching over a grave. For six days this went on, amidst tears and sighs. Edmée had lost none of her beauty even though her open eyes did not see anything any longer. Science ran dry by the side of that cradle. Only Dr. Bouillard returned; he was worthy of his name; he accused himself so that no one else would accuse him. Soon after he drove politics out of his house, realizing that his place should be at the School of Medicine or at the bedside of the sick. But the fatal blow had been struck; all his genius could not save Edmée, "his dear little cousin," he said, himself in tears.

We waited bent over her cradle. All who saw her, still so lovely, untouched as yet by the mark of death, exclaimed with a sense of hope, "That child couldn't possibly die."

But the poor child, so gay and boisterous once, could not utter anything except an occasional cry of pain. She opened her eyes but she did not see any longer; three or four times during the night or during the day she seemed to hear and even see her mother who spoke to her with so much sweetness and love.

How often in these terrible twelve days, when Heaven punished us for too much good fortune, did we save her and lose her in the same moment!

My heart was numb, or if I felt it I could not endure its anguish and revolt. We were approaching the thirteenth day: the poor little child had battled her illness to its furthest reaches. But nature fought in vain, death crossed the threshold of the house. It was night time, eleven o'clock had just struck. A few dear friends were there, saying heartfelt prayers around the cradle. Her mother held the child's hand. We gave our soul to her, bending over her, but what power has the soul over death, two blind ones meeting each other.

Minute by minute we heard the breath grow weaker. Suddenly a divine smile illuminated that dear angel's head: the soul had flown away. We had loved her so much and now we had to cover her with a shroud. I was out of my mind, and yet I remember that smile, a smile which no one on earth can imagine. And I remember that poor woman who, as broken as I, threw herself upon my heart crying, "I don't have a child any longer."

Two more days she was watched over with love. All those who had known her alive wanted to see her once more: she was dressed for her journey to heaven, a crown of white roses on her head. Death is full of strange caprices; cruelly it amused him to make that little child even lovelier; he perpetuated her divine smile, he spilled on her cheeks a tint of roseate marble. What dazzling purity on that lily cut at the first ray of morning! How did that ineffable smile come to be? Had God appeared to her, at the supreme moment, with a choir of little angels? Is that deliverance from mortal chains, then, such a great joy for the soul about to rise on high?

When the child had once more become an angel, we put her white dress on her for ever. I had burned the black dress to assuage fate. To keep her better in my heart I remained, after her death, for two days in front of her funeral cradle gazing with all my love on that vanished dream. Funeral cradle—two words which do not want to touch each other!

One by one I became aware of the transformation of death. Hédouin wondered so much at that inexpressible serenity, that angelic smile, that loveliness which was no longer a work of life, that he wanted to try and reproduce that divine expression in all its poetry.

Suddenly I saw him grow pale. "Don't you see," he said to me, much moved, "the transformation in that figure? Death is at work: The lashes move, the smile changes, the eye grows bigger, her features deepen. That is no longer a girl of three: since this morning, death means to show you what life would have shown. Your little girl would have been as she looks now, at six or seven years. Death moves so fast that she will pass through days and years as if on the wings of an eagle."

Strange labor of death! Edmée died three years old, but her twelve days of illness had already added two more. The day she died, her features deepened; more during the night. The next morning she had the figure of a girl of ten; the following day her mother cried, "Oh, my heaven! I think I see her all in white at her first communion!"

The hearse had been ready for an hour. I had laid Edmée to sleep among the only flowers which she knew by their name and their scent: violets. I spread them over her. My heart had passed into my hands. My mother, in tears, gently drew a veil over her body. All was over, then! I had become blind because I could no longer see my child. I fled, my hands still full of violets.

Lamartine

•

It was in the winter of 1845 that I met Lamartine. I happened to be seated next to him at a dinner of M. de Salvandy's. Though he was the person most in demand by all the guests, he was kind enough to turn frequently to me to chat about poetry. Poets who have become politicians always lie in wait, in the end, for a chance to turn poets once more. He talked about himself, but he also talked about me. Each book has a destiny. A booklover had once forgotten a little volume entitled *La Poésie dans les bois* on Lamartine's table. If I had sent these verses to the great poet, he would never have read them, because in those days he received a whole library every day, like wave following wave. But a volume whose pages had already been cut drew his attention; he took some time and read my poems. What did he see in them? He told me that they seemed pure Theocritus to him, especially such poems as "Le Foin" and "Le Blé." I don't recall anyone who ever read my work as closely. Lamartine cordially offered to receive me both formally and informally, in Paris and at Saint-Point. He proved to me that this was not merely an accolade of politeness: he thanked M. de Salvandy that evening for his dinner partners, not only because he had been on Mme. de Salvandy's right, but because he had also had a poet on his own right.

M. de Lamartine received on Sundays. On the following Sunday I went to his house in the Rue de l'Université, where the world of politics had already begun to extinguish the world of letters. It was something like a Prime Minister's reception, for Lamartine was already Minister of Ideas. Some people scoffed at his romantic poetry, but he ended up by imposing his will by the sheer force of his genius. It is very hard to play the role of a great man in France if one really is a great man, and it is so easy to seem one if one is not. It had been the same story for Victor Hugo. The obscure has an uncanny attraction in politics. Governments are always afraid of strong personalities.

I continued to visit Lamartine. I lunched and dined at his house in very varied and changing company. Much money was spent on entertainment, but it was money wasted because everything was mismanaged: the great wines were emptied into carafes while the ordinary ones were offered in their own bottles. His studio was a real working library, where a man would pick up the book he is not looking for because he is unable to find the book he seeks. With that exception, the hospitality was stimulating.

I can hardly describe the flames of enthusiasm that steadily rose in homage to that Olympus. The final generation of romantic ladies wore itself out with idolatry; he was no longer a poet to these women, he was a Messiah. France always has one man who is the man of the hour; then it was Lamartine.

When he was writing his *History of the Gironde*, I gave him some letters by Condorcet.

"I'll pay you back," he told me, "by giving you some pre-publication pages for *L'Artiste*."

He forgot about his promise. One day I went to see him, and though he had given orders he would see no one that day, he received me.

"I have not forgotten you, my friend. Let us talk while we have lunch, after which I'll give you the promised excerpt."

We talked. He had paper on his knees and an inkstand near the mantelpiece. He began to write without ceasing to talk, or to listen to me. He was simply one of those men who are able to do two things at any one time.

"What are you writing?" I asked him, seeing him rapidly fill the third sheet of paper in his beautiful handwriting.

"Well, I am writing the chapter for *L'Artiste!*"

I did not refer to that topic again because none of our conversation concerned the Gironde. I think that he recalled some annoying things said to him by Mme. Recamier, and we both made derogatory remarks about his neighbor at the Abbaye-aux-Bois. When lunch was announced the chapter he had intended for me was finished.

The Tears of Mme. Dorval

•

One would like to imagine that passion always remains the same. Those who, like myself, have lived among the women of the early romantic era, among the late romanticists of the second Empire, and the naturalists of today, have learned that the art of love, like all things, undergoes the changes imposed by that tyrant called fashion.

For example, could we in our day find a Dorval among those afflicted by the passions? Would that not make an interesting study of changing customs for some budding Balzac?

It was a strange destiny, that, of the actress who married twice in order to have a support in her life, and who twice became the support of her husband. The first was an actor-adventurer named Allan who sought his fortune riding Thespis' chariot. He found it amusing to wallow in misery, to marry a girl of fifteen, to deceive her the day after and to subject her to all the trials of the life of an itinerant actress in the provinces.

That hardy creature, who was to become one of the great stars of the nineteenth century, submitted to it all because she felt a divinity within herself which consoled her for everything. Allan died of overwork and of his pleasures. She then called herself

Mme. Allan-Dorval but did not keep the name of her husband very long. Mme. Dorval was good enough, a romantic name, foredoomed in verse and prose—"like mine" as Mme. Valdor, her friend, said.

Poor Valdor! She, too, died of overwork—though not of her pleasures—because her acting also was like casting hot flames at the orchestra pit, baring her very life on stage every time. Some actresses act as if they wore masks; Mme. Dorval acted from the heart.

Poor woman of genius! It was not enough to let her career become involved with her first husband. She had to take another one. Again it was Mr. Penniless; but this time at least she fell into the hands of a gentleman. All the world knew him; his very name—Merle—recalls a whole era of the Restoration when the men of spirit breakfasted and sang romantic ballads after first taking their wine. O Désaugiers! O Béranger!

Merle was handsome—"beautiful Merle," as we used to say. I first met him in 1840; I saw him again in 1850. The Théâtre Français had given him a small pension for being a second string critic, surely not to buy his praise but because he had become paralyzed. Naturally I continued the pension; but I also called on him to make sure he understood that his pen remained free.

"I am quite sure of that," he said to me, shaking my hand. "Even my wife has never had any influence on me. Haven't I always praised Mlle. Rachel ahead of her?"

"And there you have been wrong because Mme. Dorval is one of the three great actresses of the century."

"You are right. Let's say four and stop talking about it."

The handsome Restoration gentleman was no more than a shadow of his former self. Imprisoned in his bed, he believed himself to be in his shroud. Not one friend! No, I am wrong: Mme. Dorval's children watched lovingly over him as if he had brought them into the world. He found that quite natural, "that charming egotist," as his wife said.

There are actresses who, once they have left the scene, make fun of the tears their public sheds. Mme. Dorval shed tears behind the scenes. She cried in the greenroom because she had discovered some treachery. She cried at home because some vague restlessness seemed to give her an inkling of her future.

It was her tears that raised her to be the genius of drama. It was her tears that enabled her to attain that air of pale chastity, that sublime modesty, that touching tenderness, that vibrant passion of a mother, or a lover, or a lost soul.

She was in life as she was on stage, the sweetest and most unworldly of women, the most melting and the most uncontrolled, with the gaiety of a child, and the total desolation of an outcast. What lovely heartfelt laughter! What lovely glances sprung from love! What lovely cry torn from the distressed heart!

She was a heroic woman for whom nature had done nothing. A sad and vulgar figure, sea-green eyes, poorly drawn mouth, a fishwife's voice, a servant maid's body. She had to overcome all that. She was so relentless in the struggle against herself that she gained, little by little, the grace of a woman and the charm of a mistress. She did so by spreading about her that same fire which burned in her heart. Art—sacred art—adorned everything she touched.

Mme. Dorval and I were good friends when she was in love with Jules Sandeau. Sandeau was truly a man who had the misfortune both of being no longer loved and being loved too much. The one who no longer loved him was George Sand, the one who loved him too much was Marie Dorval. The most curious part of this affair was that George Sand and Marie Dorval were at that time nicknamed "the Inseparables."

One evening she asked me, "Do you think he'll love me?"

"Why not?"

"Because he still loves George Sand."

"That's no more than a memory."

"Don't you believe it; every time I talk to him about that woman he never stops me to talk about me. . . ." Mme. Dorval lowered her head. "If he loves me a little, it's because he thinks am a close friend of George Sand, it's because he finds his mistress' kisses on my cheeks."

"After all, my dear friend, love is always an old graft on a new tree. What does it matter so long as that tree bears blossoms and fruit?"

Mme. Dorval, conscious of her love, had turned sad. "Oh," she continued, "it is easy to see that you are not in love."

Two lovely tears descended from her eyes. She was so wildly in love with Jules that she often went to his room when he was not there. She told me: "Nothing means as much to me as to be at his side; there I breathe his life and his thoughts."

She ruffled the novelist's papers with jealous hands and looked at them angrily.

When I lived with Jules, the most agreeable of companions, she came one day when he was absent. While we were talking she noticed the beginning of a pen portrait which Jules had written for *Belles Femmes de Paris*. I had kept the first twenty lines; George Sand's name was not mentioned in them but Mme. Dorval recognized her and cried out: "Her, always her! That woman will be the death of me."

She had just come from "that woman" whom she had embraced tenderly. They were actually inseparable.

"Don't worry about a thing like that," I told her. "Moreover, don't you love George Sand as much as you do Jules?"

"But you don't understand that I love that woman because she loved Jules or because Jules has loved her. I don't talk to her about anything except him."

"Listen! You love her also for herself," I said with a laugh. "How could you otherwise explain that you are always together? You are her light when she is your shadow, and you are her shadow when she is your light."

While I was speaking the distressed lady in love had picked up a paper knife—there was no other dagger about—and stabbed herself violently in the chest, while still reading Jules's manuscript. A real melodrama! Mme. Dorval fainted in my arms. The poor distraught woman had struck hard and the blood was flowing. I unfastened her dress and saw a rather serious cut. Her first move was to pick up the manuscript and bathe it in her blood—not that the blood flowed in torrents, but her chest was badly lacerated.

That scene characterizes the woman. When Jules returned, he refused to believe my story because he always played the skeptic even though he had a good heart. I asked him to let me keep the manuscript among my papers.

"All right," he said, "but you'll surely show it to George Sand."

The great actress pursued Sandeau everywhere; she lay in wait for him at his house, first at the foot of the stairs, then at his threshold. She was jealous of the passing breeze. He, with his passion ended, assumed a heroic role: having left the woman, he also left his own home which I myself had left earlier because of their eternal dramas. He came to take refuge with me at 36 Rue de Bac.

I could offer any of my broken-up friends no more than a simple day bed; it was a newly invented kind of day bed, nicknamed funeral bier because at night one lifted the lid and slept in it like in a tomb.

My friend found it much more suitable than his own bed. But then witness one morning the arrival of the heroine of romantic drama, completely disheveled: "Arsène Houssaye, what have you done to Jules?"

"I have not seen him for the longest time."

"You lie!"

Upon that remark I very politely offered Mme. Dorval a chair and, on the pretext of going to look for a very recent letter from Jules, I went to the small living room and told my friend of the visit.

"Put the lid over me, quick," he told me, quite frightened.

I was forced to entomb him. No sooner had I hidden him than Dorval appeared. "I know that Jules is here!"

She cast her glances everywhere. I seated myself on the day bed and told her, "Let's talk about him! Are you really still in love with him?"

"Oh, my dear friend!"

She dissolved in tears. She began to tell me all her joys and all her sorrows.

"And yet, all he does is talk as if he had feelings. His own cleverness kills his heart. But oh, how I love him."

"Do you mean to tell me that you still can feel despair after having acted all variations of despair on stage?"

"Passion feeds on passion. And then, Jules is not a man, he is a god. . . ."

"That's saying a lot!"

"You do not understand my tears. I shall die of this."

I had risen to take Mme. Dorval out of the room because I was afraid that Jules might suffocate. But no sooner were we outside than Jules, seized once more by passion, raised the lid and threw himself at the feet of his mistress, crying, "Oh, yes, Marie, you are the only one! I am yours for life, yours to the death!"

One can imagine that Mme. Dorval was disarmed, but she was seized with a violent hatred for me.

"You are nothing but a charlatan!" she cried.

She was on the verge of attacking me physically. Jules calmed her down and suggested that they go and have fish-stew for lunch in Saint-Cloud.

The tempest passed quickly, she kissed me because I had been "a friend to my friend." She wanted me to join them for lunch but I knew women too well to be taken in by such an impulse. That romantic star needed Jules all to herself, under those green trees and that blue sky.

The journey to Saint-Cloud was the last ray of that declining passion. It ended soon. They did not see each other any more except from afar and did not talk any more except with a knowing smile. Jules said good-by to his follies, and gravely entered into a marriage of love and reason, while Mme. Dorval continued her life of adventure.

Eight years later they had a final meeting. Jules climbed the five flights of stairs to the actress's apartment, called by a note of one line: "Come to say good-by to me."

He found the door wide open and saw Mme. Dorval's daughter with her head hidden in her hands.

"Is she very ill?" he asked.

"Alas!" she answered.

He went into her bedroom. "Marie! Speak to me."

The poor actress who had had such a cross to bear had a crucifix in her hands. She had just died in the odor of sanctity, and looked pale like a marble statue.

Supper with the Muses

•

Houssaye has no need, in the following piece, to explain what kind of women he ran into at the Frères Provençaux. Not because that famous restaurant was a house of ill repute, but because he clearly indicates, by his description, that the ladies belonged in one.

In 1845 Alfred de Musset, Eugène Sue, Nestor Roqueplan, Malitourne and I often met at the Frères Provençaux Restaurant for dinner with Dr. Véron, who paid the bill: just one little item in the expense accounts of the *Constitutionnel,* of which he was the publisher.

One day when we were mounting the stairs we found ourselves inundated by an avalanche of women who had found themselves on the wrong floor: it seemed like a carnival. The ladies shouted, sang and laughed as if they were at their house. The headwaiter of the establishment intervened to make them respect the dignity of his white tie as if to say to them: order in the classroom, ladies. They passed in front of us, ogling us rebelliously. Everything about them was provocative: their hair was in disarray, their waistbands undone, their colors flashing. M. de Montoyon would not, I am afraid, have been able to distribute an award for virtue among them.

F

A great Amazon who marched at the head suddenly said, "How come Alfred is not here?"

Another shouted, "He never does his job!" Whereupon the avalanche, transformed into a tempestuous wave, disappeared into one of the big dining rooms.

Dr. Véron, always a strong one for morality, had already crossed to the other side, followed by Eugène Sue and Malitourne. Malitourne was out of breath because he had come late as usual—but he always came. That man of letters neither wrote nor dined except on the condition of being the doctor's confidential helpmate.

Roqueplan and I, more curious than they, remained on the landing. Suddenly we saw Alfred de Musset appear, humming and flourishing his cane.

"That's the Alfred they meant," Roqueplan said to me.

He joined us with a half-conquering, half-angry air. One can always manage to get out of a bad spot with a clever phrase: The poet thought he could get out with a line of poetry much abused on and off the stage:

Happy for me the place where I meet up with you

But no matter how happy the place, he passed us by without hearing our greetings and without inviting us to his festivity. We therefore rejoined our companions and made a few remarks about what we had seen. Dr. Véron said he was pleased to see that his gold coins spread joy.

"Whatever you may say, that gold belongs to the *Constitutionnel!*" cried Roqueplan.

"Yes," answered Véron. "If one never has to open one's hands when they are full to truth, then one may perhaps never have to open them when they are full of gold."

He told us that Alfred de Musset had come to him that morning to bring him the manuscript of *Carmosine*. As was his habit, Véron played the great spender: instead of giving him the agreed-upon price, five hundred francs per act, he had given him three thousand francs for the three acts. Alfred had not been that rich in a long time and now wanted to play the big spender himself by giving a party in honor of *Carmosine*. As the ladies of the Faubourg Saint-Germain had already gone on vacation, he was obliged to invite the ladies of the other world. Véron, who then lived in the Rue Taitbout, thought that they were probably his neighbors.

After some turtle soup and a glass of Château-Yquem, the good doctor applied himself to a sermon against the morals of the age, with the full authority that the austerity of his own life gave him.

All of us were much edified. We managed to comment that he had himself supped more than once in very gay company; to which he replied that custom, which makes laws—because it is an expression of the wisdom of nations—decreed an exception for the corps de ballet as well as for actresses who have plenary indulgences for the exercise of love.

During Véron's sermon we heard the cackle of our neighbors, but, no matter how we opened our ears, Musset's voice did not penetrate the partition.

Though we were all of irreproachable moral standing, we would have very much liked to cast a glance at that Amphitryon; for, if that dinner in such company was a study in morals for him, it would for us be an even more tempting study to bring to the light of day the soul of that great poet in his hours of abandon; for that reason I asked the headwaiter of the Frères Provençaux to tell us how Alfred de Musset fared at his dinnertable.

The man paid him a ceremonious visit and told us upon his return, "He carries himself very well—on the straight and narrow. He does talk with these ladies, but like a general with his soldiers."·

That was in keeping with Alfred de Musset's character: no matter what he did, he carried his head high and defied public opinion. The most troublesome inebriation did not cloud his brow. It was as if poetry, that indefatigable vestal virgin, were always guarding the sacred flame.

Dr. Véron set himself to preach a second sermon. But that evening, when he'd had his say—when Malitourne, that admirable confidant, had ten times saluted his eloquence—he relapsed into his old habit of man about town: he sent a well-chilled cup of champagne to that eternal prodigal son, that spoilt child of the century that had Victor Hugo as its sublime offspring.

Musset, touched by that thoughtfulness, responded with an equally well-chilled cup of champagne, but this time it was not the headwaiter who was employed as the emissary. We witnessed the entrance, cup in hand, of the Amazon of the regiment, a handsome creature—milk-fed, as we used to say of the women of Rubens. Unfortunately for her, she had not gone through the Conservatoire, where M. Samson would have taught her the art of striking poses. She marched like a floozy; she bowed to us like a goose; from up close she was truly the kind of magnificent and superb animal whom Goethe would have loved—to repose his spirit.

Dr. Véron took the cup and asked the girl an impertinent question: "How much has Alfred given to each of you to pay your glove maker?"

The Amazon, who had bowed to him, answered that neither she nor her friends had come "for gloves" but out of friendship for Amphitryon.

I recall Véron's question because it was characteristic of him: he had supplied the money; he wanted to know how it was being spent. He dismissed the messenger by telling her, "If I should ever become director of the Opéra again I'll invite you to become my choral director."

"Choral director?" she said leaving the room. "That's all I need!"

When I next saw Alfred de Musset, I asked him if he had had an amusing time.

"Oh, good Lord," he said with a jaunty air, "that was merely an exercise in will power. The ancients, who weren't so dumb, put nine women into Apollo's retinue. The Apollos of today are small men, backstairs poets who generally have no more than one wife and one mistress. And what good is that?"

Alfred de Musset's Case of Adultery

•

Paul de Musset, who almost always makes his brother out to be a saint, asserts nevertheless that Alfred de Musset told him about quite a number of his adventures. "He had salacious stories and romantic stories, some of them very dramatic." Paul de Musset was more than once woken up in the middle of the night to give advice "on some serious problems in which husbands were involved." He added, with his brotherly earnestness: "All these stories he confided to me under the seal of secrecy; I was told to forget them. More than one of them would have made any gossip writer green with envy." Why the devil did Paul apply the seal of secrecy to these when he told every bit about his brother's most childish tricks? We would much rather read now three or four stories from these beautiful years which had not yet been darkened by bitter passions.

Alfred de Musset was no worse a soldier than any other member of the National Guard when he deigned to wear his uniform. He fired his rifle in the June days, no matter how he despised politics; he did not care any more for Dictator II than for Dictator I, for the people any more than the King. When he was in the Guard Brigade he was no more stuck up than the others; he smoked the same tobacco and told the same cock-and-bull stories.

More than one romantic adventure happened to him when he wore National Guard uniform, and he enjoyed telling them. I well remember the one which follows, the telling of which lasted about the time it took to smoke two cigarettes. Here it is. The audience: Molènes, Bonnaire, and I. I do not make him talk here because I am afraid I would not be able to put it in his language. But, at any rate, here is that tragic-comic story.

Women were very fond of Alfred. He charmed them with his proud and appealing appearance, his gentlemanly air, his open spirit mixed with some imperceptible Byronesque impertinence. He therefore had lots of women on his hands.

One day it so happened to him, as it so often happens in the theater, that he sent a letter intended for a princess to a milliner, who was moreover the milliner of that princess; like his master Don Juan, Musset found all the fruits in the Garden of Love to his liking: it was only a question of picking them at the right time. The milliner took as true coin the first words of the letter which had not been intended for her: "My dear Princess . . ." Why not! I've made hats for so many real princesses that I might as well play a princess for fun:

My dear Princess, you are more charming than any woman, but you evidently need to put three or four hearts *en brochette* every day, as my Godmother would have said. As this seems to amuse you, I am coming to see you tomorrow. Not today, because I am on guard duty for the sake of the fatherland, "Aim . . . fire!"

But when the letter addressed to the milliner reached the real princess, it sang quite a different song.

My dear Margot,* this letter is merely intended to give you your road map; simple National Guard private that I am, I am on duty at the City Hall of the Tenth District; I shall dine at Pinson's with Chenavard unless you pass by to pick me up to go to another restaurant where you will be the spice for the stew. I present arms for you.

Alfred de Musset

* Margot can mean more than the proper name, and may be applied to ladies whose name is not Margot. It is a kind of familiarity or slang, something like "Baby" or "Kid," though much more refined.

The Princess was quite ready to have arms presented for her but not in a restaurant. Moreover, she was not on particularly intimate terms with the author of *Namouna*. What would she do?

But who was even more surprised? Alfred de Musset when, toward six o'clock, in a thin November rain, he was told that a lady was expecting him at the gate of the Guard House. A few moments later he went to her, his arms in his hands.

He recognized the Princess.

The caprices of great ladies! That particular one played untouchable and watched herself like her own best enemies, but the lure of adventure had thrown her off course. She was as curious now as Eve, though without knowing if she would go quite that far.

"Why the devil, Princess, do you come here to surprise me in this carnival outfit?"

"Didn't you write to me to come and pick you up? And, heaven knows that your letter was impertinent."

"How in God's name can I unravel that mystery?"

The Princess took out the letter. "Well, did you write this to me?"

The Princess showed him the familiar letter with its familiar language. Alfred de Musset was not foolish enough to lose his presence of mind when he could benefit from an occasion. He hid his stunned surprise. "Well then, Princess, shall we go and dine at Pinson's?"

"No, good heavens, my veil will be singed there. Once I am here, I want to go to dinner at a real wine house."

"Very well! We'll go to Montparnasse. In winter there isn't a mouse there, not even Sainte-Beuve."

Alfred de Musset took his seat in the carriage at the Princess' side, without his rifle but in a completely reckless mood.

"It does not matter," she said, "I never feel in danger with a man disguised in National Guard uniform. That's why I take this risk."

"I should have made myself a corporal for the occasion. Though that won't stop me from telling you in the best soldierly manner that I love you like the devil."

Here they were, embarked for Cythera like two pilgrims in a Watteau picture. At the gate they lightheartedly mounted, not the three steps of rose marble but the six steps of a secluded restaurant which was then famous, called "Divorce Inn" because one could well divorce oneself from the world there. They did not notice that two curious bystanders saw them enter: their friends D'Alton-Shee and Gustave Delahante.

Even though nobody is there yet, they of course prudently hide in a small private dining room. The Princess, who has never experienced a festivity of this sort, is enchanted with the onion soup and the mussels in onion sauce. She promises herself to fire her chef with his pretensions to the *haute cuisine* of Brillat-Savarin.

Alfred de Musset is full of high spirits; for the first time the Princess is to him no more than a milliner. As she is there for reasons of curiosity only, she is determined to grant him everything—except the final request.

Then, suddenly, they hear a loud noise in the private dining room next door.

"Oh, good Lord," she says, "that's the Prince. Did you yourself set up this little comedy?"

"God help me, no! He knows the place well, we've been here together."

"In interesting company, no doubt?"

"I'd say so—two virtuous maidens."

"I'd love to know whom the Prince is taking to dinner here."

At the same moment someone knocked at the door of their dining room: "Alfred!" That was the voice of the Prince who had just been informed that his friend was there with a veiled lady, "Alfred, couldn't we dine together, all of us?"

"Be quiet," whispered the Princess. Musset had thrown himself against the door.

"My dear Prince, I'll come to see you in a moment."

"Why don't you open up?" Outside, the Prince, who liked a row, gave the door a powerful kick. Musset, beside himself, told him that he absolutely forbade him to act in such a way.

"Oh, so it's that serious!" said the Prince.

"You bet it is serious. I am involved in adultery."

The situation was indeed serious, for the Prince who lived like the devil, according to the gospel of the dandies of that time, did not allow the Princess to live in the same way. If he had found her out in that escapade he would have picked up a table knife to slash her face—the face of a magnificent, unsatisfied Mona Lisa.

While the National Guard bravely defended the position and the Prince beat a retreat, though only to return to the siege, the Princess had opened the window to escape through the garden because the danger did not exactly infuse her with valor. Musset, frightened by the pallor of her face, held her back by the arm.

"No, under no circumstances will I stay here."

No matter how the poet begged her, or drew his sword, I mean to say his rifle—which in any case he did not have with him— the Princess insisted on jumping from the window. When he saw that, he jumped himself first to help her. One minute later he put her in a hackney cab, which was to take her home. As for him, he went back, furious at her husband, and determined to annoy him. Now it was his turn to knock on the door of the private room where the Prince had secluded himself with a votary from another temple.

The moment the door opened, Musset cried, "Mademoiselle Héloïse!"

He had recognized his milliner. He masked his surprise, saying to himself, "That's not astonishing; after all, the Princess is her customer."

He sat down at the table and complained that his own little devotee was boring him with her tears and that he had come to amuse himself with those who were amusing.

The Prince, without a word, went to the room whose door he had almost battered down. "Your beauty has fled!" he said when he came back.

"Oh! So much the better!" cried the poet. "I look forward to dining with the two of you now that I've lost my partner."

F*

As it turned out, however, the Princess did not want to act the schoolgirl. She retraced her steps and came herself to knock at the door of that private dining room. "Is the Prince of —————— in there?"

"No," answered Alfred de Musset.

"He is in there, I can recognize his voice. I must speak to him, on behalf of Apponyi.* It is serious. It's a matter of life and death."

The Prince decided to go out to her. He closed the door behind him but the Princess had already seen Mlle. Héloïse who, however, said to her, "I'm with Alfred."

"Yes, of course, you are reading *The New Héloïse* together!"

The Princess took the Prince away with her on the pretext of serious news from abroad. Musset, left behind, looked at Mlle. Héloïse and suddenly began to laugh.

"By God," he said to himself, "that's really beautiful. That one here was supposed to dine with me and now I am dining with her as fate intended."

Greatly animated by the adventure, he soon ended the engagement, saying that he wanted to go to the Opéra.

It was the evening that the Princess kept her salon, and she was not at the Opéra. Too inflamed to stay for the final act of *William Tell*, he recklessly went to her house where, after all, he did appear on most evenings. He found the Princess enthroned as always among her subjects. She had never seemed more serene.

"Oh, it's you!" she said, holding out her hand to the poet. "I haven't seen you in ages!"

Having reached that point in the story, Musset lit a third cigarette and added airily. "I should tell such a story only to comedians. However, if you want to know the name of the heroine, I shall tell you that it was not the Princess Belgiojoso.† "

* Rudolph, Count Apponyi (1802–1853), was both an Austrian diplomat and a major figure in Parisian society.

† The Princess Belgiojoso was Musset's mistress for a time.

The Revolution of 1848

·

On December 27, 1847, when the regular session of Parliament opened in Paris, the opposition to the Guizot government, both in and out of the Chamber of Deputies, had become deafening. Moral condemnations, many of them well founded, were thrown against Guizot, his ministers, and many of his party. It was expected that the government would fall, but it was also widely believed that these were parliamentary debates on the English model, part of a political game played according to the gentlemanly rules which had been imported from across the Channel. But France, it turned out, was not England.

For the last six months of 1847 a series of banquets had been held to carry the voice of opposition beyond the confines of Parliament. Banquets may not seem very appropriate as vehicles for radical action in the twentieth century, but in 1847 their rotund oratory inflamed the mostly rotund participants. They were not revolutionaries by nature, and the ineptness of the government was needed to turn them in that direction. Guizot banned the final banquet planned for February 22. A peaceful parade to the banquet hall turned less peaceful, and some crowds, mostly people who would never in their lives be able to banquet, began to make bon-

*fires of chairs taken from the cafés in the Champs Élysées. Barri-
cades appeared—a familiar sight in Paris—and the National Guard
was called out. The next day it became apparent that the government could no longer rely on the National Guard. Even now the
situation need not have been lost had Louis-Philippe acted decisively. General Bugeaud, the conqueror of Algeria, was placed in
command of the regular army, but his sweep of the city was called
off halfway. By noon on the twenty-fourth the King was ready to
abdicate in favor of his ten-year-old grandson. There was a touching scene in which his daughter-in-law, the widowed Duchess of
Orléans, taking her little son with her, made a last personal appeal
to the Chamber of Deputies to save the dynasty. The man who
could perhaps have saved it at that point was the poet-politician
Lamartine, but he decided for a Provisional Government and a republic. By half past one the crowds were plundering the Tuileries.*

On February 24, I crossed the Pont de La Concorde after having
witnessed the fall of the House of Orléans in the Chamber of
Deputies. I felt that I was on my way to a last salute to royalty on
the threshold of exile. But everyone had disappeared.

I went into the Tuileries Palace, in rather doubtful company,
to see from close up that bloody tyranny which called itself The
Revolution. I was not concerned about the immediate future because I had seen Lamartine assume the role of Archangel to guide
the revolutionaires to the City Hall. Thus I followed my nose,
curious and saddened, though all around me I heard the cries of
joy of the Young France of Paris. I was surprised to see so few people in that deserted palace; the victors, and the timeservers, had
gone off to the City Hall. For reasons of respect and sentiment I
did not want to mount the staircase which reminded me of the
great entertainments. But a friend insisted that I come along as far
as the Throne Room. There we saw a completely unexpected spectacle.

There was a king on the throne. That king was a small man
from Savoy with a toothy grin who said in a burst of joy, "Oh!

What fun this is!" At that moment I ran into Comte and Vicomte de La Ferrière, dragged along like myself, against their will, to witness that Shakespearean scene.

"The king is dead! Long live the king!" exclaimed the Count.

"Yes," I replied, "but if that Savoyard is condemned to be king for long, he will very quickly demand back his cap and his hurdy-gurdy."

We had not been there for five minutes when there was an invasion. Men and women of all kinds, dashing like waves up the steps of the Grand Staircase, broke with great noise into the various chambers; we were suddenly submerged, and the sack of the Tuileries began. The riffraff were looting whatever they could lay their hands on. But then a student of the College of Technology in his turn mounted the throne and made an eloquent speech about the duties of a citizen. That speaker was a prince, in fact the Prince de Polignac, son of the Minister of Supply in 1830. He had no sooner spoken than many hurled themselves violently against the looters and wrote on the palace walls the threat: "Death to looters." The riffraff satisfied itself by throwing their loot out of the windows, hoping to be able to pick up some of it outside later.

The Revolution of 1848, which was so profitable for lawyers, was disastrous for artists and men of letters. That small Republic was in dire straits in the midst of the large Republic. Toward the beginning of June I did not have a penny left; I had sold my last share in the Bank of France for five hundred francs. The fees paid by the papers were simply ridiculous. Girardin dared to talk of two pennies per line; Dr. Véron, who had increased the width of his columns by half, lowered the fee by half as well. When I reproached him for cutting his five franc pieces in half, he replied, "You can dine with me every evening." But I could not simply leave my pots empty at home, especially as I had more friends in need than ever. Fortunately, I had some pictures: I sold a Boucher, a Prud'hon and a Diaz to Anderson, an English painter who gave me ten thousand francs to get through the season. But the season was bad: I went back into the stock market and did so badly— or so well—that I immediately lost the ten thousand francs, and several more. Though hardly a gambler by inclination, I began to believe at last that my end would be disastrous. I finally became afraid and swore that I would never set foot among the money-changers again: you will see how I kept my word.

In the middle of the Revolution a son had been born to me.* He was the joy of the home—while the home was crumbling—and the mother as well as I had eyes only for the child. With great re-luctance I took my wife and child to the country. My father, even though the Revolution had not affected him, would not give me five hundred francs; but the house, thank God, was always open to us. He told me quite gently, "You ought to stay with us, too." But in those days I did not think I was alive if I was not in Paris, seized as I was both by the fever of politics and the fever of litera-ture. I only stayed in Bruyères for a few days, answering him that I was a resourceful man, not afraid of the next day. That was ac-tually true.

As it was, I had already gone through a great deal. My father was a millionaire but all he had given me for a start in the world was his curse. I had given up soldiering to become a poet; neither had made me rich. Nevertheless, after being a Bohemian for a while, I had had some strokes of luck, because it seemed to be writ-ten on high that I should encounter everything in life, from gilded misery to palaces built on sand, with the castles conjured up by champagne on the horizon.

As soon as I was back in Paris, I threw myself into my work. At one and the same time I published "Chamfort" in the *Revue des Deux Mondes*, "Plato's Republic" in *L'Artiste*, sketches of some

---

* Henry Houssaye, his oldest son, was actually born on February 24, the day King Louis Philippe abdicated. He became a historian of considerable importance, and was elected to the French Academy just before his father's death. A second son, Albert, became an officer in the French army. His father liked him, and mourned his premature death, but Henry was always the one in whom he really took pride.

famous actresses in the *Constitutionnel*, and "Hands of Roses, Hands of Blood" in the *Journal*. Charpentier was also bringing out my *Portraits of the Eighteenth Century*. In a word, I worked day and night to forget my failure in the stock market, passing from the game of money to the game of the mind. I had fired my cook, I took a genial lunch at the Café d'Orsay where I always met some friends, Gleyre and Ziem among them. I dined here and there, often at the Café de Paris, in the company of Roqueplan, La Chaise, Gilbert de Voisins, Daugny, Beauvoir, Heckeeren, Malitourne, Véron; the last, playing minister of welfare, often paid for the dinners of his gay table of writers—he did not like sad ones.

I had known Dr. Véron since he took over the *Constitutionnel* in 1844. He had called me in at the same time as Musset to fill, as he described it with his theatrical impertinence, the spaces between installments of *The Wandering Jew*. Eugène Sue was the big wheel, no doubt, and we were the extras. My sketches of actresses were published in the *Constitutionnel*. Dr. Véron liked me above all because I had close contacts with these ladies. He loved women, but as seen from the sidelines, and appreciated the moralists who studied the eternal feminine in actresses. I am everlastingly grateful to him because he came to me in the days when I did not have a penny:

"How much would you like for an article?"

"A hundred francs," I replied, "that's what Girardin pays me."

"Well, then I'll pay you two hundred."

But how he had climbed down since the 24th of February!

My wife came back to Paris and I was in despair at no longer being able to afford her luxuries—luxuries, the daily bread of women! The farther I went the vaster became the abyss I saw, because I was unable to break my old habits of living without counting the money.

That was the moment when Rachel, that tragic figure, came into my life like a smiling fate.

Pages from a Comic Novel

·

Rachel, *who inadvertently came to Houssaye's rescue in 1848, was probably the greatest French actress of all time. For ten years she had dominated the great state theater of France, the Comédie Française, thereby giving much offense to its actor members who officially controlled it.*

The Comédie Française, or Théâtre Français, is also called the House of Molière. Its proud traditions go back to the reign of Louis XIV and to Molière whose troupe of actors provided its foundation. It was, and is, not merely a theater supported by the state; like the Opéra it is a major cultural establishment in which the government has always taken a great interest. It is also a self-perpetuating bureaucracy regulated, in Houssaye's time, according to a set of rules drafted by the Emperor Napoleon. These rules are called the Decret de Moscou *because the Emperor drafted them in Moscow during the Russian campaign of 1812, while he was waiting for the Czar, Alexander I, to surrender. The* Decret de Moscou *survived better than the French army which eventually had to retreat from the city; forty years later it was still obeyed to the letter at the Théâtre Français. It provided, essentially, that its actor members, the* sociétaires, *who held shares in the enterprise, would rule the theater and employ junior actors and actresses, called* pensionnaires. *An administrator presided over the whole enterprise, but his role was very circumscribed.* Pensionnaires *could be hired only with the approval of the* sociétaires; *new plays could not be given unless they had been sanctioned by the Reading Committee, made up of* sociétaires; *stage directors in the modern sense were unknown, and the* semainier, *the man chosen to keep performances more or less in line, was a* sociétaire. *The director, or* administrateur, *was responsible to a government official, the Director of Fine Arts, who in turn was responsible to the Minister of the Interior, but these persons changed with the winds of politics while the* sociétaires *remained, conscious of their power and unwilling to be meddled with.*

As the sociétaires *were shareholders in the Comédie, their well-being depended on the box office. In 1838, not yet 18 years old, Rachel had single-handedly revived the classical drama of Racine and Corneille and saved the Comédie from seemingly inevitable oblivion. For ten years her performances had been the main financial and often artistic support of the house. She had extracted fabulous remunerations and fabulously long leaves of absence during which she toured all parts of Europe. She was tremendously resented by her colleagues.*

In 1848 the Comédie had fallen on evil days—people had concerns other than the theater—which Rachel alleviated in part by dramatically declaiming-singing the Marseillaise *from the stage at several performances. But the general whiff of freedom which the February Revolution provided meant one special thing to the* sociétaires: *freedom from Rachel. In October she resigned her membership. On December 10, Prince Louis Napoleon Bonaparte was elected President of the Republic. Rachel and he had known each other rather well for some time, mostly in England where he had spent some of his years in exile. An old revolutionary himself, he let Rachel plan a coup d'état at the House of Molière.*

A Coup d'État at the Comédie Française

One evening a mysterious individual, all in black, appeared at my door and asked me to follow him to the Élysée Palace. The Élysée is not the Police Headquarters; but as I was a friend of Thoré and Sobrier and had just saved Esquiros from the Military Tribunal, I thought that I was being picked up by the secret police.

"Who wants me, and why?"

"I don't know," answered the man in black. And to all my other questions he responded, "I don't know."

I had just been busy putting up a piece of Gobelin tapestry in my study, all that remained of some very transitory luxuries. I put a few more nails into the tapestry and went into my wife's room. I told her about the man in black; she began to cry and grasped our child to her bosom.

"Don't cry. If they wanted to arrest me, they wouldn't take me away via the Élysée." In spite of my words it was with a sense of foreboding I kissed mother and child good-by. I had not been involved in any plots against the Republic but I belonged to a group that liked Napoleon only on the battlefield.

When I reappeared before the waiting emissary, I myself was dressed entirely in black. A closed carriage was waiting for us downstairs.

At the Élysée I was ushered into one room, then another, then still another. There I suddenly met Mlle. Rachel, all in smiles. She seemed to be at home there. But, then, didn't she seem at home wherever she went? Besides, she was the "mistress" of the palace.

I did not understand her drift at once though she came to the point immediately. "Would you like to be Director of the Théâtre Français?" she asked point blank.

"Do you dislike me that much?" I answered.

"Yes, you know that a tragic actress always has to seek revenge."

"All right, seek your revenge! I am ready for anything as long as you are with me. If I can't be President of the Republic, it will at least be amusing to be President of the Republic of Molière."

A few persons with a past, and a few with a future, went in and out. Then I was presented to Prince Louis Napoleon. He first paid me a compliment about a book of mine which he had read in prison. I don't remember which, or even if it was really one of my books. Then he talked on in that vigorous bass voice that contrasted so strongly with his pensive appearance: about his determination to restore the Théâtre Français in all its splendor—and with all its tragedies; about the constitution of the Théâtre Français, about his determination not to touch the *Decret de Moscou*, its Holy Writ; but also about his decision that an authoritarian Republic should succeed the democratic Republic of Molière.

M. de Persigny asked me if I was determined to cope with the Comedians-in-Ordinary of the King who wanted a king no more; who disputed points of order all day long so much so that they had no strength left for the evening's performance; who administered their affairs so well that the box office had fallen to tragic or comic amounts, depending on one's point of view. One summer evening not long before the receipts had been fifty-three francs.

"But now that it is fall," added Commander Fleury, "they are up to one hundred and fifty-three francs."

The veiled eyes of Prince Napoleon lit up. "It seems that you go behind the scenes, Commander."

"Of course, your Grace; we must be ready for every kind of battle."

I finally said that I could not think of a more appropriate time to arrive at the Français. I thanked the President for having thought of me.

"Oh, don't thank me," answered the Prince, "thank Mlle. Rachel. She was given the names of six literary men and chose you —I don't know why."

I bowed to Mlle. Rachel.

"Do you know why I chose you?" she said. "Because I know you less well than the others."

I had met Rachel two or three times at dinner in the houses of Count Walewski, Count Obreskoff and Dr. Véron, but I was hardly one of her closer acquaintances. Like most women, she loved the unknown. Once she had asked me for a play on Sappho, in classical form. But then—whom had she not asked for a play?

The Prince spoke of the masterpieces of Corneille and Racine, but at the same time of the contemporary drama. He wanted Mlle. Rachel to play Hugo, Vigny, Dumas, Musset, and so on. Mlle. Rachel promised to prepare *Angelo* and *Mademoiselle de Belle-Isle* at once, to show her commitment to the modern repertoire. She said that she was eager to don the dramatic garb of her contemporaries.

I left the Palace with her, at peace with the world and even with myself, but above all with that great actress. She offered to take me home in her carriage and invited me to dinner for the next day to talk about the repertoire.

But the next day I was no longer Director of the Théâtre Français.

This is what happened. At the first news given out by Rachel (for I had said nothing) the actors constituted themselves as a Committee of Public Safety; * they swore on the plaster casts of Talma and Mlle. Mars that they would have a master no more. Their enthusiasm made the portrait of Molière shiver. They threw themselves into six hackney cabs and went to the Minister of the Interior. They looked like a third class funeral, dressed as they were in black clothes and white ties. They hoped to make it my funeral.

The Minister always receives the actors even on days when he receives nobody else. He is right. Those who amuse him from the stage ought to be even more amusing in real life when nature

---

* The Committee of Public Safety was set up by the leaders of the French Revolution in 1793 to organize the country against the threat of defeat by foreign powers.

drops its mask. This may be something of a mistake, however, because an actor is always acting, even in front of his mirror; that is the old story of vanity.

The Minister was Ferdinand Barrot at that time, an intelligent man, all the more so because he gave himself an air of simple-mindedness. But on that occasion the actors outwitted him. They acted so hard that he was taken in by their cries of anguish. They convinced him that it would be highly ill-advised to meddle with their republic. "It would alarm people about the designs of the Prince; he would surely be accused of starting with the Théâtre Français in order to finish with France; the newspapers would surely play the tune that both republics would not last much longer."

Though the Minister had received the order to initial my nomination, he reassured the actors and told them that he would uphold their cause before the President. He had no doubt, he said, that the Prince, who held them very dear, would leave them free to act in whatever way they wished.

All this was reported in a paper which ended the article with these words: "And that is why M. Arsène Houssaye was Director of the Théâtre Français for five minutes."

I happened to be at Mlle. Rachel's house when that article was brought to us. We were having a pleasant dinner with Rebecca. Rachel glanced at it and broke her glass.

"Why this bit of drama?"

"Read that," she said.

She gave me the newspaper.

"That's no reason to break your glass."

"Don't you know that it brings good and bad luck at the same time? Good luck to oneself, bad to the others."

At that moment Rebecca, while reaching across to take the paper, upset the salt.

"Now that's serious," I said.

All three of us took pinches of salt to throw over our shoulders.

"Yes," said Rachel, "that means a cataclysm. Wait for me here, I'll take my carriage and get some news."

Her carriage always came for her at eight. It was at her door, but she had not yet crossed the threshold when she saw coming toward her a junior Talleyrand, a genuine diplomat, a future ambassador to St. Petersburg.

"Well," she said to him, "are they trying to make fun of us?"

"No, the Prince is very annoyed about what has happened, but it seems that it is easier to get into the Tuileries in sports clothes than to enter the House of Molière. He is meeting with insurmountable obstacles."

The future ambassador and Rachel had by then come back into the dining room where we talked further.

"When all is said and done," said the diplomat on entering, "I bring you golden words on a silver platter."

"Tell us," said the actress excitedly.

"Well, the Citizen Comedians-in-Ordinary of the King, the citizen comedians of the Republic, bearing in mind that you sang the *Marseillaise* with a flag that was more red than red-white-and-blue because you managed to hide the white and blue . . ."

"On my heart," interrupted Rachel, giving the ambassador a kiss.

"The aforementioned citizens offer you an engagement of five years."

Rachel looked very disdainful: "And how much do these gentlemen deign to offer little Rachel to get them out of their misery?"

"They have left the amount open."

"I am astounded," said Rachel in a tragi-comic tone.

The ambassador smiled.

"Yes, the amount is left out because they count on your generosity. But it is understood behind the scenes that, if you want more than thirty thousand francs, they will not countersign the contract."

"That's what I expected." Rachel had sat down by the ambassador's side. "Well, my dear friend, you will take your coffee with us, even if you already took it at the Élysée, after which you will take back your golden words on your silver platter. They are not quite good enough for me."

"Is that your final word?" asked the Prince's ambassador an hour later.

"Yes," answered the actress. "Tell your master, if he has any intention of governing France as he governs the House of Molière, he won't last very long at the Élysée."

"Don't worry. His only reason for leaving the Élysée will be to go to the Tuileries." *

Why I Was a Born Theater Manager

When the ambassador had left, Rachel invited me to make a short trip around the world with her. According to her, France ceased to exist the moment French tragedies were no longer being performed. She wanted to tour America, return to England, go as far away as Russia—all sorts of adventures. I admit that with my penchant for the romantic I was almost tempted to book a seat on that Thespian chariot.

"Be that as it may," she said, "I don't want to make you lose even one day for nothing: you are going to write a tragedy for me, and I will play it, never mind at what theater. We have already talked about Sappho; well—get to work!"

We separated like friends for all time. I did not go to bed before I had written the first one hundred verses of Sappho. I intended to cast in three acts that great story of passion which mounts up, up, up until death.

"When all is said," I told myself, "I would rather have my work played by Rachel than make her play the works of others."

* The Élysée Palace was, and still is, the traditional residence of French Presidents. The Tuileries Palace was the traditional residence of Kings and Emperors of France.

For the next few days I devoted myself completely to that tragedy.

The following morning I had received a short note from Rachel which said, "There is some news; I'll come to tell you." But, as I don't care to be a perpetual candidate for anything, I did not go after the news.

A few days later I met her at a dinner of Dr. Véron's, who had constituted, at the *Constitutionnel*, or rather at his own house, a power by the side of official power: it was the hallway leading to the future Empire. At that dinner Mlle. Rachel, above all, had the most amusing things to say. When she was in form, she could go at quite a pace, dropping whole strings of pearls and bright pebbles; her wit was all-embracing, from the coarsest to the most refined. Mlle. Rachel presided at the table, in the company of her lovely friend Mlle. Rhéa, a living marvel who was later cast into the tomb of oblivion by some Russian prince. Among the guests were Roqueplan, Bolay, Malitourne, Cassagnac, Sainte-Beuve.

They spent the evening talking about a coup d'état at the Théâtre Français. Roqueplan proposed another eighteenth Brumaire.* The whole lot of them ought to be thrown out of the window.

"Where are the grenadiers?" I asked.

"We are, all of us," said Véron pointing to the journalists. "You wait and see tomorrow if we are well-armed."

"The grenadiers," I answered, looking toward Mlle. Rachel and Mlle. Rhéa, "are over there, armed to the teeth."

"Yes," added Roqueplan, "if you want a coup d'état, Mlle. Rachel is the first grenadier of France."

And more such silly things at that dinner of wise men.

But what was said was actually done. For the next several days the journalists kept up a withering fire against the actors, who were fed up with Mlle. Rachel. Their committee meetings were described in detail, their box-office receipts were published.

---

* On the ninth of November 1799 (the eighteenth Brumaire in the Revolutionary Calendar) General Napoleon Bonaparte overthrew the Directoire and made himself First Consul of the Republic.

"Moreover," said one of the newspapers, "the box office would be even worse if they had not refused Mlle. Rachel her free tickets which obliges her to take a box each evening just to annoy them."

The cause of the actors was energetically espoused by the papers on the left, which maintained that one ought to starve to death for the sake of principle.

It was necessary, therefore, to save them in spite of themselves. That is why the Minister of the Interior wrote to me in the end:

My dear Monsieur Houssaye,

Your appointment, which was decided upon a month ago, is now finally authorized, but will not take effect until tomorrow. Please come to see me at six so that we can discuss your taking up your duties.

Ferdinand Barrot

When I had got to the Minister's office he said to me, "Here is your letter of appointment. The Prince has just signed it. The actors don't know anything about it and you will start out with a war. Get that resolved the best you can. You have complete freedom of action. I don't want to see them again. You have absolute power as director until the day you make a mistake, O man of wit: no one, after all, is perfect."

His words made me realize that his main intention in making me absolute dictator was to wash his hands of the whole business; I was therefore absolutely alone to confront the tragedians and the comedians—Caesar and Pompey, Figaro and Don Basilio—the most redoubtable enemies.

We shook hands.

"Good-by," said the Minister. "We will judge you by your performance."

I went straight to Mlle. Rachel who had written me an hour earlier:

Do come and dine with me, my dear director; I have bad news for you. In spite of all I did and said to the contrary, you have got your appointment.

Rachel

"Do you know," she said, "how the whole thing came about? The Minister kept on turning it down because, as he told the Prince, the actors were set and determined to close down the theater rather than open its doors to a director, no matter who he might be. But yesterday, while the Cabinet was meeting at the Élysée Palace, our friend the ambassador slipped into Ferdinand Barrot's carriage and caught him when he came out. They traveled together back to the Ministry; our envoy spoke so well—military eloquence is still the best—that the Minister gave him his word of agreement for today. Show me your documents—I want to know if I can cry victory, because it is all my doing."

Mlle. Rachel then recited aloud for her own amusement: "In the name of the French People: The President of the Republic, upon the recommendation of the Minister of the Interior, hereby appoints M. Arsène Houssaye Provisional Director of the Theater of the Republic."

At that time the word "provisional" graced all decrees of the government—itself provisional, of course, like everything else.

"That will do," said Mlle. Rachel. "Napoleon and Barrot, two pretty signatures. Not to mention the French people thrown in. I do believe you may escort me to the Théâtre Français tonight. M. Samson, President of the Committee of Public Safety, will no longer look upon me as an outcast."

"I am quite willing to go to the Théâtre Français tonight," I answered, "but only as a simple member of the audience. I don't want to assume the burdens of office tonight. Otherwise, the ticket ladies might want to give me flowers."

"You are right. I want to enjoy the amenities of my disgrace one more time. You'll see how the poor gatekeepers play M. Samson's game and treat me like a stranger."

Mlle. Rachel lived in the Rue de Rivoli, within a short distance of the theater. We went there on foot though her carriage was waiting for her. Our entrance was clearly less than triumphant.

When we were about to pass by the control booth, the man in charge of checking the holders of free tickets motioned to Mlle.

Rachel to stop. I wanted simply to go on, but Mlle. Rachel said to me, "No, the man is right; I am no longer on the free list because I am no longer a member of the company."

The man, in fact, said respectfully but firmly, "Mlle. Rachel no longer gets free tickets."

We gaily turned around to go to the box office.

"Can I get just one seat in one of the stage boxes on the ground floor?" asked Rachel.

I was not at all sure that I had enough money to pay for the whole box, so that Rachel's words sounded golden to me.

"Yes, mademoiselle, we sell them by the seat."

"While you get ready to sell out altogether," answered Rachel.

The answer was appropriate. Seats were available in every location because the whole place was empty. I wanted to pay but the actress was too amused to let me pay for her.

Back inside once more, it is now my turn to be stopped at the control booth.

"Sir, are you entitled to free seats?"

I had not been to the Théâtre Français in some time. They did not remember me. I turned around.

"Yes," I said, "I have been on the free list for ten years."

The man asked me for my name.

"Arsène Houssaye."

The man, who obviously did not waste his time reading my books, thought that my first and last names made one word. Instead of checking under H, he checked under A. Of course he did not find me.

"You are not on the list, sir."

"Look under H," I told him.

He looked under H, expecting no doubt to find Harsène Houssaye.

"You are not on the list, sir," he said once more.

"Oh, delightful," cried Rachel, "now it's your turn to go and pay for your seat."

I did in fact go back to the box office and threw down a twenty-franc piece for two additional seats in the stage box in order to have sufficient elbow room in case any strangers were to stray into that box.

"You are going to have a magnificent box office tonight, you know," Mlle. Rachel said to the man in the control booth.

We were finally permitted to pass through.

The attendant gave us her best smile. She rushed up to us like a soul in Purgatory, living among the shades of the departed: "Oh, Mlle. Rachel, how bored we are here now that they don't act the tragedies any more! Look around, I haven't a thing to do: no more than three or four seats in the orchestra are taken. I hope and pray that you'll come back."

We entered our stage box. No matter which side one turned, the sight was heartrending. As the house was completely empty, the action behind the footlights dragged along. And yet, that evening they acted two masterpieces in prose and in verse: *The Barber of Seville* and *L'Aventurière*. The principal actors were at their posts; the whole genius of the best company in the world was struggling against a void.

As soon as the actors had noticed us in the stage box, they exchanged signs and glances. "What are they up to?" they asked each other.

Here and there we caught some whispered words. They imagined that we had come to see them for the last time before our departure for America.

"Take care," Rachel said suddenly to Got, who had come close to her. "We have paid for our seats, we have the right to hiss you."

Got did not belong to the Committee of Public Safety. He was for comedy, but he supported tragedy also.

A little later Regnier came close to us. We had met before; he greeted us with his thin smile—out of both sides of his mouth, so to say—and expressed by means of a look at Mlle. Rachel his whole regret at being obliged to fight her.

The actresses, however, were implacable; not one of them would concede with any grace the superiority of the great tragic actress. They refused to understand that her fame and her genius cast its reflection on them. Good sense is as catching as stupidity; the more talent there is in a theater, the more does all talent increase. That is also the story of beauty in the salons.

"What a shame," said Rachel suddenly. "Look how well these people can act."

"Yes, but look, too, how grey and cold everything is around them. The staging needs more color, and the auditorium needs more light."

"More light! To display all that empty space? No, thanks!"

The attendant had brought us our programs.

"I'd very much like to know the box-office receipts," Rachel told her.

A few moments later the woman came back.

"Well, mademoiselle, it isn't much to rave about: three hundred and sixty-three francs."

"Gods of Aeschylus and Corneille!" Mlle. Rachel exclaimed with consternation.

Her anger with the theater was gone: that amount wounded her in her deep affection for the House of Molière.

"Three hundred and sixty-three francs," she repeated. "The place is lost. What can we do to save it?"

One of those splendid inspirations that are the salvation of empires came to my mind.

"Very simple," I said to her. "Tomorrow I'll raise the price of seats."

She looked at me as if to see whether I had lost my mind, but then she grasped my idea and, taking my hand in hers, said, "You are a born theater manager."

·

The First Day

·

The next morning my appointment was in the newspaper. I was awakened by the women of Les Halles,* who always have friends

* The central market of Paris.

in the government departments and therefore get the news before the papers do. In that manner Fortune comes before you in Paris. At a later date, when I became director of the Opéra, I had to pay them for lots of flowers even though I was no longer interested in the limelight in which these ladies placed me. This time, however, was the first and we had to throw open the great double doors to admit the piles of autumn roses, violets and camellias.

"This is only the beginning," said the handsome spokeswoman of the delegation.

"Oh, yes," I replied, "the process servers are making me quite a bouquet, too." I had no illusions about the reception I was about to get at the Comédie.

Charles Blanc, the head of the Department of Fine Arts, had gone the preceding evening, toward the end of the performance, to inform the ladies and gentlemen of the Comédie that a director had been imposed on them by order of Prince Louis Napoleon and Mlle. Rachel. A midnight meeting had then taken place in the greenroom. All actors and actresses had resolved to resist heroically and sworn on oath in front of the busts of the gods of drama, calling upon Molière and Baron, Lekain and Talma * as their witnesses. At break of dawn all had sprung to arms. The lawyers and process servers of the Comédie were giving day and night service, and they were of course armed to the teeth for war to the bitter end.

We arrived toward two o'clock, Charles Blanc and I: the enemy. On the way we had talked about painting and sculpture; not a word about the theater. I admit that I was moved when we arrived in front of the building. Without any ado I was to enter, by virtue of a decree—one of those blind decrees of Providence and of the Republic—I was to enter a house that was not mine, the House of Molière, of Corneille, of Racine, of Beaumarchais. All these imposing figures seemed to me armed with stern expressions. The actors did not inspire me with apprehension, but the

---

* Baron (1653–1729), Lekain (1729–1773) and Talma (1763–1826) belong to the illustrious stage history of the Comédie.

seriousness of the role I was to play did. The public was waiting for my decisions because the public wanted this deserted theater once more to become the theater of France.

I entered with a firm step—a man of good will.

I was not to meet a single friendly face; even the doorman was armed to the teeth. He intercepted me, not to salute but to hand me a legal document. It was an injunction in the proper form which ordered me, at the risk of confiscation of my entire personal property, to abstain from entering upon my duties as director. I had expected this. "That belongs to the property department," I told the doorman. "You take that thing backstage at the time of the performance."

The ingenious idea of receiving me at the door with an injunction came from the ingenious M. Samson, celebrated in the realm of ingenious comedy. He has been called "sham actor, sham poet and sham man of good nature." Sham poet he was, maybe, but neither sham actor nor man of good nature. When in rage he was fierce.

In the vestibule the three ushers—La Chaume, Beaubillet, De Brie, all names fit for a comedy—had orders to keep me waiting for five minutes. But after five seconds I proposed to Charles Blanc to enter come what may. La Chaume ventured to open the door to the greenroom. I asked Charles Blanc to enter first.

"No," he said. "You have the honor to receive the first volley."

An icy silence; one could hear the grass growing on the ruins of that theater. The Comédie was in full muster, male and female. All the starring roles were cast.

M. Blanc spoke in the Minister's name. The Minister, he said, had no illusions about the gravity of the situation. A director was being imposed on the company, which had explicitly stated that it wanted to govern itself. But, while admitting fully their talents on stage, is it not possible to doubt the resourcefulness of their administration? The public had deserted the Théâtre Français—couldn't that be the fault of the repertoire? They had offended Mlle. Rachel who, together with them, had brought renown and good fortune to the Comédie. It was important to reestablish a calm atmosphere. That was the wish of the Minister, the desire of the President of the Republic.

I spoke then merely to say that I would not make any profession of faith: I wanted to speak only with my actions. I was resolved to do what I could to be useful, even to the point of being unpleasant. I had not come to the House of Molière to find an easy berth or to please my vanity, but to make the logic of Molière prevail once more.

They had expected a speech; M. Samson had told them that I spoke little but badly. As for him, he spoke much. It was as if he had made a bet; for more than half an hour he held us spellbound with his golden tongue: all kinds of stupidities gilded with all possible clichés. I was shocked: that was not Molière who inspired M. Samson; that was great art in its dotage.

"Are they all going to talk that much?" I asked Augustine Brohan.

"Yes," she said with her most winning smile. "After the men come the women. Every member of the company has the right to speak."

Even the most beautiful things come to an end. All the frock coats paraded out solemnly at last.

"Well," I said, "that's the end of the ceremony in *The Imaginary Invalid*. The Comédie is the imaginary invalid because nobody laughs."

"Yes," whispered M. Blanc. "But the invalid is not imaginary."

The actresses seemed to want to continue the conversation; as Mlle. Brohan passed by me she told me that she did not agree with a single word that had been pronounced.

"If I had spoken," she added, "you would have been absolutely crushed by my arguments."

I forgot to mention that, as his peroration, M. Samson had apprised me of the contents of the injunction I had received at the door: an absolute order forbidding me to interfere in the affairs of the Théâtre Français. That very day legal action for damages, with interest, would commence against me to compensate the Comédie Française for losses incurred as a result of my appointment. M. Samson added, no doubt to make me tremble, that these damages and interest would amount to a considerable sum and that he was pleased to know I had some worldly goods which could be used to pay the debts of the Comédie—as I was by my presence preventing the Comédie from paying its own debts.

Now, in fact, I did not have a penny to my name, but every man of good will can find a fortune under a ruin. M. Samson did not fail to remind me of Molière's saying: "Comedy takes what it needs wherever it can find it." He deigned to add that he assumed I was enough of a gentleman not to come and trouble the Comedians-in-Ordinary of the Republic. "The decree which appoints you is an abuse of power: by tearing it up you will give a lesson in good behavior to those who lay claim to govern us."

I had long ceased to listen to him. When everyone had left, M. Blanc shook hands with me and said, "A man forewarned is worth two. You are therefore not alone. Good-by."

But I felt very much alone. I took stock for a moment to consider by what strong action I could underline my appointment, but I felt so provisional that I could feel the earth giving way under me. The actors might go on strike, and I could not multiply myself to act on stage when the curtain rose. And who could know how the courts of that provisional Republic would dispose of this strange suit? For, after all, I could not hide the fact from myself that the actors had the right to consider themselves masters in their own house. Until now they had never had a director; they had governed themselves at will. They were heading straight for their own ruin, but that was their business, to use their own words. They swore up and down that they were defending nothing but their art. They cared very little for the money the public might pay and declared that they were acting solely for the sake of applause, that pure gold of the actor.

I surprised myself—I was pleading their cause. What business

G

did I have here? Wouldn't I be better off at my own hearth, in the proud dignity of a man of letters who is always master of his own mind? I had become a lowly timeserver. The Minister had told me, "You are the master there." But the Minister was my superior; above him was the President of the Republic; above the President was public opinion. Above public opinion, there was Mlle. Rachel. This struggle with the actors was dangerous; one could bet, almost, that I would be the loser. Everybody supported them: newspapermen, audiences. If I brought the public back to the theater, the actors would say: we did it. If the public refused to come, the actors would say: he did it.

It was getting dark, a cold grey night. I felt a shroud descend on my shoulders. The fire had gone out in the greenroom and I could not distinguish anything any more except the bust of Molière, the grave melancholy of its features accentuated by the gathering darkness.

"And yet," I went on thinking, as if speaking to Molière, "what could be more magnificent for a man who loves the old masters than to revive this illustrious mansion, to act those masterpieces in all their brilliance, to draw to himself all those great minds: Hugo, Dumas, Musset, Vigny, Balzac, Augier; to contrast the work of the living with the work of the immortals, to prove that France has not fallen and that her life of the intellect shines as splendidly as ever?"

The marble Molière was a skeptic who gave my beautiful ideas no encouragement; but I went into the Director's office with renewed determination.

A gentleman of about fifty was writing at a mahogany desk in the austerely furnished Director's office.

"This, then, is my kingdom," I said sadly to myself.

The gentleman rose, bowed to me, and turned imperturbably back to his writing. I did not understand why he was there, and to whom he was writing.

"This is the repertoire for next week," he told me, pushing his spectacles up on his forehead.

"I see. And who decides the repertoire?"

"I do."

"I would be grateful, sir, if you gave me your card. Here is mine."

"I am M. Sevestre."

"I see. Yes, M. Sevestre. You are the director of the Montmartre Theater and you come here to make your repertoire?"

"No, sir. I am no longer the Director of the Montmartre Theater. I am Director of the Théâtre Français, now referred to as the Théâtre de la République."

"I see. As a result of what appointment?"

"I was appointed by the ladies and gentlemen *sociétaires* of the Théâtre Français at the same time you were appointed by the Minister."

"And that gives you the pretension of taking up room at this mahogany desk?"

"Yes, sir. I am merely doing my duty."

"Very well, sir. You will allow me to have this mahogany desk carried to the Montmartre Theater."

"No, sir. First of all, because this mahogany desk is the sacred property of this house. It is here that M. Buloz corrected the proofs of the *Revue des Deux Mondes* and that M. Lockroy corrected the spelling of Mlle. Rachel."

"My dear sir—and colleague—you have experience as a comic actor. That is very evident. I assure you that I shall not argue with you about that piece of mahogany. But now," I added, dropping the banter, "I represent the Minister of the Interior who has given me the right to this particular domain. You have, I am sure, learned enough about manners when you acted the heavy fathers not to oblige me to resort to armed force."

He continued to write his repertoire. I rang the bell. La Chaume entered.

"Monsieur de La Chaume," I said, taking care to put in the "de," "would you please be good enough to rid me of this mahogany desk. As one disputes me in everything here, even the right to write, will you please send to my house and have them bring me the small inlaid desk which is now in my study."

La Chaume appeared undecided for a moment; there he was confronted with two men, two superiors, two authorities both of which seemed legitimate to him. But La Chaume also thought, like Louis XIV, that youth should always be served, and above all, that the House of Molière had become an old age home. He therefore took my side, at any cost, even at the risk of being fired. It was an act of heroism and La Chaume remained my friend.

When M. Sevestre saw that I was quite prepared to blow up that desk as one blows up a fortress, he looked at his watch and decided, like a sensible man, that it was time to go to dinner. I remained in possession of the fortress.

Half an hour later my little writing desk, the handiwork of Boulle himself, was brought to me, the desk on which I had written nearly all my books. Now it was my turn to make out the repertoire. I believe that it was not very much like the one made out by the other director. I replaced M. de Wailly by Alfred de Musset, and Wailly came that very evening, enraged, to find me. His first words were: "Monsieur le Directeur, as you are determined to take my life, take my head as well."

He had a small round head that would have made a good bowling ball.

"Dear sir," I replied, "I would not know what to do with your head. I have come here to play the comedies that please me, not to play at bowling. I am fair haired but quite pigheaded. Keep your dark head for a better occasion."

From here on Houssaye met up with a steady procession of protesters and enemies.

One man who entered without offering me his hand was M. Empis. That man of society, that scribbling civil servant, had become a member of the French Academy as the result of a bet by Dr. Véron, who had rather extraordinary views of the power of the press. Dr. Véron wanted to prove that the *Constitutionnel* could get someone elected to the Academy in opposition to public opinion. When Véron's enemy Alfred de Vigny became a candidate, the *Constitutionnel* cooked up the candidature of M. Empis. Politics had already penetrated the Academy. The *Constitutionnel* forced M. Thiers, M. Molé, all the enemies of the Guizot administration with whom it was fighting, to vote for M. Empis, and M. Empis was elected. May he rest in peace.

That evening he entered my office almost as impetuously as M. Brindeau before him. M. Empis always wanted to prove that he was a real daredevil. He was indignant at having been kept waiting, he declared that an ordinary actor like Brindeau should not keep a member of the Forty, like M. Empis, waiting.

I asked him to sit down in the chair that Brindeau had just vacated.

"Monsieur," he said to me, "you appear not to know who I am."

"I know who you are, monsieur, and I know why you have come."

"Monsieur, I am here to request a meeting of the Reading Committee for tomorrow, to hear a comedy which I have—destined—for the Théâtre Français."

"Sir, who can answer for destiny! But you will not read tomorrow or the day after tomorrow. I carry the responsibility here for my actions. I have literary ideals which do not at all correspond to yours. I have not come to the Comédie Française to put on comedies I don't like. I speak openly to you to avoid any misunderstanding, and your own openness will therefore prevent you from bearing me a grudge. We both have our principles."

My calm behavior exasperated the Academician. He looked at me with contempt; one could see that he was taking stock of his own literary worth and found me miles below himself—he, one of the Forty!

"But, Monsieur, I am a member of the French Academy."

"I know, Monsieur, but you know also that M. de Molière

was not, though he wrote—considering his time—some pretty good comedies. You are one of the Forty, but if you were one of the ten thousand you would not scare me."

Empis absolutely bounded out of his chair. "Monsieur, if I did not have such self-control, I would throw you out of the window."

"Good heavens, Monsieur," I answered, remaining seated by the fireplace. "You are not the first to come here with that in mind. M. Brindeau came here just now with precisely the same intention. As he is an actor, I was well aware that he was acting. As for you, if you say that, I am sure you do it out of love for hyperbole. But if you, a man of the world, persist in your intent, I shall politely conduct you to the door."

And when M. Empis, unable to contain himself, advanced threateningly toward me, I gravely rose and went to open the window. The fresh air calmed him at once.

"I am going, Monsieur, I am going," he said.

He left with tragic dignity, telling La Chaume that it was truly unheard of that a man like himself, who, when he was in the Tax Office, had exempted the Comédie from the tax roll, was now no longer permitted to set foot in it.

When La Chaume told me what he had said, I felt very sorry for having opened the door. I could not deny the moral rights of M. Empis. I wrote to him at once that he would be welcome to read his play at one of the next meetings of the Committee.

He read it, and it was turned down unanimously. He was awaiting that decision in my office, the same where he had almost opened the window. I went up to him and told him straightforwardly that his play had been turned down. He looked at me without saying a word. I told him why it had been turned down: it was a historical comedy with a very undramatic subject; I showed him that with all his talent he could not hope to make a comedy of a subject with which Scribe—to him the great master of historical comedy—had failed. I convinced him. I had feared to arouse his fury but found him quietly acquiescent. He was quite charming once he had recovered from a violent outburst. He had been spoiled in a bad dramatic tradition: if he had come a little later he might have been a great success because he had considerable original wit. I remember one thing he said. When he had become director—the reader will remember that he was my successor—he patiently listened to a perfectly terrible play, a poetic comedy that was neither poetic nor comic. All at once a particular line struck him.

"Upon my word, that's a good line," he said. "I wonder how it got there?"

An unexpected visit consoled me for the departure of M. Empis. It was Alfred de Musset. He came to tell me cordially that he would be on my side in this extraordinary war. Didn't we have the same ideas and inclinations as far as theater was concerned?

"Unfortunately," he added, "the theater is not making any money and money is the life blood of genius."

"You are right; yesterday's and today's box office would together not be enough to give a supper for the actresses. In spite of that—if you write me a comedy in five acts, in verse or prose, I shall give you at once a note on the Bank of France for ten thousand francs. And it will be cheap at that price because while the Comédie plays your play, it shall not have to play the grandsons of Andrieux who always write the same comedy because the public likes it."

The great poet had always been badly paid for his masterpieces, and that was spoken at a time when the one franc piece still had some buying power. Ten thousand francs seemed to him almost a fortune. He picked up his hat, saying, "Good-by, my dear Houssaye, I am going to start writing."

Unfortunately he passed by the Café de la Régence, began to play chess, and, in his own words, "absinthed himself until morning."

Augustine Brohan, who enters next, is won over. She is followed by Anaïs, another actress whom Houssaye charms or convinces to turn from enmity to support. The men are less easy to convince Provost is still stiffly hostile when La Chaume enters.

La Chaume announced Mlle. Rachel. Provost rose to leave.

"You may stay, M. Provost," said Rachel patronizingly: "M. Houssaye, my spiritual and temporal director, is aboveboard in his administration. No more star-chamber meetings at midnight."

"Mademoiselle," answered Provost, "we are protecting the dignity of the Comédie Française."

"Is that why Harlequin Samson is your leader? He is culpable, in my opinion, no matter that he was my teacher. I feel free to say that to you because you refused to admit me to your course, on the pretext that I would never amount to anything—which of course does not prevent you from being a great actor."

At that last hit Provost bowed and left.

"Well then, Director, have you raised prices?"

"Tomorrow."

I rang the bell and dictated a simple press release: "The price of seats at the Théâtre Français is raised."

Victor Hugo entered. Mlle. Rachel and he exchanged somber greetings; until then romantic drama and classical tragedy had not embraced each other.

"To see the two of you together in my office," I told them, "is a great event. Together you symbolize my ideal of theater: the antique world and the new world, Aeschylus and Shakespeare."

They finally embraced each other quite cordially; but it seemed to me that it was the charming woman named Rachel rather than the daughter of Aeschylus whom Victor Hugo kissed. In the beginning people said that she was not beautiful; but by sheer genius and strength of will she had become beautiful, not merely with intellectual beauty but physically as well.

The conversation lasted more than an hour. Rachel, ever lavish with promises, told Hugo that she was going to act *Angelo, Marion Delorme, Hernani,* even *Lucrezia Borgia*. She had already mastered the role of Thisbé in *Angelo,* and acted out the great scene from it with such strength and passion that Victor Hugo told her, "You bring Mme. Dorval back to life—but with real style."

He held out his hand.

"Farewell, Thespis, take good care of your chariot."

"And do not fear to break the spokes of the wheel," added Rachel.

·

The Actors Go on Strike

·

At midnight I went home without knowing if the illustrious Old Guard would deign to descend from Olympus onto the boards of the stage. I had made my decision, come what may, to organize a new company drawn from all the theaters. In addition, if the *sociétaires* resigned, I still had the *pensionnaires:* Got, Monrose, Delaunay. There was also a whole swarm of fugitives from the Conservatoire, like gaily colored birds from an aviary, who could not care less for the tradition of that school: Fix, Rebecca, Favart, Théric, Luther.

How many actors would be immediately available like Bocage and Rouvière? It was not too late to enhance the glory of the Théâtre Français with the great Frédérick Lemaître. I could recall Menjaud, call in Bressant. Mme. Plessy was about to return from Russia, Mlle. Doze wanted to return to the stage. The debut of Madeleine Brohan was already talked of. The unforeseen, after all, plays a prominent part in all things.

The next morning the papers reported that the *sociétaires* had left the Théâtre Français to form a company at the Théâtre Ventadour. The field was now wide open and I put together the most magnificent company in the world—on paper. To the Minister I wrote:

Yesterday the greatest need at the Comédie was a director. Tomorrow it will be actors: we must prepare for all contingencies. I

G*

am still convinced that all will have a happy end; still, I want to be prepared against the menace of *Messieurs les sociétaires* whose plan is to create a second Comédie Française.

I have absolutely no doubt that I can assemble, within twenty-four hours, a magnificent company of actors not at present associated with the Théâtre Français: for example, Frédérick Lemaître, Bocage, Rouvière, Mélingue. Mlle. Rachel will be responsible for the women. In addition we have a brilliant group at the Comédie quite apart from the *sociétaires*. Frédérick Lemaître would be excellent in *Tartuffe* and *The Miser;* Bocage would arouse great interest in a wide range of repertoire. Rouvière is a genuine tragedian and Mélingue is a genuinely creative man. These are actors who bear the mark of Shakespeare, and who have until now lacked nothing except a good theater to show them off. Nobody admires more than I the subtle, traditional—too traditional?—almost legendary—too legendary?—acting of the *sociétaires*, but that does not mean we should wring our hands at their whims. If they persist in the madness of going to act at the Salle Ventadour, they will perhaps carry the rockbottom conservatives with them and continue to make one hundred and fifty francs a day, but they won't displace the House of Molière. I don't expect them to be able to play truant for more than six weeks.

I could not run a theater without actors and I had no intention of giving up without a fight. Come what may, I was determined to keep the Théâtre Français open with the cream of French actors just as I had already decided to put on, in addition to the classical masterpieces, nothing except the works of Hugo, Dumas, and Alfred de Musset, and of the new group. I would refuse to have one bit of old-fashioned stuff just because it was still in fashion at the Comédie.

I quickly went off to see Frédérick Lemaître. On the way I ran into Offenbach.

"Do you want to help me with my revolution at the Comédie Française?"

"Yes," he answered. "I am a man of noise."

"Good! I appoint you music director. At present the Comédie has only two violinists. I'll let you have four."

That evening Offenbach was majestically enthroned in the

orchestra pit. (It proved to be to his advantage: at the Théâtre Français he composed some of his freshest music. In the same way I was instrumental in the debut of Gounod, who composed the choruses of *Ulysses* there.)

Frédérick Lemaître embraced me at the thought of playing *Tartuffe* at the Théâtre Français, but to his great regret he was not free: he could not break his present engagement from one day to the next. He asked for three months' delay.

Bocage did not want to enter the House of Molière without the most arrant red-carpet treatment. He saw himself as Molière because he looked somewhat like him, though he had not yet written a *Misanthrope*.

I was getting nervous. To be director of the Comédie Française without actors! The galleries would have a field day.

But that evening the Comedians-in-Ordinary of the Republic, realizing that I meant to carry on without them, were all at their posts.

[After a few days] I asked my friend Roqueplan, the Director of the Opéra, whether he would lend me his corps de ballet to appear in *Le Bourgeois Gentilhomme* or *The Marriage of Figaro*.

"I shall be delighted," he said. "But your old fuss-pots will refuse to act if personnel from the Opéra shares the stage with them. I know their stubbornness."

"What the Devil! They'll simply have to change. Molière liked lavish productions. Moreover, he may even have danced himself in the ballets with Louis XIV."

"Yes, but M. Samson never leaves off seeing himself as the drama professor. Even behind the footlights he professes—and all with the object of getting the Legion of Honor. He'd scream bloody murder if you'd dare to play Molière the way Molière would have liked it."

Verteuil, whom I had called in, added, "These gentlemen are already making quite enough noise about Offenbach, who now has six violins in the orchestra. Provost calls upon heaven as his witness, and Ligier dashes off in all directions asking if Offenbach will be asked to fiddle in the background during his great speech in *Phèdre*."

"Never mind," I said to Roqueplan. "You promise to lend me your corps de ballet, even if it is only for one evening?"

"With all my heart: I like desperate measures."

Of course one cannot stage either *The Marriage of Figaro* or *Le Bourgeois Gentilhomme* in a day.

"After that," I said to Verteuil to give him heart, "who knows if Offenbach won't become a drawing card."

One can simply not imagine the indignation of the *sociétaires* at the appointment of Offenbach. My main reason was precisely what they feared—the return of lavish productions. The Comédie had become a morgue peopled only by shadows of the past; it needed noise, light and movement. A few days later, for the revival of *La Coupe Enchantée*, I invited all the press; the public came— because I had raised the price of admission—and the President of the Republic, at my request, occupied his box. The theater was transformed: all the gilt had been touched up, the curtain had been repainted, the great chandelier and all the candelabra were ablaze with gaslight; crimson carpets covered the staircases and each member of the audience received a program bound in satin.

The *sociétaires* were terrified at the lavish expenditures; to them it was the last straw to see me take my seat quite unconcern- edly in the first floor stage box, a thing which had not been done since the days of M. de Rémusat, Lord Chamberlain and Superin- tendent of Theaters under the Emperor Napoleon I.

I did all this as a simple act of courtesy toward the audience: I wanted them to understand that on the night of Mlle. Rachel's return to the stage, or at the opening performance of a new play by Hugo or Dumas or Musset or Augier, the House of Molière would once more be the House of Molière. The public liked the spectacular: it decided that evening that our theater would rise from its ruins.

Roqueplan said to me: "The Theater has had seven years of lean kine; you will give it seven years of fat kine."

"I should say so!" cried Brohan. "We already have three." And she named three corpulent beauties.

·

Comte d'Orsay and Comte de Morny

·

Enemies surrounded me on all sides in the battle, but I gained one ally who saw the President almost every day: the Comte d'Orsay. And in that same week I made a friend of an enemy: the Comte de Morny.

One day the Comte d'Orsay was announced at my office. I had seen him at Lamartine's at dinner, but we were at different parts of the table; he left immediately after dinner, to my great regret, because he was one personage who attracted me.

"Oh, I have met him," said Rachel, who happened to be in my office. "I'll present you to him."

He entered. He bowed to her with his friendly smile and asked her most politely to present him to me.

He had immense natural charm. Nature had been very bountiful to him, making him a clearly superior being in whom grace and strength were combined. His features bespoke his intelligence, but softened by that smile which came from the heart and went to the heart. Here was one man who had no need of a coat of arms: his nobility was so evident in his bearing. One might have said—a page taken from the book of heraldry.

He was still very handsome and lively at that time though death had already marked him. "I expected to find you here," he said to Rachel, "because I came to see Houssaye in order to see you. You play *Phèdre* tonight, and I would consider myself fortunate to be there, but there is not a single seat left in the house."

"That's true," I replied, "but there is still my own box which I am most happy to offer you."

"Very well, I accept it in the kind way in which it is offered.

It is the best box in the theater. I shall offer it to the Duchesse de Gramont who will come with Guiche." The Duc de Guiche was Gramont's heir.

D'Orsay and de Guiche did in fact come that night with the Duchess, who insisted that I take my seat in the box. It was a delightful evening. The Duchess, like d'Orsay, was very witty. Guiche had the natural manner of a gentleman—completely self-assured. Rachel signaled her pleasure to us from the stage. She was very pleased with us because we certainly applauded her magnificent acting with complete enthusiasm. A small door opened directly to the stage from my box: we went to congratulate the great actress; even the Duchess herself went onto the stage to tell Rachel how much she admired her. Phèdre was used to all that adulation; one can safely say that she was the actress of society, even at the time when she intoned the *Marseillaise* from the stage.

To the compliments of the Duchess, Rachel, who never missed a cue, replied with great charm: "How could I help acting well when I saw two Hippolytes * in the box before me?"

From that day on d'Orsay and I were genuine friends. He was a frequent visitor in my office or in my box: I often visited him in his studio or rather his great hall because he was the first man to give Paris society a notion of those large suites drawn together making up salon, studio, study, smoking room and conservatory—filled with sofas, couches, window seats—all in one.

D'Orsay was then occupied with sculpture. He made a small bas-relief of my head in which he somehow made me look British. We talked at length about Lord Byron and he read me parts of Byron's letters to him, letters which were remarkable for their tortuous style. These letters made me feel that Lord Byron had constantly lived in fear of being caught in an act that betrayed either genuine feeling or a lack of intelligence. He compared d'Orsay and Gramont: "Why have you made yourself over into an Englishman? I love my country but not my countrymen; but at the age of twenty, one has no self-doubts: one plays at being

---

* Hippolyte is the man whom Phèdre loves.

Lovelace, one thinks that the women of this fog-shrouded land are angels; take care to note that those eyes raised to heaven are more likely raised by drunkenness than by ecstasy." And another letter: "If I were to start my life all over again I would go and live obscurely in Paris, and watch the passing show. I would not write one word, not even to women. But no one starts life over again, which is a good thing."

Morny was not one of my friends when I took over the Théâtre Français, because he was an ally of the actors; perhaps I should say "although" rather than "because" he was their ally, considering that I came to save them from disaster. I had met him at parties given by the Comtesse Le Hon, but we had never exchanged more than a few words.

Persigny told me one day, "Beware of Morny! He is furious at you because you have made fun of the Theater Commission."

The best way to meet the fury of man or beast is to go straight at them. That is why, one morning, I went to Fidele's Nook. That was the name of the exquisitely small mansion Morny had built in the shadow of the great palace of the Comtesse Le Hon, at the Rond Point des Champs Élysées.

"Oh, so it's you!" he said, looking very official. But he did offer me his hand. "You are making revolution at the Théâtre Français."

"Yes, and it's because I want to carry it through to the end that I've come to talk to you."

"Very well; you will take lunch with me. A very scanty lunch, I warn you."

The ice was broken. The Comte de Morny had received me in his picture gallery. In going through to the dining room I did not fail to express my admiration here and there about his paintings. My admiration hit the mark. It went to his heart.

"In the last analysis," he said, taking his place at the table, "I am much afraid that you are right about the Théâtre Français. But I stand on principle: as a member of the Theater Commission, I refuse to allow you to make fun of us."

"Now really! Are you really such a stickler for principles? There are no such things as principles, there are only men. If I am not man enough, then I shall burn myself like a moth at the legendary candles of the Théâtre Français."

"Well, then. Tell me what you intend to do."

"I have only one intention. It is very simply to have the public on my side even if it means continued war with the actors and the Theater Commission. Am I not there at my own risk, as they have already sued me for one hundred thousand francs in damages?"

"Aren't you afraid that you might have to pay?"

"Not one penny."

"Aren't you afraid of the actors?"

"Even less. They threaten to found another theater. So much the worse for them. I shall be at the Comédie Française with Rachel. It will still be the Comédie Française whether they are there or not because I shall engage Frédérick Lemaître, Bocage, Rouvière, Mélingue, Fechter, Bressant. As far as women are concerned, I am not worried at all. Give me ten women and I shall make ten comic actresses of them. The accomplishment is merely to put women in their proper setting."

M. de Morny, who had drunk two glasses of Haut Sauterne, exclaimed, "Bravo, I'm on your side!"

That was the death knell of the Theater Commission.

We became such close friends that this brother of the future Emperor invited me to lunch twice a week, always to talk about theater, plays and pictures, and sometimes, if I remember correctly, also about women.

.

The Two Directors

.

Gradually the fact that the audience was returning to the Théâtre Français overcame the resistance of the actors. Many of them became Houssaye's friends and worked with him to restore the brilliance of the Comédie. The next blow was to come from the outside, from the new Minister of the Interior, Baroche, who wanted to placate the parliamentary opposition.

One evening, when I thought that I had finally mastered the situation, Regnier, still in his costume as Figaro, came into my office looking completely distraught.

"My dear director, I am in despair! M. Mazères just left my dressing room where he showed me the copy of a decree appointing him Director of the Comédie Française."

Mlle. Rachel followed Regnier a moment later. She had met M. Mazères at the door of the theater.

"I barely escaped his embrace," she said shuddering, "but don't you worry, my dear Houssaye."

She gave me a kiss, took a pen and wrote to the Minister:

Monsieur le Ministre,

I have just learned that, thanks to you, M. Arsène Houssaye will remain Director of the Comédie Française.

I immediately went to embrace and congratulate him.

Allow me, sir, to thank you most humbly for having so graciously preserved for the theater in the Rue Richelieu a man who has the support of my colleagues and the complete devotion of your most grateful and obedient servant

Rachel

"Servant is overdoing it," I told her.

"Nothing is overdoing anything today; tomorrow the servant will be a queen in front of the Minister."

Regnier suggested to Rachel that she would do better if she wrote to the President of the Republic.

Beauvallet had just entered. Rachel showed him the letter. "I don't understand," he said. "Do you mean to tell me that Mazères is appointed and you thank the Minister for letting us keep Arsène Houssaye?"

"Look, Beauvallet, it is much nastier than if I wrote to him stupidly: You are giving us Mazères and we don't want him! And now I'm going to write to the Prince."

"It's too late for that," said Regnier.

Rachel threw down her pen.

"Very well, then I'll go to the Élysée." I wanted to stop her, but she was gone in a flash.

When a man has a stroke of good fortune few people come to wish him well; but when his pride receives a blow, the whole litany of mourners arrives on the scene, happy to behold another man thrown overboard and eager to see what figure he cuts as he descends. I cut a rather good figure for the benefit of the numberless friends and enemies who came.

"Oh, my dear friend! That was hardly worthwhile to be director for such a short time! But, what can you do? Everything is provisional nowadays."

"Not that provisional. I want to stay here for a Biblical span of seven years, the seven fat kine, according to Roqueplan's prophecy."

"But M. Mazères has already been appointed to succeed you!"

"Who cares? You go and tell him that I am not going to leave except at the point of his bayonet."

"But you must realize that he has been appointed by the Orléans faction: M. Baroche supports him, and him only."

"M. Mazères has merely a cabinet member on his side—a mere man. As for me, I have a woman: a man is always beaten by a woman."

Mlle. Fix comes in, deathly pale. "M. Mazères has just done his bit for me. He wants to change the whole repertoire for this week. He intends to give my role to Mlle. Favart. I said to him: 'You can't do that! I'm going to the Director.' And he yelled at me: 'The Director—I am the Director!'"

It may be worth recalling how M. Baroche appointed M. Mazères to take my place without consulting the President. The Minister was in the hands of the Orléans faction in the National Assembly who were determined to prove that Prefect Mazères was a jewel of a man; but they could not get the better of Mlle. Rachel with this maneuver. At the Élysée, where she was immediately admitted, the Prince gave her authority to convey his sentiments to the Minister. He also let her have a note written by Persigny and countersigned by him, which said:

My dear Minister,

Let us keep M. Arsène Houssaye as well as Mlle. Rachel.

But the appointment of M. Mazères had been made official and the Minister decided that he could not go back on his word. He had already received a letter from Alexandre Dumas, which said:

Monsieur le Ministre:

I find myself at Mlle. Rachel's house at the very moment when she has the honor of writing to you to give you her opinion of M. Arsène Houssaye as Director.

I have no right whatever, sir, to make any kind of recommendation to you but I have the right to tell you this: In the Comédie Française, I have never seen anyone do more for art or treat artists better than M. Houssaye.

My opinion in this matter has the more real value, sir, because it is completely disinterested. I have my own theater where I can produce my plays and I therefore have absolutely no need of the good will of this or that director in the Rue Richelieu.

Moreover, sir, it is for the sake of art, of the artists and of your own person that I felt it necessary to tell you: No one has ever managed the Théâtre Français better, and no one will ever manage it as competently, let alone more competently, than M. Arsène Houssaye.

Alexandre Dumas

Victor Hugo that same afternoon accused M. Baroche in the National Assembly of intending to turn the Comédie Française into a house of ghosts by his appointment of M. Mazères. But M. Baroche held his ground because the appointment of M. Mazères was, I am pretty sure, his first official act after assuming office. He had just replaced M. Ferdinand Barrot as Minister of the Interior and thought that this concession to the Orléans faction would give him more elbow room in other matters. Politics makes a mess of everything because it makes power the arbiter of everything. M. de Rémusat and M. Vitet were my friends much more than the friends of M. Mazères, but because the Orléans faction wanted to get back into power, they made that move and laid siege to that small outer fort, the Théâtre Français. That was clearly why M. Baroche, who perhaps had one foot in their camp, refused to give in.

For the whole of the next day M. Mazères was the Platonic director of the Théâtre Français. In vain did Alfred de Musset, Émile Augier and Ponsard write to the Minister asking him to tear up his letter of appointment. M. Baroche held firm. Three times Mlle. Rachel went to the Ministry of the Interior without being admitted to his presence, though he did find time to receive three or four authors of the School of Mazères in order to accept their felicitations. I had made my decision and had already given an order for my little Boulle desk to be taken back to my house, when Rachel told me, "All is not over yet. I have sworn that I'll see the Minister, and I absolutely will see him."

At the dinner hour she bravely went—not to the Ministry any more, but to his house. M. Baroche brusquely sent her word that he was on his way to dinner with the Minister of Justice and that he had not even one minute to spare. What did Mlle. Rachel do? She jumped into the carriage that was waiting for M. Baroche. The coachman thought that this was prearranged, so much so that he did not even mention it to the Minister.

When the footman opened the carriage door, M. Baroche, who did not recognize Rachel, was astounded. She told him her name, her age, and her profession.

"Oh, your profession, mademoiselle, I know."

"Well, then obviously you have no need of my professional services because you are forcing me to leave the Théâtre Français."

"On the contrary, M. Mazères will give you a better contract than you have."

"Perhaps, but I refuse to have anything to do with him at any price. If M. Houssaye leaves, I resign. I have the Prince's word that he does not want M. Mazères any more than I do."

"Where are you going, mademoiselle?"

"Place Vendôme."

"Very well, I'll take you there."

"Yes, my carriage can follow yours."

M. Baroche explained to Mlle. Rachel that it would cause a major crisis to revoke an appointment which had already created such a sensation in Paris.

"The Prince," he added, "will surely bow to political necessity."

"Maybe, but I won't."

In a few minutes they had reached the Place Vendôme. Mlle. Rachel opened the door herself. M. Baroche fairly threw himself out of the carriage through the other door in order to come around and help her out.

"That is your last word, M. le Ministre?"

"And yours, madame?"

"You know it. Good-by."

The Minister was between the Devil and the deep blue sea, between M. Mazères and Mlle. Rachel.

He decided: "Well, then—I do not want such a novel sort of audience to end to your dissatisfaction. Give me the letter from the President of the Republic and tell M. Houssaye that he remains your director. And to prove to you that I am for him as well as for you, I shall be happy if both of you will come to dine with me on Saturday; I know that you don't act that night."

Thus ended the Mazères management. The ex-prefect consoled himself by reading to us a comedy in five acts or five disasters.

M. Baroche collected in a file the whole correspondence pertaining to this somewhat strange affair, and I had the following letter about it from him:

I thought it my duty, a few days ago, to protest against a public sale, unauthorized by me, of certain letters from my term of office. (*Catalogue Charavay* #142.)

I have heard that you have expressed the wish to own two of these letters, one by Mlle. Rachel, the other by M. A. Dumas, both of them addressed to me on the occasion of your permanent appointment as Director of the Théâtre Français.

I am pleased to be able to offer them to you, being aware of the value you must attach to the judgment of such a great artist and such an eminent writer regarding one of the actions of my time in office, an action of which I myself have a truly agreeable recollection.

J. Baroche

A Day in a Theater Manager's Life

•

Arsène Houssaye had the seven years of fat kine at the Comédie which Roqueplan prophesied for him. The Second Republic became the Second Empire; Mme. Houssaye sickened and died; Rachel left, first to go to Russia, then, in 1855, to go to the United States. (Her health gave way there and she never acted again.) Yet Houssaye's tenure at the Français was brilliant, lively, full of accidents and incidents—in a word, exactly to the Director's taste. Clearly these seven years with their frantic pace were the best of his life.

In that period I could not afford to waste time. If you are curious to know how a director of the Comédie Française lived around 1850, here it is.

I lived then in the Rue du Bac, at the corner of the Rue de Verneuil, on the first floor, with a balcony. There were flowers on the balcony, roses, and I believe that I even tried to grow strawberries there, so great was my desire always to have a corner reserved for nature in my life. The apartment was handsome, the salon red, enlivened with contemporary paintings: Delacroix, Théodore Rousseau, Diaz, Decamps, Meissonier, Marilhat and

Théophile Gautier. Two busts, one of Mme. Houssaye by Jouffroy, the other of my sister Cécile, by Clésinger. Two bedrooms, one leading to the other, a cradle on one side, a small bookcase on the other—but not one book in it. Only some miniatures, some fans, some chinoiserie. A handsome dining room hung with Gobelins representing human beings.

It is eight o'clock. I arouse myself from sleep, find my slippers, take up my pen; for the next two hours it steadily glides across the paper. Why? For no very good reason. There are intermissions: our boy comes to jump on my knees, my wife appears like the morning star in a cloud of blue.

I love beauty and hers enchants me and fills my heart for the whole day. Then I depart, with mother and child, for a journey around the world: I open the window and lead them to the front of the balcony; a rose is picked, the strawberries are in bloom. We hope for fruit in the following week if the boy does not pick the blooms. Five minutes later we return from our journey, and I pick up my pen once more, believing that I am obeying my destiny. Fortunately there are occasions when I get nothing done.

Ten o'clock strikes and Zizi takes my hand and leads me to the dining room; the table is tastefully set, breakfast is a feast for the eyes as well. Moreover, it is a real breakfast because one or two friends are generally expected. Why is breakfast more pleasant than dinner? Because morning is springtime: the beginning of the day recalls the beginning of life. Unfortunately I am often rash enough to ask for the mail and the newspaper; then the clouds obscure the rays of light. But my boy pulls all of it out of my hand when he sees the shadows cross my brow. A friend comes, then another, a joke here, a serious thought there, the breakfast is a pleasure. We rise from the table in pleasant high spirits and leave for town. At eleven-thirty my carriage leaves me off at the Théâtre Français and waits for me. I read more or less official, more or less private correspondence three lines at a time, promising myself to read the latter more thoroughly later on. If we have a gala evening there are at least fifty requests for boxes and orchestra seats. Prudhomme asks for a box, no matter how bad; Roque-plan asks for a box, no matter how good. A journalist writes: "It's for Mme. X, who has only recently recovered from illness." An editor writes: "It's for me." Mlle. A + B from the music hall: "It is in order to take a lesson from Mlle. Brohan." Mlle. C + D: "It is to throw a bouquet to Mlle. Rachel." Dumas and Janin always ask for boxes without telling why or for whom. M. Mazères writes like a schoolmaster; Verteuil throws his letter into the fire but immediately snatches it out again: "We must be careful about refusing him a box, he may take it into his head to read us one of his comedies."

No session of the Reading Committee today. Reading rehearsals of a half-forgotten old play are beginning, and Rachel is beginning to rehearse *Angelo*. I go over to the auditorium and settle a few points about the staging. I convince Provost that he does not have a cold and Samson that he is younger than ever. I confer with Geffroy and Beauvallet about some scenery that has to be painted or touched up. If the rehearsal seems to go well, and if it is not one of the very last ones, I leave and go back to my carriage. I feel I ought to go and see my journalist friends: Armand Bertin, Dr. Véron, Émile de Girardin. And I also ought to see my friends at the Presidential Palace.

The Comédie Française is a state within a state; for, though the actors confine themselves largely to their own circles, the actresses go everywhere—into the world of sports, the diplomatic world, the literary world. An affair of state is always under way in Mlle. Rachel's life. In France, if tragedy is well, all's well. But if the great tragic actress should suddenly turn the public against herself by some capricious act, everybody becomes quite upset.

I must also call upon the Minister if he is my friend; and if he is not, then I must go so as not to arouse his antipathy or his prejudices. After that come visits to the gentlemen who review plays—such men as Janin, Gautier, Fiorentino, Thierry, Saint-Victor; but these men are my friends, they are at my house more often than I am at theirs. The others I simply don't go to see.

When I meet them I pretend that I take their unbounded enthusiasm for my theater, plays and actors for granted. Nothing disarms criticism so much as to take an unfavorable article as a hidden compliment.

I am back at the theater at two o'clock, a fatal hour for anyone who would like to be alone. As soon as I enter the waiting room I am waylaid by three or four impatient visitors, male or female, for in that kind of society little things like politeness or social grace are not much attended to. At the Théâtre Français, thanks to the repertoire and to the actors, one does not have visitors of social unimportance. Most of the time I open the door wide and let everyone in, holding audience in the conference room, standing in a window recess by the fireplace. That is the best way for high officials to receive callers if they do not want to waste time and be bothered with a lot of irrelevant speeches. That, incidentally, was the method of the Comte de Morny when he appointed himself Minister of the Interior on December 2, 1851. All callers at the Théâtre Français are persons of importance: ambassadors, *sociétaires*, stars of the opera or of other theaters, Ministers, deputy ministers, foreign princes, playwrights, critics, journalists—in one word, the most significant people in Paris.

With all of them I have informal and relaxed conversations. Many of them come to ask for impossible things. Most of them leave in good spirits even though they have not received what they came for; one feels himself rewarded by a wise word of Dumas' or Gozlan's, another feels more than paid by a smile of Mlle. Rachel's or Mlle. Brohan's.

It is now four o'clock, everyone has left, and I call in Verteuil; my other two secretaries are never there. They are no doubt safeguarding the virtue of some young novices whom their mothers have forgotten: Mlle. Luther is so pretty, after all! I love to see my two secretaries, Armand Barthet and Adolphe Gaiffe, and to listen to them in prose or verse, but when work is to be done I call for Verteuil, who is the real secretary of the Comédie. To him I dictate my official correspondence while I write some private letters. When that is done we take up the question of free tickets. I am politeness itself when I am unable to offer a box and have to turn down a request, which of course does not save me from making at least one enemy per day. That is the spice of life, the pepper in the stew. Naturally I have also had fallings out with some of my best friends in that way, especially those who simply cannot understand how anyone can refuse them the moon.

It is five o'clock, and I have an hour's breathing spell. I go where I like, happy to walk in liberty. Ah! Woe to him, for example, who stops me in my flight in order to gossip. So it goes until six when I meet my wife on the Champs Élysées in her carriage or at the Tuileries among the orange trees. The Tuileries were still in fashion then. We return to the Rue du Bac together, but unfortunately we cannot take dinner there; that is one of the least pleasant aspects of the Director's duties. Practically every evening I have to dine almost any place except at home, in a more or less official capacity, with members of the Cabinet, noblemen, publishers, theater managers. One simply has to do one's job; but how often have I recalled Racine's escape from the dining room of Mme. de Maintenon, where the King was expected, saying in order to get away: "Mme. Racine is waiting for me with such a marvellous carp *fricassée à la Normandie* that she would be in tears if I were not home." I often followed the example of Phèdre's poet; at times I even stayed home to dine with my family after accepting an invitation to some big government dinner where there would be so many people that my absence would pass unnoticed amidst the ministerial festivities. Apart from that, one of my sisters always stayed with us so that my wife would not feel too lonely. Almost every evening she received a bouquet to tell her that she should come and join me at the theater in the small stage box in the first tier where we had a salon for her friends.

I never lingered long after dinner. On the pretext of going to the smoking room with the smokers, I escaped as fast as possible in order to get to the Théâtre Français in good time. I was on very good terms by then with the actors and actresses, and they liked to see me in the house when I did not have to be in my office. There are days in the theater when an actor does not seem to see a living soul. It is known that his audience, to be a really good audience, should not consist entirely of strangers; here and there it ought to contain a well-known face, a friendly glance. Actors don't act well unless they feel they know someone in the house. In my box I therefore generally had a well-known political or literary figure with me. I was obliged, for reasons of fairness, to put on comedies occasionally that I did not like; on such evenings I did not have the philosophical fortitude to be in the audience— it would have been torture. On these occasions I remained in my office where I always found much to do. Though I had a horror of paper work, I was often obliged to look over administrative matters. But I put them aside as quickly as possible. Budgetary details always jostled each other in a corner of my memory. I always made mistakes when I wrote things down, but never when I kept them in my head. Perhaps I was a born mathematician just as I was a born writer. For that reason I never fell asleep over accounts any more than over stories.

This particular night *Marion Delorme* is being given, with Judith in the title role. Victor Hugo comes backstage to kiss her on the forehead. That is the extent of his compliment, but she feels herself sanctified. Alfred de Musset in passing by her kisses her arm.

"To whom should I offer my other arm?"

Her words do not fall on deaf ears: Alfred de Vigny bends over her hand.

Judith does not miss the opportunity. "You'll let me act Kitty Bell, won't you?"

But Alfred de Vigny never says yes.

The clock strikes nine and Baciocchi races in like a whirlwind. "My dear Houssaye, will you be my witness in an affair of honor? It's going to be terrible because I am going to kill my adversary!"

"What in heaven's name has he done?"

"How do you mean, what has he done? Didn't you read

L'Indépendance Belge this morning? It calls me the Superintendent of Presidential Pleasures. I have already seen Nieuwerkerke who will be one of my seconds." "How very unfortunate," I say to Baciocchi, "I am already committed to Roger de Beauvoir in a similar matter. The duel is to take place tomorrow. Moreover, your opponent is a friend of mine. It was wrong of him to publish that tasteless joke, but I think that it was also wrong of you to read it; if you fight, that duel will create such a stir that the title Superintendent of Presidential Pleasures will stick to you for life."

"Nonsense! Blood washes out everything!"

"On the contrary. Blood stains everything."

Baciocchi refuses to give in. He is determined to fight. He does fight; two valiant swordsmen: the two champions nick each other, but if enough blood is not shed to wash out everything, enough is shed to stain. Until now Baciocchi has been a more or less official friend of the Prince; from now on he is the Superintendent of Presidential Pleasures at the Élysée Palace. Well, the truth is that he is no more than the superintendent of his own pleasures. The Prince does not need anyone else to cast his nets in the ocean in order to catch his Aphrodites; they come all by themselves to the shores of the Élysée. Isn't everybody nowadays talking, for example, about the beautiful Marquise de C———— T———— who went to ask the President for a prefecture for her husband? She looked most provocative with her beautiful breasts clearly outlined under her scarlet velours dress, and the President, in casual conversation, put his hand on one of them as if it were a lovely fruit. She waxed indignant, the Prince resumed his role as Chief of State and concluded the audience with a rather indefinite promise. She came to ask me for a box right after that audience and told me the story, concluding with the thought that is its moral: "Do you think I acted foolishly?"

It is ten o'clock, the evening's receipts are reported to me, and for a moment I feel like a gambler. If receipts are up, is it because one has played his hand well, or is it because one had a lucky hand? If receipts are up, nobody worries about tomorrow;

if they are down, everybody claps his hand to his head and tries to dredge up a bright idea. Don't we have some good trump cards in reserve in that game called the repertoire? I hold a conference with Verteuil, or with an actor who happens to come in, most often just with myself. The Director is the best judge because he is impersonal.

At eleven comes some bad news. One actor has lost a relative, another is hoarse. But there is also good news. Mlle. X has just been abducted, which does not upset me at all; she can be advantageously replaced. Moreover, her abductor will be only too glad to bring her back with her talent enhanced by a great passionate experience. On the other hand, there is Mlle. Y, who cannot get over the departure of Ulysses and comes to ask for a leave of absence to run after him. For a moment tomorrow's performance is in doubt but I have been in worse trouble before. Tomorrow, when the curtain rises, everybody will be at his post.

It is now eleven-thirty, and the last intermission. I go to my box for a moment; the little salon is full of people eating ices and talking about the performance.

"X has been excellent, Y has been sublime, but for God's sake get rid of some of the others."

"I can't, they are *sociétaires*."

"Just like the Academy, where M. Victor Hugo and M. Viennet sit side by side; they are both classified as immortal, no matter what."

At midnight I have the right to go home, but a lot of late suppers take place nowadays in very lively and reckless company. I often escape from these improvised festivities, more content to stroll home by way of the Tuileries and the Pont Royal, with only the chaste company of moon and stars.

Beaujon

•

In 1852, more than ten years after his marriage, Houssaye at last
has the money for what he calls "Parisian luxury." His presentation of that fact to Mme. Houssaye is worthy of a theatrical manager in a male-oriented society.

Mme. Houssaye is informed one morning that her carriage is
at the door. As she does not own one she at first refuses to believe
it and is not entirely happy to be confronted with luxury in this
peremptory manner. Houssaye meets the carriage in the Champs
Elysées and first of all apologizes handsomely for having taken ten
years to give it to her.

"Where are we going?" Mme. Houssaye asks.

"To the Bois, like everybody else, but first we have to pay a
call."

"Where?"

"At our house."

And off they go to a small Gothic château whose half-Chinese,
half-French architecture astonishes all who pass by—as well it
might. This, her husband informs her, is her new home. She is
enchanted with the gardens (she does not mention the house) and,
in tears, embraces him.

The new home consists of two small châteaux on the heights of Beaujon; Houssaye is proud of their strange charm and their history, which he details at length. He is a rich man by now, not through the Comédie, but through playing the stock market with fabulous success, part of the wave of speculation and financial confidence which did much to pave the way from Republic to Empire. Houssaye is pleased with the way in which he came to Beaujon.

How did I get to Beaujon? This was the way: one morning when I lunched at the small mansion of the Comte de Morny, the conversation turned to an affair of money: the sale of two châteaux built by the Comte de Lanscombe, on the highest point of Mont Beaujon. Morny said to me, "Houssaye, you must buy those two houses."

That seemed rather far-fetched to me, but after lunch he took me there, as he owned land in the area. I was enchanted by the half-Gothic, half-Chinese architecture of the châteaux for sale. Morny proved to me that they were a great bargain: less than two hundred thousand francs, for one and one quarter acres and two châteaux.

I needed not to be asked twice. On my way to the Théâtre Français I stopped in the Rue Castiglione, at Delapalme, the agent for the seller. I did not bargain and signed that same day.

Morny told me, "If you don't sign today, I'll get them myself; ten years from now that property will be worth a million."

Everyone had started talking about millions after the Coup d'État, everyone dreamed of making them. Reality surpassed the dream. I myself had two million. I was not proud of it; money is a bad thing for a man of letters.

His friends coin the phrase: "Happy as Houssaye," but the pleasures of Beaujon do not last. After two years Mme. Houssaye falls ill and dies, a brave and charming lady sincerely mourned by husband and son. Yet the mourning, as he describes it, is pervaded by a tone of guilt which indicates that he must have sinned frequently during marriage. As a gentleman, Houssaye does not tell a single personal anecdote of love that the reader of the Confessions *could definitely associate with the period of his marriage. There are many undated anecdotes, and it is hard to associate them exclusively with the young bachelor or the widower between marriages.*

After Mme. Houssaye's death he leaves Beaujon and takes the apartment from which Mlle. de Montijo had recently moved to the Tuileries, to become the Empress Eugénie. The lovely gardens of Beaujon were mostly destroyed by the urban redevelopment in which Baron Haussmann cut the great boulevards through Paris.

H

Here and There

•

A Dirty Trick

•

When one writes his confessions, one must have the courage to reveal even the more risqué pranks.

Rachel arrived one day, very cheerful and gay, when I was in the garden at Beaujon. Before saying anything she broke into a peal of laughter.

"Are you laughing at me?"

"Not in the least; I am laughing at myself."

"You have said something horrible."

"No, even better: I have done something horrible." She showed me a diamond and pearl bracelet worth at least twenty thousand francs.

"Where did you take that?"

"Take is exactly the word. I took it from the hands of Dr. Véron, and I am going to act a comedy for him in my peculiar manner."

Rachel assumed a serious face. "Are you my trusted friend?"

"For life and death."

"Very well then, you are going to play the role of a man who has just resigned as Director of the Théâtre Français."

"Why?"

"Because the good doctor will be appointed tomorrow to take your place."

"I am not sure I understand—tell me the punch line of your comedy?"

"That's rather simple and rather complicated: I saw a bracelet in the Rue de la Paix on my way to dinner with the doctor, and so I said to him: 'Why aren't you director of the Théâtre Français? Houssaye gives me no more than bouquets of flowers—you would give me bouquets of diamonds, O Maecenas!' Whereupon I told him about the bracelet I had just seen. Gallantly he sent for it, found it beautiful, but did not want to give it to me. I told him: 'I made Houssaye director of the Théâtre Français; tit for tat, I'll make you director.' You won't believe it—he did answer, 'Tit for tat.' But he started off by giving me the bracelet on my word of honor. I immediately ran to Fould, who is as much of a pig as I am, and said, 'My dear Achille (that name from the *Iliad* never misses to have its effect), I have appointed Véron director of the Théâtre Français in return for that bracelet here which is dazzling your eyes.' Fould asked me if I were on my way to the madhouse. 'No,' I told him, 'but if you love me (a phrase that also never misses), you'll call in Véron, you'll tell him that he has been appointed director—the whole comedy will last twenty-four hours after which he will not dare to ask for the return of his bracelet.' 'But,' said the Minister, 'if I give him my word and don't keep it, he will screech like a peacock, and the whole cabinet will talk about the scandal.' 'Well then, you'll say that Houssaye, who had resigned, took back his resignation after twenty-four hours!'"

Who would believe that Rachel, Fould and I played such a comedy? Véron came to see me and said: "Don't be downcast, you'll be appointed Director of Fine Arts."

"What does it matter," I replied, "so long as I please Rachel and you?"

All went well: Rachel was the first, after a few days, to drop her mask, expecting that he would forgive her. One always forgives a woman who has played her role well. Rachel, in order to obtain his forgiveness, returned the bracelet to the jeweller, but Véron flatly refused his money back. However, he sentenced her to kiss him, being an old admirer who had never managed to be any more than that. Véron was also reconciled to Fould who swore by all the waters of Jordan that he had acted in good faith; but he never forgave me, nor did I him. All that happened in 1854, at the very time when Véron had just had Geffroy paint a copy of his own group portrait of the members of the Comédie Française, in which I spread myself between Mlle. Rachel and Mlle. Brohan. He gave the picture to Janin in order never to see me again.

That was not all. He had out of friendship written ten pages about me in his memoirs. His cook Sophie asked him for them in order to throw them in the stove. Rachel invited us both to dine the following winter. She joined our hands on that occasion but Véron preserved his hatred for me. I never saw him again except at a distance, but I never forget—having forgotten it that one time—that he had once been my friend.

.

A Comedy by Mérimée

.

In 1849 Théophile Gautier wrote a feuilleton in which he said, "Mlle. Rachel, who will soon return to the stage, will perform *Mademoiselle de Belle-Isle* and *Thisbé*. Between these two major works Musset's *Le Chandelier* will be given. As M. Arsène Houssaye displays such a strong determination to break with the banal and the commonplace, why does he not try to put on one of the plays of Mérimée, for example *La Carosse du Saint-Sacrement?*"

I decided to follow Théo's advice when Mérimée came to see me. He seemed to like the idea very much but told me that he did not want to read to the Reading Committee. I went along with that somewhat lightly, which set all the gentlemen of the Committee against the play. Mérimée, in love with Augustine Brohan, wanted her to play the main role; she was the actress I had also in mind. The play was produced with great care.

Mérimée came to the rehearsals three or four times and found that things were going well, always adding that he did not know anything about the theater. As for me, I was not without concern; I felt that the play would turn out to be more noise than substance. I would not have been upset if the author had decided to withdraw it. I went to see him one day to talk about that possibility; but Mérimée was like a child who was flying a kite for the first time and who therefore insisted on seeing it up in the clouds. He would not be headed off.

The play was put on, and it was booed. The Théâtre Français had not had such a festivity in a long time. Most insultingly, the boos came from all parts of the house. I believe some people even hissed from backstage. In vain the great actress deployed the resources of her acting with all its unexpected wit, gaiety and intelligence—the people hooted, the people booed and kept on booing. The Minister of the Interior, all flustered, decamped. Dr. Véron, that libertine who considered himself a Holy Roman, exclaimed that it was an absolute scandal to insult the Sacred Faith in that way. I saw myself being burned alive. Alfred de Musset said to me, "Look, there's Mazères using Empis' housekey in order to whistle louder." Théophile Gautier said he was sorry not to have worn his red vest.

But here is the best point. One belated spectator did not arrive until toward the end of the performance. He had a very well located box in which he was being awaited by two bluestockings going on forty, two unfashionable ladies who thought they belonged to the Faubourg Saint-Germain just because they lived there.

"He is not coming!" they said impatiently. At last he came. While the attendant took his overcoat, after having opened the door to the box, he said to her, "Who is being booed so nicely?" He thought he had arrived before the performance of *La Carosse du Saint-Sacrement*.

"Oh, sir, don't even mention it, one would think we are at the Odéon."

Mérimée, who liked to see others hissed, seemed to relish the adventure; but then, seeing the stricken figures of his two friends, he cast a glance at the stage. He could not believe his eyes. What, they are hissing me—me, Mérimée!

He consigned me to the deepest pit in hell. Since that lovely evening we have not greeted each other, not even at the palace of Princess Mathilde where we often ran into each other and where he never stopped hissing at my prose and my poetry.

Many times he was asked, "Do you really imagine that the whole thing was a conspiracy by Arsène Houssaye?"

"No, but he should not have put the play in performance."

Perhaps Mérimée was right, but he did not know that the playwright of the evening always ought to have a lot of friends in the house. Experienced men of the theater know that well: those are the friends, who, as if with an electric shock, light the straw fire which often saves opening nights.

·

Monsieur and Madame Ingres
·

It was in 1850. I was in my office at the Théâtre Français when M. Ingres wanted to see me. I had never met that great artist whom I had at one time admired, at another criticized, for his skillful drawings and his calvinist palette. I received him as a prince of the arts. He immediately admired the bust of two eighteenth-century actresses which I had on my mantlepiece. Then he raised his eyes to my ceiling, a tapestry of Apollo leading the Muses. There was a violin in it which really moved him. In vain I tried to talk about painting; he replied with music and poetry. Racine was his god;

there he agreed with Delacroix. Only Racine could make these so very different painters agree.

M. Ingres ended up by telling me why he had come. It was on account of Mme. Ingres. "The Académie des Beaux-Arts has its [free] tickets to the Théâtre Français, which I am very glad about. But Mme. Ingres and I are like one person, which is the reason why I am knocking at your door."

"I understand, I'll immediately list the name of Mme. Ingres [for free tickets]; you will continue to be as one; this is so beautiful that I am really moved; but though you are as one you will still have two seats each time Racine is performed even when Mlle. Rachel acts Phèdre or Hermione."

M. Ingres held out his hand. "The Comédie will not lose by this. I don't want to give you a finished picture for the foyer, I want to paint one especially for it. I already thought about it on my way here: for example, Racine hurt to death by a look from the king who wants to punish him for mixing in politics; or, better still, Louis XIV serving breakfast to Molière."

"Two legends," I replied. "But what is history other than legend? Moreover, when you have created one of these paintings it will become a true event."

"Very well, I'll start work tomorrow, but you won't get the painting until the day after because I am not like the fashionable artists. I don't improvise."

That same evening M. Ingres brought Mme. Ingres to the Comédie. *The School for Wives* was being performed. I went to welcome him in the dress circle and offered him a box, which he declined. He presented me to Mme. Ingres. Those who live together resemble each other: man, woman, both completely alike; to achieve such likeness one has to live together some fifty years. The old lady—one could see it in her looks—had made a god of her husband. Otherwise one could have taken them for two good bourgeois from the provinces, M. and Mme. So-and-so, dedicated to black clothes. Clearly they were following fashion at a respectful distance. The woman gave the impression of being dressed like a man. As a matter of fact, the dear lady was nothing more than a good companion.

"Do you know what makes me angry?" M. Ingres suddenly said to me. "It's that the audiences of 1850 refuse to see all the beauty of that masterpiece even though it is acted by the best actors in the world." And turning toward the orchestra seats he shouted to some young people who were ogling the boxes, "You wretches, be respectful."

As M. Ingres had told me, he did not improvise. He started and abandoned six versions of "La Source." He started on "Molière," left it aside, continued it, forgot about it, returned to it and ended up by giving it to the Théâtre Français. That was in 1857, one year after my resignation. My departure of course prevented me from giving him the beautiful seventeenth-century frame which I had promised him.

Let me describe how M. Ingres painted that legend of Molière's breakfast with Louis XIV. He understood the scene with a profound sense of history. He was too great a genius himself to try to put genius in its proper perspective. That scene, while elevating Molière to the level of a *grand seigneur*, made the king even greater because the king is giving a royal lesson to his courtiers. He saw the door opening to the future, when the high born no longer would lord it over the poor devils of genius who had come into the world in a tapestry-maker's shop. There is not a great scene in the Versailles Museum more eloquent then this small page of art.

When I met M. Ingres after having seen the painting I shook his hand thanking him for having done so excellently. "Very simple," he replied. "I took my time, genius is patience." I replied, unconvinced, "Genius is genius, look at Molière who never could afford to be patient." "So much the worse," murmured M. Ingres, who never liked to be wrong.

Of Musset, Scribe and Others

Alfred de Musset, that embodiment of the French spirit, showed here and there also the humor of a Lord Byron or Lord Lytton. His wit could cut to the quick. I shall only record one of a thousand instances.

An actress—perhaps it was Mlle. Figéac, who had her heyday around 1855—had an obsession for wanting to be thought impeccable, which she was not. Alfred de Musset had paid her two fingers' worth of courting as one drinks two fingers' worth of port. He had committed himself to the arms of one of her fellow actresses; however, this did not hush the backstage chatter—that the beautiful actress had once been entirely too devoted to the poet. As she was moreover jealous of her more successful colleague she gave herself great airs in front of Musset, speaking to him in a haughty manner, or not speaking to him at all.

One day she ran into him in my office at the Théâtre Français. "Oh, is that you, Monsieur Alfred de Musset?"

The poet looked the actress full in the face while bowing to her coldly.

She resumed: "Tell me, Monsieur, we need to have an explanation before witnesses, and here, as luck will have it, is one worthy of you."

The actress turned to me but I replied, "Not at all. A gentleman and a lady should not have explanations except in private."

But she refused to let go; she flatly asked Musset, hoping to embarrass him considerably, "Monsieur, have you really boasted of being my lover?"

Musset, not in the least embarrassed, answered her smilingly, "But, Madame, I have always boasted of the opposite."

The actress turned out to be the one who was trapped.

That same evening, in the greenroom, she had her revenge. Her rival was a very pleasant woman but as large as the Tower of

Babel. Some people who had seen Musset backstage asked why he was not in the greenroom.

"Don't you know," said the outraged actress, "that he is circumnavigating his mistress?"

Scribe was a famous man in his time, with his town mansion and his country château, his one hundred and one plays and his one hundred and one thousand francs per annum. In his great days I was often a guest at his table. Though his dinners were magnificent, his guests were rather bourgeois. Roqueplan once told me, "I don't go there any more, everything is simply too proper."

Scribe was a charming man, always in good humor, always spirited, always interested; he had only one fault: he had a mania about not wasting time. If he had ever had the ability to worry less about losing time, he would undoubtedly have produced a masterpiece, for masterpieces are like good fortune, they come to knock at the door of the idle.

During the second performance of *Le Chandelier*, Scribe met up with Musset telling paradoxes to Mme. Allan. He asked him point-blank, "Monsieur de Musset, I am absolutely entranced by your comedy. Tell me—how do you manage to write so well? What is your secret?"

"And what is yours?" asked the poet.

"My secret is that I want to amuse the public."

"Well then, my own secret is that I want to amuse myself."

Rachel loved to play jokes on Véron. One day she came to his house when he was absent and told Sophie that Dr. Véron had sent her to take along a silver tea service and the portrait of Adrienne Lecouvreur. In spite of some uneasiness Sophie did not dare to say no. Véron was enraged when he returned home and quarreled bitterly with the Muse of Tragedy; but after a few weeks Rachel, seeing her friendless state, arrived bravely at the dinner hour which

as usual united the doctor's intimate friends, most of all Roqueplan and Gilbert de Voisins. Sophie announced her.

"Advise Mlle. Rachel," said Véron spreading himself in all
his girth, "that only honest people are received here."

"Well then," answered Rachel who had entered, "the master
of the house ought to start by leaving."

Mlle. George had been granted a final farewell benefit. She
wanted to perform at it one more time, but I begged her to remain behind the scenes.

She answered with a bitter smile: "Oh! If I were ten years
younger, you would sing a different tune, because I would give
you the sort of hour which a man will always remember."

She was then eighty years old.

How Alfred de Musset Failed to Thwart His Destiny

·

Alfred de Musset was capable of inspiring extraordinary affection and friendship. He produced no work of any significance in the last ten years of his rather short life, but many friends and admirers attempted to draw him back to poetry and drama, and away from the Café de la Régence where he divided his time between absinthe and chess. Houssaye records several such attempts, including one by Augustine Brohan, whose power as the great star of comedy at the Théâtre Français around 1850 was hardly second to Rachel's, the star of tragedy.

I mentioned before that I had hopes of getting a comedy from Alfred de Musset just as Rachel had hopes for a tragedy. He had made a start on *Frédégonde*, but he did not even begin work on *Les Enfants du Siècle*, a title which recalled his novel. As women had been his undoing, I believed that a woman's love could also save him—but which woman?

Alfred de Musset, Rachel and Augustine Brohan were in my office one day. Suddenly I said to the tragic actress, "Why the devil did you, a year ago, take a comedienne and a poet to La Chaumière, and in broad daylight?"

"That was a silly thing," Rachel answered with a laugh; "certainly it was not to marry them off to each other. I had gone out to —well, just to go out. By force of habit I drove by the Théâtre Français. Alfred de Musset was smoking a cigar in the doorway. As I am very fond of him, I invited him into my carriage, but I also said to myself: 'What are you going to do with him?' Mlle. Brohan appeared on the scene right then and I was saved. I called to her, I hauled her into the carriage, I made much of her; and at once I cast both of them upon the waters, that is to say I threw them upon each other's company by driving them to La Chaumière, from where I made my escape laughing like a fool. That's the whole secret of that tragedy."

"Is that really true, that lie of yours?" asked Mlle. Brohan.

"It is as true as my friendship for you and your friendship for me."

"Now I know at last," said Brohan.

"Give each other a kiss!" cried Alfred de Musset.

"What a mess," he continued. "Augustine barely escaped doing a good deed, and I barely escaped writing a good play."

With which Alfred de Musset poured himself a glass of water and looked at Brohan with a benevolent smile.

"You won't take that glass and throw it at my head, will you?"

"No," she answered, "but I dare you to drink it."

Heroically Musset downed the glass.

"At last," Rachel said to me, "he is mixing water with his wine. Unfortunately he is also mixing it with his poetry."

But here is the whole edifying story of the ride the poet took with Tragedy and Comedy:

One fine day, at the door of the Théâtre Français, Alfred de Musset doffed his hat to Rachel, who had just got into her landau.

"My dear friend, where are you off to, so beautiful and smiling?"

"My dear friend, you are too inquisitive. I fly wherever the wind takes me."

"You are absolutely right. Would you like me to fly with you?"

"Why not? I am not at all averse to traveling in such illustrious company."

"You speak for yourself."

"Let's speak for each other."

Alfred de Musset dropped his cigar and seated himself at Rachel's side. Just as the horses were starting, one of the three stars of the Comédie waved to them. Which star? The liveliest? Each of the three had been the liveliest at one time, but this was Comedy's shining hour. Clever phrases issued from her lips like flaming swords. Everyone was afraid of falling on the battlefield stabbed by her words, but her lips were so red and her teeth so white that everyone who was worthy of it sought out that battlefield.

Rachel said to Musset, "There's Brohan, who will say fine things about us."

"Madame," answered Musset, "she won't say anything worse about us than what we are thinking."

Tragedy had already extended her hand to Comedy. "We have room for one more," she told her.

"Oh no," cried Comedy, "I don't want to be dog in the manger."

"I order you to get in," answered Rachel, "because you are the one we need for our festivities."

"Oh, if there are festivities, of course I'll come."

And she got into the landau.

The carriage had a fourth seat, but only an Edgar Allan Poe could have sleuthed out where Tragedy was going to take them.

"To the Observatory," she told her coachman.

"Bravo," cried Musset. "I am not at all afraid of discovering my star—for though I am out in starlight every night, I never manage to see it."

"That's not its fault," said Tragedy.

While the poet smiled and continued the verbal sparring,

Brohan said to herself: "Rachel is obviously not going to the Observatory to search for her own star but for a comet; moreover, she is not going to find him because I saw him just a short time ago around Mlle. X."

"Evil to him who evil thinks," said Rachel. "I told the coachman aloud to go to the Observatory because I did not want the people at the stage door to know where we are really going."

"But I don't have a passport," said Brohan, acting frightened.

"And I don't have a shirt," added Musset.

"And I don't have a nightgown," concluded Rachel.

They had reached the Place du Carrousel. Rachel, pleased with Musset for having thrown away his cigar, offered him an even better one which had not been intended for him, but which he lighted with great pleasure.

Amid the smoke the battle of wit and laughter went on. When Rachel enjoyed herself, she really enjoyed herself, and her two companions did not hang behind. In that way they were in the Avenue de l'Observatoire in no time. Alfred de Musset was delighted not to know where he was going, and Rachel enjoyed the curiosity of Brohan, who, however, was not in the least impatient.

"We are going to La Chaumière," Rachel said suddenly.

"To La Chaumière? What the devil are we supposed to do at La Chaumière in broad daylight?"

"We'll walk about like a group of undergraduates."

"Where are the violins?"

"Oh dear, I've forgotten the violins! But the birds will sing to us romantically."

Soon they were at the door of La Chaumière and entered the battlefield of the dance where at that time of day only a few medical students were smoking their pipes and drinking grog. There the three of them wander about the thickets, pluck some roses and promise each other to venture to return there one evening when both Rachel and Brohan are not occupied on stage.

Meanwhile Musset has ordered a bottle of beer, a bottle of absinthe and a bottle of cognac. The hour has come: Tragedy tells

Alfred to watch over Comedy. She asks Comedy to watch over
Alfred. Then she disappears, telling them that she would be back.

The poet presents a rustic chair to Comedy and seats himself.

"My dear, can you tell me why Rachel plants us here face to face?"

"My friend, can you tell me where the illustrious tragic lady
has gone?"

"Is she trying to make us play extras?"

"Oh, no doubt you'd prefer to play the part of Hippolyte!"
And Comedy declaims some of Tragedy's best lines.

"No," says Musset, "that is not what I want. You know that
tragedy is not my line; if I ever fall in love with Phèdre, it will be
as a woman of the world."

"Oh, indeed," says Brohan mockingly. "Your tastes and habits
are well known."

"Surely you are not holding it against me that I pass my
evenings with ladies of a different world?"

"Yes, in the land where virginity is mended."

"I am not joking. If innocence had been banished from the
earth, that place is where we could find it again."

"I have no doubt, but you would do better to find it in your
own home."

"Nonsense. Do you insist on preaching to me today?"

"And why not? You know very well that the stage is a school
for morals. Jesus Christ changed water to wine at the Wedding
Feast at Cana. I would rather like to change the wine to water at
the feasts which you hold every night."

"Well," cried Musset, "here's another one who keeps telling
me that I am a lazy good-for-nothing."

And Apollo-Musset, mounting the Pegasus of paradox, set out
to prove to Brohan that Bacchus, the son of Jupiter, is the second,
if not the first, of the gods.

"Has he not a barrel for a throne and a wreath of grapes for
a crown? Can you find a more even-handed king? Semele, his
mother, was a greater poet than the nine muses put together because hers was the poesy of love. Bacchus is cheerful: is not cheer-

fulness the chief mark of a gentleman? All those who drink water —what do they sing? What do they know of the world? The gods were always feasting. I hold with the ancient sage who reports that the gods were drunk to the gills when they created man—and especially woman. I act like the gods when I must bring one of the children of my imagination into the world. Look, my dear, you must throw away all these prejudices."

"I hear wisdom speaking," said Brohan with a smile.

Musset and Brohan felt a friendship for each other that came close to love. She had already tried to tear the poet from his nocturnal wanderings. Each time he became attentive to her she wanted to make him as attentive at night as he was in daylight.

"My dear," Musset resumed, "when someone has flaming eyes and a laughing mouth, she should not preach, she should love."

"Very well. So be it. I shall love you if you are willing to be locked up at my house."

"I ask for nothing less."

"Fine, but you will have to go through a probation period of six weeks."

"Agreed."

"You will write a comedy for me."

"Agreed also, on condition that you dictate it to me with these lovely clever lips."

The poet bent over the actress and kissed her hair.

"What would Rachel say if she came back now? She surely did not plan this rather singular meeting."

At that point the waiter of La Chaumière rather belatedly brought a small glass of cognac, a middle-sized glass of absinthe and a big glass of beer. Though Musset frequented cafés—and worse— every day, he had not lost his good manners. In one instant he had flung the three glasses over the head of the waiter who had served them.

"I told you to bring me a bottle of cognac, a bottle of absinthe and a bottle of beer."

When Alfred de Musset's anger was aroused he assumed an imposing air of authority. Drenched as he was by the contents of the three glasses, the waiter obeyed. .

This time the poet complacently composed his well-known recipe: he poured out the beer, the absinthe and the cognac in the exact proportions he had long ago determined. He was about to put that elixir to his lips, like Apollo at an intimate party with Daphne, when Brohan seized that ideal cup and hurled it in turn over the head of Alfred de Musset.

He seemed not to understand because he said to her, "Would you like a glass of water?" He thought that she was offended because he had not offered her anything.

"What do you mean?" she cried. "Don't you realize that I have thrown your alcoholism into that garden?"

Alfred de Musset raised his cane as if to strike her. His eyes flashed, he grit his teeth, completely caught up in his anger.

"Hit me, my friend," she said with complete calm.

Disarmed, he let his cane drop and threw himself at her feet, sobbing and kissing her hands. She raised him up at once and took his arm to move away from the curious bystanders.

"You are saved!" she said with great tenderness.

"Yes, you have accomplished a miracle. But tell me that you love me too."

"If I did not love you I would not have accomplished that miracle."

That minute was the high point of their love: he, because he believed that all the blooming, singing boughs of his youth were rising once more from the abyss; she because she wanted to sacrifice herself in order to save a soul in anguish, the soul of a great poet. More than that, she was truly capable of loving him, and he of loving her. More than one woman had burnt herself at his flame, more than one man had been hurt by her.

The force of circumstance, however, put a spoke in the wheel. There they were, wandering like two lovers in the garden amidst a profusion of roses. Alfred de Musset's thirst had left him, except for the thirst for love, for passion, for the ideal. He walked more proudly, breathed more freely, he felt a horror at his past squalor. One great love had undone him and now he had found himself in another love. Theater-love, said those who don't know the theater. Augustine Brohan is not well-known now, or rather no longer well-known, though she is still young; but she did abandon the theater that day in order to make a valiant attempt at that rescue. She was a young actress then who had all the aspirations to greatness. She acted magnificently, with a great natural talent, entering into the spirit of her roles. But her own intellect did not stop there; she wrote like Mme. de Sevigné, so much so that Musset, reading some of her letters, considered her superior to Mme. Sand as a letter writer.

He had first been taken with her body; now he was taken with her style, at once smiling and passionate, penetrating, full of laughter and tears, with sudden stabs at the great horizons of thought. She was a strange but charming woman, somewhat hidden by her laughter, which was for her often a mask of grief. This, then, might have been the right woman for Musset because he could find heart and intellect in her, a poem and an ideal.

It was, however, not the first time that someone attempted to tear Alfred de Musset from his nighttime peregrinations. His sister had tried to play the role of the consoling angel who chases away the clouds. A lady of society, who wishes to be anonymous, had compromised herself in an attempt to rescue him; she had been too serious in her almost religious zeal. Alfred de Musset wanted a tête-à-tête only when it was amusing. The actress of the Théâtre Français had the requisites for her role more than any other.

Rachel, meanwhile, had not returned. Musset gently placed Augustine's arm in his, saying, "I am yours; let us go. If Rachel comes back, all the echoes of the place will tell her that we are happy to have come with her, but that we are even happier to return without her."

Musset quite naturally did not want to go back to his own place. He swore to the actress that she would in effect be able to save him only on one condition, that of offering him the hospitality of her own home.

"What will they say at the Théâtre Français?"

"Let them talk. A poet and an actress are not beneath each other. And moreover, you are not bound by anything any more than I am."

"I should think not! Very well, come to my house. The die is cast. I'll say that you are writing a comedy for me."

"Very well, I shall write you a comedy in fact!"

So said, so done—almost. The actress shut Alfred de Musset into her apartment and he at once began work on *Louison*. The apartment was strictly divided up, with doors locked in-between. They lived like two friends, not at all like lovers. Each had the right to invite his friends or to give a supper after the theater. These little parties had great charm because everyone who came to them was as witty as he was intelligent—even though one met the misanthrope Mérimée there and the philosopher Rémusat. Everyone was beginning to remark on the new life of Alfred de Musset. Augustine gave her word of honor that the author of *Le Chandelier* was none other than a new La Fontaine to her La Sablière * —both of them merely being younger.

Alas! This happy existence did not last more than three weeks, a mere interlude in the half-somnolent, yet radiant, orgiastic life of the great poet. One night after supper and after midnight, Musset suddenly developed a platonic desire for Anaïs, that persistent ingenue who kept man's illusions afire until the end of her life. He saw her to her door, he took her to the staircase, he conducted her into her apartment without even realizing that he had forgotten his hat.

The next morning Augustine sent him, by a messenger, his hat and his play with these simple lines: "My dear friend, you lost your head with Louison; it is Anaïs who will play that role because I am not willing to play the part of Caprice."

---

* Jean de la Fontaine (1621–1694), best remembered for the fables he translated from Aesop, enjoyed Mme. de Sablière's hospitality for twenty years.

Mlle. Anaïs did in fact act *Louison* at the Théâtre Français with her carefully rehearsed simplicity. Mlle. Brohan threw a bouquet to her on opening night.

That is the story of how Comedy almost managed to bring Alfred de Musset back to his poetry but failed to cure him of his nightly wanderings. In place of a comedy he wrote her the merest trifle—and gave even that to Anaïs. As for myself, I wasted my time talking to him of a premium of five thousand francs, a thousand for each act, while he was writing, and another five thousand on opening night, exclusive of royalties. He promised me a hundred times to get right to work, but always the next day.

A Supper at Rachel's

•

It is midnight, the right hour for a supper, arranged on the spur of the moment and ordered from the best caterer.

We all leave the Comédie Française together, some in a carriage, some in a cab. A prince is the first to arrive, in Rachel's company in her small coupé, the gift of another prince, and drawn by two English horses, the gift of an ambassador: Rachel refuses nothing to the poor but accepts everything from the rich.

The Prince would have done well to bring two servants with him because the service is no better than at the famous supper of Mlle. Rachel and Alfred de Musset.* It is not the actress' fault, who is in the hands of Rose, a servant of the old school, devoted to her to the limit. What a tyranny, though, is in that devotion! Rose is the mistress of the house; she does everything so that it will be done just right, but as she has only two hands the guests must, on busy days, lend a hand if they want to be served.

On that evening there are about a dozen guests who have come, impromptu, from the theater to celebrate the success Rachel has just had in *Lady Tartuffe*. She herself is not particularly satisfied.

* A supper of which Musset has left a charming description. (*Oeuvres Posthumes*, Paris, 1867.)

She needs to be plied with compliments, and to ply herself with champagne to forget some poorly conceived scenes.

Mme. de Girardin, the author of *Lady Tartuffe*, is present. For the first time in several months she has prevailed on Émile de Girardin to come also. He is her friend but no longer her husband and, like Louis XV, he is every woman's husband except his own wife's. Mme. de Girardin keeps her home as virtuous as Penelope. Many are in love with her, none are lovers.

Jules Janin, Théophile Gautier, Paul de Saint-Victor, Albéric Second, Fiorentino, and I are also part of the company.

But what brings Princess Rhéa among us? She is so beautiful that no one holds it against her to have come. The mistress of the house presents her to Mme. de Girardin as if she were a fairy rather than a foreign princess. It is pure joy to rest one's eyes softly on that delightful half-Greek, half-French figure, to see that image of ancient Athenian beauty with the voluptuous smile of a Parisian in love.

Girardin, who knows Rhéa well, seats himself by her side at the table and launches into an interview.

"Why, Madame, are you called the consolation of the afflicted?"

"It is easily explained, Monsieur: because I console them by weeping with them."

Behind his napkin with its crown of laurels embroidered by Rachel's sister, Fiorentino thinks he is spreading Neapolitan sunshine with some more or less unedited pieces of malice.

The pewter spoons of Rachel's early days would look out of place here. The brilliance of the chandelier is instead reflected in a magnificent set of handmade silver.

The conversation first turns loudly to *Lady Tartuffe*, but one can only wish that Molière were present. He would explain to Mme. de Girardin, in the most charming manner, how she just missed her mark, for *Lady Tartuffe* is not the work of a mere amateur.

Janin explains, "Everyone will wish to see the battleground where Mme. de Girardin and Mlle. Rachel have met up with such dangers! Villemain himself said to me during the fifth act that this is comedy which combines all talents."

"That Janin is terrible," murmurs Paul de Saint-Victor. "In a moment he will be talking about the *Iliad.*"

And Janin, only half hearing the others, fairly shouts on, "Yes, when I see Mlle. Rachel lay aside the veil, the cloak, the golden cup, the scepter and the dagger, then I liken her to a disarmed Achilles. But Mlle. Rachel's arms are not in the hands of the enemy. After *Lady Tartuffe* she must play *Phèdre* *."

Rachel, who is kind, talks about reviving Mme. de Girardin's two tragedies, *Judith* and *Cléopâtre.*

Except for Mme. de Girardin everyone shares the same opinion of *Lady Tartuffe.* The title had seduced Rachel who had more than one Lady Tartuffe in her acquaintance. She wanted to immortalize that despicable character on stage, as Molière had done for its male counterpart. Mme. de Girardin, who could rise to the challenge of tragic verse, never had the talent for laughter. It showed considerable fortitude, therefore, for Rachel to manage to play that mirthless comedy twenty-seven times. The public let her know that it was pleased with her, but she was not pleased with herself. Rachel was Rachel's best judge. She was never blinded by illusion.

She let her friends talk that evening, thinking that they were so many amiable Tartuffes. She continued to play the role of Lady Tartuffe at her supper table but her eyes showed her real feelings. To the friends who really knew her she said, lifting her glass, "Oh! I wish I could drink a little truth."

Fortunately the conversation turned to another topic. We had just begun to attack a game pie and a *pâté de foie gras;* all the food, it seemed, was to be cold. Rose had not lit the kitchen stove; the York ham had been served cold, and the partridges as well. And in

---

* *Lady Tartuffe* was one of Rachel's very rare excursions into comedy, for which she laid aside the accouterments of the classical tragic drama which Janin mentions.

addition, Rose, tottering about the table, was being called to task for not icing the champagne.

Suddenly Girardin addressed Jules Lecomte, the chronicler of northern courts and stage queens. "Is this like the suppers you had with Marie Louise * ?"

The Prince, completely surprised, turned his eyes toward the journalist who replied, "More or less. We always supped helter-skelter, because there was no order in her house."

"But you were the one who gave the orders!"

Lecomte smiled. "Right, right. I told everybody to go away."

"You supped tête-à-tête, then?"

"Yes, I was studying the woman under the Empress."

"A devilish woman under that anointed Empress," said the Prince. "She might have saved all, but she ruined all."

"Tell me," continued Girardin with unconscious impertinence, "whom did Marie Louise love in you, the clever man or the tenor?"

"Oh, I had no illusions. She had already made beautiful music with Mario, and she wanted me for the same purpose."

"Well then," concluded Rachel, "if I ever make you my Master of Ceremonies, it will not be in order to make beautiful music with you."

Théophile Gautier chimed in. He never liked to miss the opportunity of tilting against tenors and all others who "make noise on the pretext of making music."

"You better keep quiet," said Mme. de Girardin. "When you were in love with Julia Grisi, you would have metamorphosed yourself into a nightingale at a glance from her eyes."

The Prince gave as his opinion that one ran into a tenor or a baritone in almost all houses of society nowadays.

"All women let themselves be caught in the act of making music."

"Not at my house, or Mlle. Rachel's," said Mme. de Girardin.

---

* Marie Louise, Archduchess of Austria, became the Emperor Napoleon's second wife. After his banishment in 1814 her father, the Emperor Francis, gave her the Duchy of Parma in Italy.

"Yes, of course, because in your houses it is the men who are caught making music."

Someone remarked that Saint-Victor was not expressing his opinion on the art of seducing women. The reason was that on that evening he was devoting himself assiduously to Rachel's third sister, the one who, by virtue of her figure and dramatic voice, was most like her great sister.

Suddenly the door was flung open and admitted a noisy and dishevelled man, a former cavalry officer who had become a great sculptor, but who behaved everywhere as if he were still in the regimental tavern.

"Lord have mercy," cried Rose, "there'll be nothing left over for breakfast."

"A thirteenth guest," shouted Gautier, throwing a pinch of salt over his shoulder.

The newcomer planted himself behind Rachel and delivered himself the following speech, in a piping voice which contrasted with his great size and rakish manner:

"Well, yes, I am Clésinger the sculptor. No party is complete without me as long as my wife is not around. Do you know my wife? Very sweet and very pretty! A real angel as long as her mother is not present: because she is the daughter of George Sand. They say I use her as a model. What nonsense! The Academy of Fine Arts is the one that spreads such rumors. But don't you have anything to drink? Have you lost the keys to the cellar, like at the Last Supper?"

Rachel turned to him with a smile. "Sit down next to me, you mad genius. We don't lose the keys when you are here. Would you like a bit of supper?"

"But I want lots of supper and you don't have anything left except pie crusts. What a cheap winehouse you keep! Do you think that I feed on chips of marble? Oh, divine Rachel! I am going to make you a statue as the Muse of Tragedy, then the Muse of Comedy, then the Muse of Love. But you'll never do for the

Muse of Gluttony. Come on, Rhéa, you pose for me, won't you, Rhéa?"

Clésinger sees that Girardin is at the twentieth paragraph of his love interview with her. "Come on, tell me, you great writer, why don't you people your garden on the Champs Élysées with statues? I'll make you half a dozen for thirty-six thousand francs and throw in your bust as well."

"Why not my statue?" asks Girardin.

"Because you are not big enough yet. What an age this is, all the statesmen are tiny. Napoleon III, Thiers, Guizot, Girardin—dwarfs, every one of them."

Mme. de Girardin points out to Clésinger that all great states-men were small.

"Indeed," answers Clésinger, "one can easily see that Charle-magne did not give them a hand up—he was a big one."

With that he rose, turned and left saying that he would eat in a tavern.

"What a relief," cried Rachel. "I was afraid he might like it here. Last time he liked it so well that we found him the next morning asleep on a couch in the library."

Dessert was being served. Gautier had asked for permission to smoke, but Mme. de Girardin, sitting next to him, extinguished his cigar as soon as he had lighted it.

"Who'll cut up the pineapple," asked Rhéa.

"Be still," said Rachel in high humor. "That's a sacred pine-apple, no one must touch it. The Comédie Française lends it to me on festival days."

"Well, pass us at least those magnificent grapes."

"You know very well that they are made of marble. I brought them back from Naples with my coral tiara."

Someone asked Rachel if she herself did not turn to marble when someone wanted to bite her.

She smiled and said artlessly, "Evidently not, for the Prince has not broken a single tooth."

Mme. de Girardin judged the conversation in need of improvement. She rose to depart. M. de Girardin accompanied her—as far as her carriage.

The string was broken and the beads scattered quickly. Soon nobody except Rose was left in that Pompeian dining room. She looked over the table which was really not very disheveled, "God of Israel!" she exclaimed. "What an orgy! And those are supposed to be clever people. Gargantua was an angel from heaven compared to these voracious beasts! I hardly dare to think of the bill. A supper of twelve francs a head! Not counting the wine and fruit! Twelve times twelve is one hundred and forty four! And it took them no more than an hour to make such a massacre!"

One must be just to Rachel—she never counted the cost of a supper.

Today that supper of one hundred and forty-four francs would cost ten times as much—and without Rachel!

From the Élysée to the Tuileries

•

*The transformation from Republic to Empire is reflected in the
Confessions. When he recalls 1849, Houssaye sees Napoleon, the
Prince-President, as a democratic head of state, jockeying between
the political parties to make his policies prevail. Within a year the
tone has changed. The Élysée Palace subtly assumes the aura of a
court—Houssaye calls it that with unconscious naturalness—and the
drive toward autocratic monarchy is on. Soon censorship is en-
forced again, and the Director of the Théâtre Français has his polite
battles with ministers who are imperial well ahead of the Empire.
Eventually the Empire becomes a fact and the Emperor moves
across the Place de la Concorde to the Tuileries.*

•

A Conversation at the Élysée Palace

•

Though the Prince never let himself go, even in the most intimate
circle, he was never stuffy with his friends. Court etiquette was not
rigorously observed at the Élysée; after all, he had lived the life of
a simple citizen in the United States not so long before, without any
court to trail after him. He was too glad to be back in France and

to breathe his native air not to be pleased with things as they were, except for the Orléanists who, disguised as republicans, made fierce war on him in the National Assembly.

One morning when he had asked me to see him—I do not remember why—I arrived at lunch time. He had just entered the dining room when I was announced. His first impulse was to ask me to take a walk in the garden, but he changed his mind and invited me to lunch.

Most of the guests were already in the dining room: Persigny, Toulongeon, Fleury, Prince Murat, Baroche, Baciocchi were standing and waiting for him. They had preceded him at his request because some diplomatic business delayed him. They left off talking more or less as he took his place, in case he wished to say something, but he remained silent as if engrossed in thought.

Prince Murat began to talk to me about Rachel, which brought the Prince back into contact with us. In his deep bass voice he began to speak in praise of the great actress, which in turn led him to praise tragedy, no doubt because tragedy is the apotheosis of princes. For him everything counted that helped him to govern. It was well-known that art as such meant little to him. Though he had composed some poems and searched for eloquence in solemn prose, he was no more endowed with poetic than with artistic talents. The heir of Napoleon I was a utilitarian. What he loved most in the firmament was his own star; what he loved in the forest was the hunt, what he loved in the valleys was the smoke of the railway engine, what he loved in the magnificent gardens of the Élysée was the view of the Tuileries.

I admit that I did not answer the Prince without some trepidation. We were no longer merely at lunch; we were having an open meeting: everybody was looking at me. They had hardly had time so far to judge my performance as Director and now they wanted to judge me by the way I responded to the Prince. If I uttered no more than some elegantly empty platitudes my spell as Director would be at an end. The spreading silence boded me ill. Fortunately I had something to say.

I began by reminding the Prince that there were several kinds of theaters in Paris. It was very well to open the doors of the Théâtre Français as wide as one could. People would not come because people don't go where they don't expect to enjoy themselves. They are afraid of tragic poetry, they reject the noble lessons of the masters. Therefore, the Théâtre Français should not address itself to the general audience. When art is at everyone's beck and call, it is not art any more; democracy does not love the heights: when it ascends the mountain it does so only to level it. The beautiful is not always the greatest good—the people love what is good but greet real beauty respectfully, at a distance. No matter what we do, we are in need of two kinds of performance: the kind that pleases the intellect and the kind that pleases the emotions. One can shatter the aristocracy which rests on coats of arms but not the one which rests on nature. The descendant of a Montmorency may go to a mere crowd pleaser, while the ragpicker's son will seek out the most intellectual fare if God has put His mark on his front. We must therefore leave the Théâtre Français its intellectual preeminence. To lower it would be a crime against the world of letters. It is up to the spectator to rise continuously to a challenge. Let us give him the ineffable experience of *Le Cid* and *Le Misanthrope*, let us remind him of Aeschylus and Shakespeare, let us show him his own moral condition in a mirror, let us make him laugh after having made him cry—that is the right thing to do. But to turn the Théâtre Français into a school for politics, rather than a school of beauty and truth—that is the wrong thing to do. The real genius of the stage is to elevate the soul to all the great feelings of heroism, of virtue, of patriotism, but of a patriotism divorced from all partisanship.

Here I was interrupted by one of the guests who maintained that there could not be any patriotism without partisanship because the genius of France was always represented by a man.

"That is exactly the danger," I said, "because the Parisian scene always consists of a battle against the powers that be: under Napoleon I everything republican or royalist was applauded; under the Bourbon Restoration, everything imperial or republican was applauded; under the Second Republic, Mlle. Rachel has sung the *Marseillaise*, but it was Mlle. Rachel and not the *Marseillaise* that was applauded."

The Prince, who was not obstinate, said, "Perhaps you are right."

•

Trying to Kill Charlotte Corday

•

The actors still did not want a director at the Théâtre Français. One day I managed to obtain universal harmony by resigning.

Here is the story. One morning Mlle. Rachel said to me, "Ponsard has just finished his *Charlotte Corday;* according to Augier it is beautiful. I want to play that Angel of Murder. Ponsard must give his play to the Théâtre Français but I am not on very friendly terms with him and I think that you too are not in his good books."

"Why?"

"Because both you and Méry have published something about the School of Good Sense *."

"What was it?"

"Of course, like all critics your offenses slip your mind. Méry said, 'The most outstanding characteristic of the poets of the School of Good Sense is that they don't know how to write poetry.' That would have been enough, but you added, 'If they don't know how to write poetry it's because they don't know how to write prose.' "

"That's right. Well, I may have said that, but in a battle one does not pull his punches; apart from that I think I am closer to the truth than Méry because I have never found any good prose in Ponsard but I have applauded some beautiful poetry in *Lucrèce.*

---

* Ponsard (who had been Rachel's lover) was the chief playwright and spokesman of the School of Good Sense, a group that opposed the romantic drama of Hugo and Vigny. The success of Ponsard's *Lucrèce* had been considered a defeat for Hugo.

He has a talent for the epic and knows how to put his characters on the stage; I am quite prepared to perform *Charlotte Corday*."

I promised Rachel to go to Ponsard that same day. I found the poet in a tiny apartment, unworthy of a master, in the Rue des Beaux-Arts. He behaved like an absolute gentleman. Though old enemies, we shook hands cordially and right then became lifelong friends; no friendship was ever more fully observed. He believed at once that I would dedicate myself to the success of *Charlotte Corday* if he were to give it to the Théâtre Français. But he had already promised it on the Right Bank and the Left Bank, to the Porte Saint-Martin and the Odéon; his friend Bocage was to play Robespierre, Marat or Danton. I promised to hire Bocage, I urged on him that he would nowhere in the world find a Charlotte Corday like Rachel. "Oh, I know all about her," he said, "she'll do the play three times, if that much. Besides, who knows if the Reading Committee of the Théâtre Français won't turn down the play."

"Don't worry about that. If they turn it down I'll put it on all the more because the public will prove me right."

I pleaded my cause so well—really pleading his cause—that he said in the end, "Take my play, read it, and play it if you find it worthy of the House of Corneille." He was right in calling it the House of Corneille, for later on the House of Molière refused his comedies.

Well, here I was, master of *Charlotte Corday*. Before going to Rachel I went straight to the Minister.* As I governed the Comédie autocratically while waiting for the Council of State to limit my powers, I told the Minister that I had decided to go ahead in any case even if the Committee did not want *Charlotte Corday*.

"But you haven't even read the play."

"I have given it a quick glance, I believe that it is an extraordinary drama, a work that will make a stir."

"Too much stir, perhaps, my dear Director. Just think—Marat on the stage."

* Ferdinand Barrot.

I

"Yes, and in a bathtub. Shakespeare wouldn't have been afraid of such a scene. Haven't you seen David's marvellous picture 'The Assassination of Marat'?"

"Yes, Marat in a painting; but when people see Marat himself taking a bath, which, after all, was not his habit `. . ."

"Well then, we'll put the scene off stage like in those everlasting French tragedies. Would you like to read the play?"

"I don't have a moment."

"Ponsard will come to read it to you. Invite three or four of your political friends to back us up."

"All right," answered the Minister with a smile. "I don't want to die a sinner. I have some twenty people for dinner tomorrow; I'll have places laid for four more. You come with Mme. Houssaye, Ponsard with Rachel."

"I see; and after dinner Ponsard reads *Charlotte Corday*."

"Agreed; you go and invite Ponsard and Mlle. Rachel for me."

On the following evening everyone was at his post. The dinner, though official, was excellent, and the conversation superb; the moment everyone rose from the table, the politicians, who had left their seriousness at the bottom of their glasses, crowded around the actress like schoolboys who had escaped from their teachers. Though she was smiling, she had the aura of a duchess about her by reason of her ceremonious simplicity—one needs to combine these two words here. Ponsard's audience seemed to me the best he could have; as soon as coffee had been served the poet turned to his work. I had offered to read it for him, but he considered himself the best reader in the world: I have never heard a worse one; he murdered his best lines and effaced the best dramatic moments. In spite of that his listeners quickly concluded that they were hearing a strong and daring work, one that was worthy of the Théâtre Français. No one wanted to leave. Interest followed the author from act to act without lagging for a moment, moving through all the scenes and all the characterizations of this unique work which has remained Ponsard's greatest achievement.

I am wrong. There was someone in the room who was not

happy. Rachel. Though she had chanted the *Marseillaise*, flag in hand, with revolutionary passion, she was afraid to be on stage in the midst of all these bloodstained figures. It offended her to be an angel on condition of murdering someone, even a Marat; besides, she concluded that the central role was not that of Charlotte Corday. Therefore, as soon as Ponsard had spoken the last line, she extended him her hand in silence, and came up to me saying, "I have no intention of playing that madwoman." I wanted immediately to prove to her that she had not really understood it, but she had already walked out.

Everyone congratulated Ponsard, except for Ponsard himself. "You see for yourself," he said to me. "Rachel asked for the part, and I told you that she'd play it three times at most. Well—she won't play it at all." I tried to reassure Ponsard that Rachel would play it and spoke to him of the Corneille-like beauty of the work. The Minister also spoke very kindly to him. M. Ferdinand Barrot was enthusiastic about three parts in particular: Danton, Robespierre and Marat. "In the whole Assembly there is not one man who can evoke the spirit of history like you, except Lamartine and Hugo. Your play will cause quite an uproar when it is performed but, as Arsène Houssaye says, the adventure is worth it."

Ponsard went away sick at heart; he had hoped that Rachel would return with him to the Rue des Beaux-Arts. But if the actress had promised him a love song the night before, she was not in the habit of remembering such things for very long.

The next morning I convened the Reading Committee; Rachel was included though she no longer had a vote. They already knew that I was determined to put on the play even if the Committee turned it down.

Charlotte Corday was not accepted unanimously. A few red balls * attested the hostility of the unreconstructed *sociétaires*. Samson and Provost were among them, in part because they saw that they would not have parts in this beautiful work.

---

* The Reading Committee voted by casting white or red balls—yea or nay—into a container.

When I went from the reading room to my office in order to give Ponsard the good news, I found that Rachel had already congratulated him. "The only thing we need still is your vote," I told Rachel. She embraced Ponsard, and at the same time gave his hope the death blow: "I won't play Charlotte Corday because I would be horrible in that role; I am a daughter of Antiquity. Go get your peplos, the galleries would shout. They would hiss me for my judgment, past, present and future. Take Judith for the role, she has neither personality nor opinions."

She was completely right. Rachel had made such a strong impression on the public with her acting of Phèdre, Hermione, and Émilie, that it would have been almost impossible to see her transformed into this flag-waving peasant who came from the country for the sole purpose of striking a blow against the Revolution. Moreover, many republicans bore Rachel a grudge for having put down the flag of the *Marseillaise* and gone to supper at the Élysée Palace.

All eloquence faltered against Rachel's determination. I gave the role to Judith. She was not a tragic actress but she knew how to create a stage character. She was more believable as Charlotte Corday than Rachel would have been.

The distribution of the other roles made quite a story. Who would get Marat? No one wanted it until the great Geffroy decided not to be afraid of everyone's enmity. I saw from the first rehearsals that he would be excellent. As good a painter as he was actor, he made Marat into a portrait that David could have signed.

Meanwhile the hurricane was building up. As soon as I had decided on the date of the first performance, the President of the Republic called me in. We took a stroll in the Élysée gardens. He told me that he liked bold adventures, but was afraid that *Charlotte Corday* would offend all parties. He told me he wanted to read it, and did so that very evening. I went to see him again early the next day; we took the same stroll under the huge trees planted by Mme. de Pompadour, who could hardly have foreseen that so much politics would take place in her garden in the nineteenth century. The

Prince told me once more that the play would offend all parties and please no one but the intellectuals. I pointed out that it would be more dangerous not to play it because that would turn it into an affair of state. Ponsard, who was now a Corneille, would be turned into a Brutus; the people would surely say that Caesar wanted to banish all those great personages of the Revolution.

"Good heavens," said the President, "the best reason for performing the play is that it contains so much great poetry. When all is said, you are responsible: if there is a hurricane, it will sweep you away."

"I count on that," I answered in a decisive tone.

The Prince shook hands with a skeptical smile which seemed to say: "Your reign won't last long." He realized his veto would turn against him all the friends of Ponsard, who were quite numerous in the National Assembly. He would have liked Ponsard himself to withdraw the play or for me to table the whole thing. But I don't like to retrace my steps and Ponsard wanted the play performed no matter the cost. That same day I told him of the rising danger, but he told me that the real danger was not in the Elysée. The National Assembly, where the reactionaries had a louder voice than the republicans, was very upset about the play. Many members had forebodings that Ponsard would reawaken the revolutionary fervor even among the most lukewarm; the matter had almost become subject of official debate. In the end they contented themselves with a warning to the Minister, who smiled at first; but when he encountered the force of the opposition in committee, he began to be sorry that he had been for, rather than against, the play. I do not know if he, in some Machiavellian manner, put the Director of Fine Arts on his guard by telling him that Ponsard's was a reactionary play. Charles Blanc acted through the Office of the Censor who, to my great astonishment, called a halt to our plans. The moment there was a spoke in the wheel, someone quickly put in a second, then a third. Now the republicans in the Assembly also became aroused against *Charlotte Corday* and condemned her to death for the second time. Rehearsals continued as before even though the newspapers declared that the play would surely not be performed. All was going well at the theater, where we counted on a hundred performances, but the politicians yelled so loudly in a time when everything had to give way to politics that I expected an order from the Minister to end it all.

The first performance was two days away. A friend at the Élysée came to tell me that the play would not be performed—not by action of the President but by action of the Assembly. I knew that the Minister, a loyal man if ever there was one, would move heaven and earth rather than reverse his decision. I decided to relieve him by resigning myself, thereby assuming all responsibility.

My letter had just gone when Victor Hugo appeared. I told him the story. "I know all about it," he said to me. "What pleases me is that you have the courage to resign. That will kill the censorship. Now, your resignation will not be accepted, fortunately for Ponsard and for all our playwrights. I am determined that Ponsard's play shall be given: it is said that I am his enemy: you'll see if I am."

Victor Hugo began to give battle that same day. He went to see the heads of all the parties in the National Assembly. He spoke so well, and so feelingly for Ponsard and said so many intelligent things against censorship that he convinced even the strongest opponents. "Now really," he said to the Left, "there you have a true poet who recreates the great moments of the Revolution. Now really! Are you afraid to view the work of your forebears? At that rate you look as if you'd put a ban on Aeschylus!" "Now really," he said to the Right, "do you want the *History of France* rewritten in the style of Father Loriquet? Let the truth take its course, only in that way will you confound traitors and monsters."

Victor Hugo had no trouble convincing the Minister, because he was already on his side. "Here, see for yourself," the

Minister said to the great poet, "I have already written to Arsène Houssaye that he does not have the right to resign."

When Victor Hugo came to the theater the next day, he told me happily to put up the notices for the first night of *Charlotte Corday*. Ponsard, deeply touched, went that same evening to thank Hugo who replied graciously, "That's the kind of enemies we are." This ended the war of the School of Good Sense, a war that had owed its very existence to the Romantic School.

But my war was not over yet. The stir caused by my resignation had strongly reinforced my position: most of my enemies had given battle solely because they wanted to tumble me from my bed of luxury, to use their term. When they saw that I was ready to leave voluntarily they half sheathed their weapons, though only with the intention of stabbing me in the back. In the army the privates take pride in the successes of their officers, but in the literary corps no man is forgiven for taking the lead because in it every man is just a private. Why should X have a job which pays twenty-five thousand francs while Y has to slave with his pen every evening just to earn half as much? Equality, yes, but not fraternity. I am not speaking of those who are guided by their star or who will be stars themselves one day.

One remembers the success of *Charlotte Corday*: some noisy outbursts in the auditorium, but also battles at the door to obtain tickets. It was the only occasion on which the Revolution was shown on stage in its proper character.

·

Corneille's Shoes

·

On June 6, 1851, the anniversary of Corneille's birth, I decided that the Comédie Française would hold a gala performance: *Le Cid* and *Le Menteur* would be played, by an all-star cast. Between the two works a major poet would read his own verses to the glory of Corneille; that would be either Victor Hugo, or Alfred de Musset, or Théophile Gautier.

Victor Hugo, completely embroiled in politics, said that he had no poetry in hand and expressed his regrets at not being able to glorify his master. Alfred de Musset slipped away for a game of chess. Théophile Gautier forthwith composed some admirable verses.

Everything was going well. The expectations for the night were excellent, but suddenly M. de Guizard, Director of Fine Arts, at the behest of M. de Rémusat, asked to see Théo's poem. At that time there were still two powers which warred with each other, the Élysée Palace and the National Assembly. Guizard was considerably upset that the poet reproached Louis XIV for having left Corneille without shoes, and Molière without a grave. And, would you believe it, under a republic a poet dared to write such verses as:

> And in the future, though now we cannot know
> The fame of kings will lessen but the poet's grow

Guizard dashed to the theater and told me immediately that the Minister would never consent to such sacrilege. I wanted to make a light-hearted response, but he chose to take it all very seriously.

"If you refuse to suppress this piece of verse, it will be my duty to inform the Minister."

"Very well. Let us both go to see him."

And so we went. The Minister at that time was M. Léon Faucher, a very newly minted republican, who found it quite extraordinary that Théo would side with Pierre Corneille against Louis XIV.

"Please note," I said to the Minister, "that this is not a gala in honor of Louis XIV but of Pierre Corneille: who in heaven's name could put it in his head to find that this is an impertinence against the Sun King! When all is said, this is after all part of history, but if anyone gives you trouble in the Assembly you can tell him that this is poetic licence."

The Minister got on his high horse, "You don't really imagine, do you, that I would risk a challenge to the government for such a trifle?"

A trifle! I was indignant but managed to hide my anger.

"There is, as you know," continued Léon Faucher, "a Censorship Commission."

"Oh, yes," I answered, "but the Republic promised to rid us of it."

"Now then, that Censorship Commission is responsible; it will decide if these verses by your friend will be read out or not."

"Do not forget, M. le Ministre, that our Louis XIV of today is the public. The public is waiting now. In the eyes of the public it isn't the censor who is responsible, it is I alone. I am not able to change anything in that performance; I prefer to hand in my resignation rather than submit to an order by the censor."

"Very good, that is fine; you have resigned, which exonerates you with the public, the actors and Théophile Gautier."

With which Léon Faucher picked up his briefcase to go to a cabinet meeting. M. de Guizard convoked the Censorship Commission. These people were afraid of everything. Undoubtedly they were afraid of Louis XIV, because they decided to suppress all passages relating to him. Naturally neither Théophile Gautier nor I consented to cut the most beautiful passages of the poem.

I prepared to leave the Comédie. Beauvallet enthusiastically improvised a few stanzas in honor of Corneille which went some way to save the dignity of the evening. The most curious fact, however, was that the Emperor, believing it to be his duty to honor the memory of a man whom his uncle would have made a prince,* applauded those verses as if they had been by Gautier. The next day, however, there was a great outburst of anger in the political and literary circles of Paris.

I was completely ready for my departure, but the President, after reading Gautier's poem for himself, decided that I had been right to demand that it be read as it was written.

---

* That is, Napoleon I would have acted much better toward Corneille than Louis XIV.

1*

"That is really quite astonishing," Roqueplan said to me, "because he sees himself, like his uncle, as a direct successor of Louis XIV."

The Prince shed a tear over the misfortunes of Corneille without giving a thought to bestowing a pension on Théophile Gautier who, at any rate, wore very fine shoes.

•

The Second of December

•

In their first election the citizens of the Second Republic had chosen the Bonapartist pretender as its President and selected a Chamber of Deputies in which monarchists of Bourbon and Orléans persuasion outnumbered republicans. The foundations for the speedy demise of the Republic thus laid, it was left to the Prince-President to choose the time of its formal end. The Coup d'État of December 2, 1851, was carefully prepared. In the coups he staged in 1836 and 1840 during the reign of Louis Philippe, Louis Napoleon had always insisted on avoiding bloodshed. Some of his devotees maintained that he could have assumed power much sooner except for that peculiar squeamishness. Clearly he hoped to avoid bloodshed in December 1851, but did not succeed. The opposition reacted in the streets of Paris, barricades were thrown up, and the insurrection was suppressed with great brutality on December 4.

By the end of 1851 Houssaye was firmly on the side of Napoleon, but he could not suppress his own qualms about the events. Victor Hugo, whom Napoleon wanted on his side as an adornment of his impending reign, turned against him for good. Hugo's History of a Crime: The Deposition of an Eye-Witness *is a superb account, written in the white heat of furious indignation, of that brutal slaughter of December 4 in which, according to the London* Times, *eight hundred men, women and children, mostly of the working class, were killed by the army. Hugo thereafter refused*

all blandishments—some of them described by Houssaye—and
exiled himself to the Channel Islands for the duration of Napoleon's
rule.

In September 1852, the Prince-President toured the country
and found it receptive to the next logical step. In Bordeaux he gave
a speech which contained the famous line: "L'Empire c'est la paix,"
and on December 2, 1852, the Empire became a reality. Within less
than a year the Empire which meant peace was involved in its first
war, against Russia in the Crimea.

When a man talks politics to himself he acts like a dictator; when
two friends conspire with each other they have tyrannous designs; but if lots of men meet, republican sentiments flash out like
fireworks. Look at all formal assemblies—don't they always move
toward the extremes? Only the most heroic men are not afraid
of being caught red-handed with royalist sentiments. Weak
shoulders cannot bear the purple, and have turned kings into no
more than the humble servants of their people.

When one talks alone to an actor, he is dictatorially or im-
perialistically inclined, but when all the actors are together in the
greenroom, they are republicans. At the Théâtre Français, therefore, the gentlemen *sociétaires* and *pensionnaires* had two ways of
looking at the Coup d'État, now being for Augustus, now for
Cinna.

Some of them said to me in the morning, "We must close, we
cannot act in the face of such a catastrophe."

I replied, "Let us be above all politics. The Assembly wanted
to imprison a President who is a socialist, and the President im-
prisons the Assembly which is more reactionary than republican.
History will judge. While we wait let us play some comedies, for
that is our business."

"But there are going to be some terrible allusions—we are
supposed to play *A Glass of Water*."

"If we were to play *The Marriage of Figaro*, *Tartuffe* or *Cinna*
there would also be allusions. But though there are storm clouds

there will be no storm: you are much too skilled to be afraid of a catcall."

The play went on and there were some murmurs; but the public, which is much more sensible than one thinks, understood that it had come to enjoy itself and not to take lessons in politics.

On the first day of the Coup d'État all went well or all went badly depending on one's opinions; at any rate, people did not kill each other. On the next day the demagogues and revolutionaries, who liked a disturbance merely for its own sake, wanted to stage a counter-coup; a number of people got killed on a few barricades. An extra who had not come to rehearsal got hurt while looking at a skirmish on the Boulevard Bonne-Nouvelle. His wife, all in tears, came to see me to ask if the theater would make him a special allowance.

"What do you mean—an allowance because he went in search of a bullet instead of coming to rehearsal?"

I gave her something, however, to look after her husband.

Samson was present. He recognized like me that art is above politics because the only revolution for great minds is the revolution of creativity.

"One Collot d'Herbois * is too many," he said.

Provost, joining us, added:

"Very well, Rachel will sing *Partant pour la Syrie* †."

"You are unfair, my dear Provost; you forget that Rachel more or less saved the Comédie by singing the *Marseillaise*. In those days, moreover, we all sang it because we imagined that we were marching toward the Promised Land. But not one of us, it turns out, knows the way. Let us respect all those who have lost their way and let us wait patiently for a second Moses."

---

* The actor Jean Marie Collot d'Herbois (1750–1796) became heavily involved in politics after the French Revolution and pursued the actors of the Comédie Française with implacable hate. The actors were saved by the fall of Robespierre and the end of the Terror, and Collet d'Herbois himself was deported to Devil's Island, where he died.

† The Bonapartist anthem.

"Oh," exclaimed Provost, "I do not believe in a second Moses. I believed in Lamartine and that was my final illusion."

"And mine," I added.

"And mine, too," murmured Samson.

End of Comedy.

Enter Rachel: "Well, there are some who have gone over to the Blues, others to the Whites and others to the Reds. Victor Hugo is at the head of the revolt."

"Yes, because he has not been given a Ministry," exclaimed Provost.

"And they made a mistake in not giving him one," I added.

"He will end up in exile like all the radicals," said Samson.

"Perhaps," I answered, "but we won't exile him, will we, Rachel?"

"I should say not. I'll play *Tisbè, Dona Sol, Marion Delorme.* But I'll start out by asking for his pardon at the Élysée."

"His pardon—he is not the man to accept a pardon," I replied. "He ranks too high to come down to that, but there will be an amnesty within a month: Louis Napoleon has spent too much time in exile and in prison to allow Frenchmen to be exiled or imprisoned for reasons of policy."

At that moment enter Brindeau, completely distraught: "Gentlemen, all of Paris is a sea of flames and blood, we must protect our theater."

"Where have you been?"

"At the Porte-Saint-Martin. They say a hundred thousand are involved in the uprising."

Leopold Le Hon, who was always pursuing Rachel, had come in behind Brindeau.

"Don't get upset," he said quite calmly. "They are pretending to fight, they are not really fighting. I have just come from Police Headquarters where no one is afraid of anything."

"Let us go to see Morny," said Rachel.

The three of us left—Rachel, Le Hon and I.

Would you like to know what the Comte de Morny was

doing when we came to the Ministry of the Interior? He was calmly taking a bath which, however, did not prevent him from dictating orders to two secretaries.

"And aren't you afraid," said Rachel, "that a Charlotte Corday is hiding in me?"

He laughed and showed us a revolver.

And that is all I saw of the Coup d'État.

But I forget: On the first day I saw the President, on horse-back, riding along the Rue de Rivoli and stopping at the Place du Palais Royal a few feet from the Théâtre Français. He carried his head high; his expression was as impassive and fatalistic as ever. On the following day I also saw the disturbances on the boulevard and, in fact, became involved in a duel with Clésinger, who had changed his opinion four times since the previous evening—without finding a single valid one.

Historians who profess to have seen everything have generally seen nothing much: they are like the character in a comedy at the Théâtre Français who boasts to have been present at the taking of the Bastille.

"What, you were?" someone answers.

"Yes, just as you see me before you."

"Oh, tell us all about it."

"Very simple. I was at my notary's office to make my last will, and suddenly a man rushes in, shouting, 'The Bastille is taken.' With these words he showed us a small stone from the Bastille and then fainted dead away. I took that stone and kept it as a trophy: and thus I had my part in the taking of the Bastille."

I put on a cheerful face, in these days of deliverance to some, of mourning to others, but inwardly I felt sad. Where was it all going to lead? My beloved France, still ravaged by the June Revolution, torn apart by the sterile battles in the National Assembly—was she ever going to rise again in all her strength, in all her superiority, her glory? How many of her best sons would have to take the road into exile because they refused to see the same light as those who retained power? After so many volcanic eruptions, with so many craters still open, after so many tears, so much sacrifice and bloodshed, why did we have to launch into still more political adventures?

While we wait, let us make comedies and act them.

.

The Empire Means Peace

.

On the eve of the Empire, after the famous speech at Bordeaux, "The Empire means peace," the Comédie Française and the Opéra gave gala performances in honor of the President about to become Emperor. I composed the following program:

COMÉDIE FRANÇAISE
GALA PERFORMANCE

Cinna
or, the Clemency of Augustus
Tragedy in five acts by Pierre Corneille

The Empire Means Peace

Stanzas spoken by Mlle. Rachel *

There is No Telling What May Happen
Comedy in Three Acts by Alfred de Musset

"No, indeed," people said, "there's no telling what will happen with regard to the Empire meaning peace and Augustus being clement."

.

---

* The stanzas spoken by Rachel, and based on the Prince-President's speech, were written by Houssaye. He mentions elsewhere that both Rachel and Mme. Houssaye received bracelets worth ten thousand francs after the event, as tokens of the future Emperor's esteem. When the Comte de Persigny told Houssaye that the Emperor would now bestow the Legion of Honor on him, Houssaye politely requested that the government wait until after the appearance of his next book. Evidently he felt that he wanted to be rewarded as a writer, not a flatterer.

When I went to welcome the Prince upon his arrival, he said to me, half angry, half smiling, "Monsieur Arsène Houssaye, you have a strange way of composing programs."

"Monseigneur, I included *Cinna* because I know that you will remind us all of the clemency of Augustus. The stanzas *The Empire Means Peace* are nothing other than a translation of your magnificent speech. Finally, *There is No Telling What May Happen* is the immutable comment on the future."

The Prince never lost his temper but I was somewhat apprehensive that the program I had so light-heartedly composed—with that incorrigible French tendency to jest—would put the audience in too good a humor. But as soon as the performance got under way, a solemn feeling pervaded the house and everything was applauded.

·

Victor Hugo, the Emperor and I

·

After the Coup d'État I continued to play Victor Hugo because I believed that one should not confuse literature with politics. Men like Romieu, who were more imperial than the Emperor, raised an outcry against me. Romieu was Director of Fine Arts, but I was not afraid of him. After the publication of *Napoleon the Little* the situation got worse, but I nevertheless announced routinely a performance of *Marion Delorme*. Even after the publication of *Les Châtiments* it was still *Marion Delorme*, that masterpiece which gives expression to some of the most telling ideas on clemency. Great uproar at the theater and at the Ministry of the Interior. The actors tell me: "You wouldn't dare!" At the Ministry busy hands are preparing my dismissal.

At midnight, when there was still time to change the announcement for the following day, my friend Romieu came to tell me with a smile, "You will be dismissed tomorrow morning if you do not change the play because *Marion Delorme* will definitely not be performed. That is an act of defiance toward the Emperor."

I answered him that this was a purely literary matter as far as I was concerned; that I had a duty to keep the work of the greatest dramatic poet of the century in the repertoire of the Théâtre Français; and that I would sooner have my hand cut off than change the announced program.

"Moreover," I continued, "I know the Emperor; he is above all these partisan quarrels because he is the kind of man who does not get angry for one moment—and because he has great political sense."

The announcement of the performance went out, my dismissal was signed, and the Théâtre Français was in a fever of excitement; would *Marion Delorme* be played or would it not?

It was played. At about noon, at the very moment when M. de Persigny raised his pen to sign my dismissal, a message came from the Emperor. It simply said that Napoleon III wanted to attend the performance. Total confusion.

I went to see Persigny, who handed me my notice of dismissal with one hand and grasped my own with the other.

"I am very much afraid," I told him, "that Romieu has wasted his ink because the Emperor has informed me that he will come to the theater tonight to see *Marion Delorme.* I came to ask you to attend also."

"I certainly will."

If ever a man felt pleased to be right, I was that man. When I returned to the theater everyone fervently shook my hand and congratulated me. I received notes and letters like the one from Mme. de Girardin:

> Your conduct toward the exiled Victor Hugo is noble and good, and I want to thank you for it in this time of systematic ingratitude and glorified cowardice. It does one good to know that there still is somewhere a brave heart, a friendly soul who is rash enough to be steadfast.
>
> *Delphine de Girardin*

"You ought to frame that letter," said Alfred de Musset, who also stood by me as a friend.

Everyone who counted in Paris was at the theater that evening. How did the Emperor react? Napoleon III arrived before the rise of the curtain. Almost all his ministers were with him, Baroche and Persigny among them. M. de Morny and M. Rouher joined him in the Imperial box.

At his arrival the Emperor had told me, "Please come and see me in the course of the evening."

The performance began amidst glacial silence. Everyone was on the lookout. The Emperor was like a statue. No one around him uttered a sound; everyone always waited for him to speak to catch the right tone, everyone except Morny and Persigny. I was not worried because I knew very well that nobody could witness a play by Victor Hugo without being swept up by its beauty and its ideals. It was not long before the Emperor was moved and gave the signal for the applause.

And what followed was magnificent: the entire audience rose as one man and the most thunderous ovation swept the theater, both for the poet and for the monarch.

The ovations started up again at each act. Victor Hugo never had a more stupendous triumph and the Emperor never seemed happier. It seemed as if he were saying to Hugo, with a line from Corneille:

> Let us be friends, Cinna, it is I who ask you.

But Cinna refused to accept the seat which Augustus offered him.

Just before the fourth act I went to the Imperial box. The Emperor asked me to sit down by his side and said in his bass voice, "How beautiful it is!"

"Then, Sire, I did right in putting on *Marion Delorme?*"

"Yes, absolutely."

"Yet I am dismissed for having put on this great play?"

The Emperor looked at Persigny. "Yes," he said, "I have been told about that, but it is a mistake."

And, turning toward me, he added, "If you had not had the courage to play *Marion Delorme* after having announced it, then you would have been dismissed."

·

Alexandre Dumas' Plays on Louis XIV and Louis XV

·

In 1853, Dumas, tired of playing outlawed opposition to the Empire, called on me one fine day, put his arm around me and told me point-blank, "My dear friend, you play too many forgettable plays. I am going to give you two which will do wonders: *The Youth of Louis XIV* and *The Youth of Louis XV*."

"My dear Dumas, you overwhelm me. But you are going to wear out the actors; don't you know that some of them don't have it in them any more?"

"Don't worry. Moreover, there are lots of female roles in these plays; and all your actresses still have a full set of teeth. Just think of the stir we'll make: one day we'll give *The Youth of Louis XIV* and the next day *The Youth of Louis XV*."

"And the day after that we'll give *The Youth of Louis XVI*."

"Let's be serious. Louis XVI's only dramatic function was to mount the guillotine. No trilogies for me! Do you want me to read you *The Youth of Louis XIV?*"

"Tomorrow, if you like; I'll call a meeting of the Reading Committee."

"Tomorrow is perhaps a little too soon. I have not yet started to write my two plays."

We both had a laugh about that. Then I suggested that he read a week later.

"That's fine. If you want to read the play before the rest of them, I'll give it to you on Sunday. How much advance are you going to give me?"

"Five thousand francs for each play."

"That's fine. I'm getting to work."

And so he left.

But one moment later he was back with two young actresses in tow whom he had found on the stairs, saying, "Two magnificent parts for these darlings." And he embraced them with a devilish glee.

"Oh, by the way," I asked, "who will play Louis XIV and Louis XV?"

"I am not such a fool as to tell you the names of the actors. Let's wait first to see how they * like it."

And he was off once more. This time I stopped him on the threshold. I had not seen him since the Coup d'État and asked him why he had played that game of exiled opposition as he had never been exiled. He was about to give me a major Roman speech, but then laughed instead and answered, "A lady of high principles spirited me away to the waters at Spa."

A week later Dumas read *The Youth of Louis XIV* to us. The play was approved unanimously and immediately cast. But some troublesome creatures in the Committee went and sounded the alarm at the Ministry of State. The Censor threw himself into the breach. Dumas did not waste a moment in giving battle, he was in such haste to write the five acts of *The Youth of Louis XV*. He was about to read us that second play, when, as a preamble, he asked me to give him his ten thousand francs advance. I had already given him five thousand francs from my small Civil List. I tried to give him five thousand more from the general funds of the theater pending approval by the Minister. But the gentlemen of the Censor's office were too much for me. They determined, as they also did later in the case of *The Sun King*, that kings could not be put on stage without tainting the majesty of emperors. Dumas was furious but gallantly returned me the first five thousand francs and went off to put on his plays in Brussels.

---

* *i.e.*, the *sociétaires* of the Comédie Française, who first have to approve the play. If they know in advance who will have the major roles, those who are left out may object to the play.

·

Four Monarchs at the Tuileries

·

For some time Alfred de Musset had not written anything. His mind was becoming more and more clouded, and a miracle would have been needed to set him right again.

The Empress Eugénie's liking for men like Octave Feuillet and Victor Hugo extended particularly to Alfred de Musset. She refused to give up her hope of seeing the author of *Rolla* finish his tragedy *Frédégonde*.

"Rachel would be so magnificent and so awe-inspiring in it," she said, asking all her gentlemen-in-waiting to press Musset's golden pen once more into his hand.

Count Baciocchi carried the Empress's greetings more than once to the Rue du Mont-Tabor, at the very early hour when one could find Musset at home, but he was no more successful than Rachel or I in pulling him back to those Merovingian legends, although the graciousness of the Empress touched him.

Though she finally despaired of ever seeing *Frédégonde*, the Empress did not give up hope of getting a comedy from Musset. In vain everyone told her that he no longer produced anything of value; she was sure, and rightly so, that such great intelligence could not just vanish completely. She also knew that Musset's nighttime exploits at times produced some shining hours in which he regained his youth.

I was asked to be the ambassador. The Empress not only promised to pay all royalties; in imitation of Queen Marie Antoinette acting in a play by Beaumarchais, she promised to act in his play.

I might have waited until the poet came to the theater or gone to find him at the Café de la Régence, but I wanted to do things in style. At an early hour the next morning I had my carriage made ready in order to create a stir in the very quiet street where he lived. When I rang the bell Alfred de Musset himself came to open.

"Are you going to a wedding?" he asked, seeing me in a formal black suit with white tie.

"No, I have come, sent by an empress to see a great poet."

Alfred de Musset was touched by that bit of comedy. If I had said any more he would have embraced me as he had after the first performance of *Le Chandelier*.

I informed him that the Empress wanted to act a role that he would write for her.

"And what in the devil's name do you want me to write?"

"Oh, very simple: something like *The Barber of Seville* or *The Marriage of Figaro*. Didn't Marie Antoinette act Rosine and Suzanne in Versailles?"

Alfred de Musset cast his eye toward the entrance. "Then, since you've obviously brought M. de Beaumarchais along with you, he will have to collaborate."

And as he never lost his presence of mind he asked me what he would be paid for such a masterpiece.

I had unlimited powers. It was well-known that everything was generously paid for at the Empress' court, but Musset wanted more than a promise; as he doubted himself, he doubted everyone and everything. Nevertheless he began to look through his old manuscripts.

"Well then," he told me, "here is a comedy which is neither finished nor unfinished, but which has two very good female parts. It is called *As You Like It*."

"A very pretty title."

"Yes, but that title is not much good to anyone except Shakespeare. I will have to call my play *L'Âne et le ruisseau* [*The Ass and the Brook*] because the idea of it is this: a man is in love but he is afraid to cross the Rubicon."

"Well then; call the play simply *The Rubicon*; that always goes down well with an emperor *."

---

* The Rubicon, a small river at the head of the Italian peninsula, marked the line in the Roman Republic which generals were not to cross with their armies. Julius Caesar crossed it, disobeying the law, took over Rome and established the dictatorship which became the empire of his successor, Augustus.

"No," said Musset, annoyed like a child that had been teased. "It will be called *L'Âne et le ruisseau.* All the kings and queens of the world won't make me change the title."

I knew him too well to contradict him.

"How many acts?"

"Only one."

That was too little, even if it was as good as *Il Faut qu'une porte soit ouverte ou fermée.* At the Tuileries, where self-confidence reigned, talk had been of a full-size comedy, but as Musset was unlikely to be able to improvise five acts, I asked him to spread his act into three.

"Why?"

"Because, if they are supposed to pay you ten thousand francs for five acts, they are not likely to give you ten thousand francs for one act."

"Well, that's where they would be wrong. Let them go and get M. Scribe to write them a comedy in ten acts."

Nothing was harder than to discuss things with Musset in an amiable way. I promised him all he asked for: one, he would receive five thousand francs in gold minted especially for him. Two, if he decided to make his play over into three acts, the Empress would have the option of increasing that sum. Three, the play was to be given first at the Tuileries, and thereafter at the Théâtre Français, with the presentation at Court relieving the author of the duty to read his play to the Reading Committee.

Alfred de Musset set to work. The following day he asked me if the Imperial Mint had yet set to work on his napoleons. We had not been together for five minutes when La Chaume, my marvelous assistant, completely distraught, rushed in thinking that we had come to blows.

We were having verbal blows only, speaking too loud to be able to listen to each other: he had consigned me to the pit of hell, I had sent him even farther; but we had not opened the windows to do what we were threatening. And the whole uproar came about because I had most politely asked Musset to come with me, a few days later, to read his play to the Empress. In vain I told him that there would not be more than three or four people, all friends of his—the Emperor, Nieuwerkerke, Persigny, Baciocchi, perhaps Morny and Fleury.

All these names ending in i or y had provoked him.

"Ni-Ni, not for me, I am through, I am going to burn the play."

When I passed him a match to light his cigarette he took it to mean that I wanted him to burn his play.

"There, you see," he said, "you agree with me."

He became completely obstinate on this point. He stamped his foot. Our voices rose. When La Chaume entered the scene, we must have looked as if we were performing a play.

I was sure that all was over as far as the play for the Empress was concerned, because Musset snatched up his hat and stormed out of the room.

I immediately wrote him the following note:

I do not quite understand, my friend, why you refuse to read before a woman who admires you when you consent to read before a committee of actors almost all of whom make the mistake of judging you only by your flights of imagination.

That piece of diplomacy reached Musset at the Café de la Régence. His anger must have subsided rapidly for he scribbled a line saying, "I'll read tomorrow." And to prove to me that he bore me no grudge, he added, "Yours, with all my heart."

I went immediately to the Café de la Régence, but he had already left to finish his play.

At two o'clock the following afternoon Musset arrived at the theater, manuscript in hand.

"Look at me," he said gaily, "don't I look like the starving poet of the age of Louis XIII who is about to read his tragedy to the Cardinal?"

"Don't be silly; you look like Prince Charming who is about to read a fairy tale to Sleeping Beauty."

I did look at him: he was dressed perfectly, a gentleman of high society; pearly grey gloves, deftly tied cravat, faultlessly fitted dress coat, beard carefully trimmed, not a hair out of place.

"That's great," said Beauvallet, who saw us leave. "Here's Alfred de Musset on his way to Court, stone sober."

The truth was that he had fortified himself for the occasion with a rather small dose—or rather with the dose of the previous night.

When we entered the carriage my hopes vanished once more. He kept on telling me over and over that it was absolutely ludicrous to read one's work to all the world, even to empresses.

"That's a job for gentlemen-in-waiting," he said suddenly. "I'll ask Nieuwerkerke, who is as clever as I am, to read the play in my place."

Count Baciocchi came to the foot of the staircase to receive Alfred de Musset, by express order of the Empress. But the poet was so temperamental that, far from being pleased by that mark of esteem, he immediately wanted to turn around.

"What does all this mean?" he said.

Fortunately Baciocchi was a perfect catalyst with his brisk liveliness and courtly clichés.

Once we were in the Empress' salon, the poet was a completely different man. His head high, he stepped forward proudly to bow to his sovereign and addressed her with the most consummate courtesy.

The Empress turned to the Emperor. "What did Mérimée say to me?"

"This is how history is written," murmured Napoleon III.

After clenching his teeth and producing that gritting sound which he habitually made, Musset opened his manuscript and read the first scenes very fast. But soon he began to make the Emperor and the Empress uncomfortable because of the entrance of another Majesty: King Gold had come into the salon without being announced.

I had never seen a thing like that in the Tuileries, but this is what happened: James de Rothschild crossed the threshold without the least ceremony. That he was able to enter so freely was due, a little too much so perhaps, to his being treated as a sovereign by a sovereign, but also because of his ability to tell stories well and to amuse the Empress. Storytellers have always made their fortune at court, where there are too many public speakers and too many silent bores.

M. de Rothschild had learned outside that M. Alfred de Musset was reading a comedy. He had not originally come to hear that play, but he thought that a listener like him would not be amiss.

So he came in. Some slight commotion in the salon; the Baron makes a sign not to mind him: he spreads his arms as if to appease the flood.

"Who's that?" exclaims Musset, jumping up and turning toward me.

"Another monarch," I tell him. "Don't you recognize M. de Rothschild?"

The situation was turning into a drama. M. de Rothschild, who was leaning against the fireplace, now spoke up.

"Monsieur Alfred de Musset, you may continue."

The poet misunderstood the tone: he believed that M. de Rothschild was patronizing him. He turned to me. "But he has not paid for his seat! By what right should he hear my play?"

He folded up his manuscript.

"What does it matter to you?" I said, while the Empress rose to appease him.

But like a gentleman who had drawn his sword, he would not retreat.

"Madame, you are as gracious as you are beautiful; I raised no objections to reading before your Majesty, but no human force will oblige me to read before M. de Rothschild."

"Don't you know that he is a very witty man?" said the Empress.

The Emperor saw that nothing would appease Musset. He, too, had risen; he went straight to M. de Rothschild, who had no intention himself of retreating before the poet.

"I am very sorry to create an intermission," said the Baron, "but M. de Musset is wrong if he is afraid of boring me with his play; just yesterday I saw a play of his with great pleasure: *Il Faut qu'une porte soit ouverte ou fermée.*"

The Emperor smiled.

"Yes, M. de Rothschild," he said, "a door ought to be open or closed."

The Baron understood, but he was not a man who could be thrown easily.

"If I were not afraid," he said loudly, "of being impolite to M. de Musset, I would not stay until he had finished reading his play. I would content myself with applauding it at the Théâtre Français."

As the Baron spoke loud enough for everyone to hear, Musset murmured, through his gritted teeth, a line from Boileau:

"That's a right that one buys at the door when coming in."

All of us pretended not to have heard that, but M. de Rothschild, who heard it very well, wanted at least to make a good retreat. He went straight up to the Empress and took her hand. After that he bowed so low to Musset that it seemed to turn to mockery. Then he asked me, "When are you going to perform that masterpiece?"

"Never," I replied.

"Never?"

"The play was written for the Tuileries Theater."

Monsieur Million thought he could now have his revenge: "Oh, so much the better. There one does not have to pay when coming in."

If he had left at that moment M. de Rothschild would have had laughter on his side, but he made the mistake of asking for the title of the play.

Musset told him with silken mockery: "*The Ass and the Brook.*"

"Oh, I understand," said the Baron. "The ass does not cross the Rubicon: a very wise ass."

With that M. de Rothschild bowed himself out of the salon. The Empress told Musset, "You can see, M. de Musset, that everyone obeys you here and that you infuse wit into everyone."

The poet bowed and opened up his manuscript. From moment to moment he himself was saluted by those welcome words that, like bird-song, floated across the salon: "How beautiful! How charming! How adorable."

When he had finished he asked me smiling whether his play would be accepted. The Empress, who had heard him, answered for all to hear, "Unanimously."

Yes, the play was accepted, in proof whereof Musset received his author's fee.

Why was it not performed? Because at court woman proposes and accident disposes. Those who are masters of all they survey are masters of none. One thing happens, or another. At court, above all, plans are subject to the unexpected.

When we were leaving the Tuileries, Alfred de Musset suddenly said to me, "I have just read a comedy in public, but I wonder if that public was not the one who performed the comedy around me. Are you quite sure that we are not departing from the theater just now?"

"The theater of the world," I answered.

"No, a real theater. All these people there played roles they had carefully learned, that's the whole tragi-comedy. While I was reading my play I watched the Empress, full of apprehension of what would be tomorrow. They say she is Spanish—don't you believe it! I saw her very well. Look at her hair, her eyes, her lips—that's another Austrian, like Marie Louise and Marie Antoinette. She has charm, but I tell you that she plays a role fate has given her. All's well today, but I wouldn't bet two pennies on the final act."

I asked Musset if he would bet two pennies on the final act of
M. de Rothschild.

"Yes, because with his Majesty Money two and two make four
—and sometimes five."

·

The Torchbearer

·

My dear Houssaye,

His Majesty will attend the Théâtre Français this evening. I hope
that this time you will be provided with the two legendary candlesticks, like Roqueplan, Perrin and Montigny.

Baciocchi

My dear Baciocchi,

You are determined on my being a torchbearer; I am determined
not to fall into that trap.

Please recall the origin of this two-hundred-year-old tradition.
Formerly one of the assistant stage directors came to greet royalty
carrying two candlesticks, but that was not a mere pretence of courtly
obsequiousness or formal courtesy: the candles were not lit for
pleasure; gas had not yet superseded sunlight, and it was necessary to
prevent their Majesties from breaking their necks in the tortuous passages of the theater.

Today those tortuous passages are replaced by a brilliantly lit
grand staircase where no one runs the risk of stumbling. What difference, do you think, would two candles make in this wealth of illumina-
tion? It would be a silly comedy before the real comedy gets under
way.

You say quite correctly that this is a sacred tradition, but
Napoleon III does not dance in the court ballet disguised, like Louis
XIV, as Apollo.

Do not therefore make me do what the other directors do of their
own free will. The Emperor has always been so gracious toward me
that he will surely not think I am trying to offend him by this revolt
against old customs.

When the Emperor comes to the theater he shakes hands with
me; if I held a candlestick I would have to forego that mark of friend-
liness. The Emperor often invites me to sit with him in the Imperial

box; do you think he would condescend to talk to a torchbearer? Even more, I myself don't want to find myself no longer worthy of that conversation with him.

Houssaye

I don't know if Baciocchi, somewhat annoyed, showed that letter to the Emperor. I continued to receive Napoleon III—without torch—and he continued to be as gracious toward me as before, perhaps even more so.

·

In the Imperial Box

·

The conversation in the imperial box during intermissions at the Comédie Française was always very spirited and amusing. One day the Emperor complained about a new play. "Good Lord, Good Lord," he said, "what an awful play. But—at least there are the intermissions."

On another occasion the Emperor said to Romieu, the Director of Fine Arts, "People accuse you of being more often backstage than in the museums."

"Your Majesty, the great works of sculpture and painting get along very well with each other, but the great works of the stage are always at war with the great actresses and singers."

"I see; but you must admit that you prefer a conversation with La Cerito or Mlle. Rachel to one with the marble gods and painted goddesses."

·

How to Improvise a Tragic Actress

·

M. Achille Fould, the Minister of the Interior, sent me word one day to come to his office.

"Do you know Charles Ledru?"

"Very slightly, he is an attorney who has been debarred."

"In an act of consummate injustice, because he is a man of honor. I would like to render him a service."

"You don't mean to suggest that he should make his debut at the Comédie Française?"

The Minister offered me a cigar as he usually did when the conversation became very private.

"You are not very far from the mark. Charles Ledru has introduced me to Mme. Dartès who sees herself as a born tragic actress. She talks only in heroic verses; she strikes poses like a goddess. She should be given the chance of a debut."

"Yes, some Sunday," I said, not being entirely convinced.

"No, not at all. I want an absolutely brilliant debut."

Though the cigar was good, I reminded the Minister that debuts at the Comédie Française did not come about in the same way as at the Follies. It was necessary to start with an audition and to obtain the consent of the *sociétaires*.

"Very well, you will get the consent of the *sociétaires*. If you don't, you will have to do without it because I am determined to give you an official order for that debut."

"All right," I said to the Minister. "If you have a star on your hands, we will be lucky."

I collected the *sociétaires* the next day for the audition. The future star of tragedy came to my office. As she was very beautiful, I sounded encouraging, but I saw at once that she did not possess the particular talents which had dazzled the Minister. Nature had wrought very well, but art had done nothing for her as yet. At the audition the beautiful tragic actress was quite incredible. I let the actors speak for themselves; all of them opposed a debut. When I told the Minister, he had already seen the lady, who had come to tell him that her royal audience, that is her audience of actors, had interrupted her with a thousand wisecracks. The Minister was furious; he told me that he would stand against their judgment and that Mme. Dartès would have her debut forthwith. In vain I pointed out that it would be in his protégée's own interest to take lessons from Beauvallet for a few months. He reminded me that Rachel had been turned down by the Conservatoire and declared that he would override all objections.

It is well-known that under Napoleon III, who was a very good sort of man, not at all dictatorial, the Imperial Ministers were first class despots—as if they themselves had earned their laurels in the great victories of Napoleon I.

I had given M. Achille Fould my resignation several times before, and did not think it worthwhile to do it again in this case. So I told him that I would arrange the proper debuts for Mme. Dartès. And I did so in completely good faith. I asked that semi-tragic actress to come to see me and tried to get her up on her feet. She was a very decent creature, completely spoiled by flatterers. Her feet no longer trod the ground, she saw herself as a princess of tragedy—what do I say—as an arch-goddess on Mount Olympus. Beauvallet himself, sarcastic as he usually was, tried with the greatest good will to give her some advice. But she paid not the slightest attention, for she believed only in her own inspiration.

A lady of society may, quite without knowing it, act excellent comedy in a salon, because in the last analysis that is all she has ever done since entering the world of society, or even since entering the world as such. But take a thousand of them and tell them to act Phèdre or Roxane then and there, and not one of them will be able to do it; they will all be caricatures. That is the reason why there are so many good comic actresses and so few who can do tragedy. I begged Mme. Dartès to act Célimène or Sylvia, to revive the glories of Mlle. Mars, but she persisted in telling me that she carried within her the sacred fires of Champmeslé and Adrienne Lecouvreur.* I tried once more to warn the Minister before announcing the performance. He seemed to me to be the more blind because he was otherwise usually a good sort. Why was he so

---

* Mlle. Mars (1779–1847) was a great comédienne, and Adrienne Lecouvreur (1692–1730) and Marie de Champmeslé (1642–1698) were among the greatest tragic actresses of the Théâtre Français.

obstinate? Heaven knows. But he had to climb down a peg or two when he saw the performance. He was in the imperial box and asserted that all the actors in the tragedy that night performed detestably. He accused me of not having given his novice enough of a chance.

And the novice? The less said the better. When she realized that the Court and society had come to her debut, she was seized by a holy terror; Racine's lines began to choke her. She asked Beauvallet what Mlle. Rachel did to enable her to face the audience.

"She drinks!" thundered Beauvallet.

In reality Mlle. Rachel drank beef tea, not an act of treason against poetry. Mme. Dartès sent for a flask of brandy, which did calm her. Until then she had acted her role like a good middle-class lady who wanted to put on a show for friends and family; but when she was three sheets to the wind the audience witnessed the most lamentable comedy in many years.

People wanted to laugh, but many in that audience, myself among the first, were sorry indeed to see the career of this beautiful creature so destroyed. I was more magnanimous that day than M. Fould. The Emperor had asked me to come to his box, which would have enabled me to assume a victorious attitude in front of the Minister, to say, "I told you so."

I confined myself to the explanation that Mme. Dartès had lost her head at her first entrance.

"And besides," I added, turning toward the Minister, "M. Achille Fould knows well that there is not more than one great tragic actress in a century."

·

The Purple Heart

·

The Order of Saint-Helena was conferred on those wounded in the service of the first Napoleon. For the story which follows to be true, Houssaye would have had to be born in 1814, not 1815. In early March of that year the armies of the Allies fought the Emperor in battles around Laon and Soissons on their way toward Paris.

The Emperor once bestowed on me the Order of St. Helena for having been wounded in the service of Napoleon I.

The story is quite well known. In 1852 I was lunching at Saint-Cloud with King Jerome, Prince Murat, Fleury, Baciocchi and some imperial aides-de-camp. Napoleon III, for reasons of some military affectation, was conspicuously wearing the Order of St. Helena. "What are you looking at?" he suddenly asked me.

"Sire, I think that Order of St. Helena would be almost as appropriate on my lapel as on yours."

"Why?"

"Because I was wounded in the service of Napoleon I."

The Emperor looked at me searchingly. He had been told twenty times at least that I was too young to be Director of the Théâtre Français, that land of tempestuous passions whose ruler ought to have white hairs. I was hardly more than thirty and was generally accused of being no more than twenty-five.

"Nonsense," he exclaimed, "you'll never convince me that you are one of the Old Guard."

"Oh, yes! Perhaps I look like a drummer boy, but I was wounded in the service of Napoleon I just the same!"

"All right, let's hear your story. If it isn't a fairy tale, you shall receive the St. Helena."

Thereupon I told the following, which is a true story and not a fairy tale:

In 1814, during the first invasion, a cloud of Cossacks descended upon the little town of Bruyères where my grandfather was mayor. In that day Bruyères was still surrounded by its high city walls, its moat, drawbridge and gates, a true medieval town all prepared for its proper defense. My grandfather, who had been military commissar under the Directoire, after having been a soldier under Louis XVI, ordered the gates closed and wanted to defend the town; every young man was away in the army and the resistance was a joke, though a bloody joke that nearly cost him his life. When the enemy penetrated the walls nearly everybody fled to the nearest vineyards; but my mother remained valiantly near the main gate where the mayor, with the bravest men, wanted to make a stand. She had our house key in her hand and the Russians thought that it was the key to the city hall. One Cossack wanted to negotiate, with his lance at the ready; she answered back bravely and defied him with key and haughty looks. The Cossack, tired of negotiation, gave her a blow with his lance which threw her to the ground bathed in her blood. The blow had barely been struck when a Russian officer dashed up to help her, though not without first killing the Cossack point-blank with a pistol shot. My mother had fainted, a stretcher was improvised and she was carried to the house of her mother where she gave birth on arrival, even though I had not yet given the customary three taps. The doctor had no hope of saving her; he stated, throwing me on a couch, that I, too, did not have long to live as the lance had touched me. My mother recovered. I need not say that I recovered, too.

That is the reason why Napoleon III, at that luncheon in Saint-Cloud, before two noble witnesses, a king and the son of a king, took the Order of St. Helena from his lapel and gravely gave it to me. I immediately affixed it to mine even though I had presented my side to the enemy's lance without any awareness of my great deed. That order pleased my mother more than the cross of the Legion of Honor: it was, after all, her order.

·

I Am Appointed Director of the Opéra

·

One day Baciocchi came to see me and said: "The Emperor has decided to make you director of the Opéra. All of us are for it and, moreover, you are officially appointed."

"How do you mean, officially appointed?"

"Yes, don't worry, everything is so carefully arranged that the only risk in it for you is to make your fortune, because the three clubs * guarantee you against all reverses on condition that you get rid of the monsters in the corps de ballet."

"Oh, on that condition I accept!"

"You'll come with me to thank the Emperor."

Baciocchi took me to the Tuileries. The Emperor, always gracious to me, told me that he wanted the Opéra to become splendid. If it was necessary to raise the level of state support to achieve it, he would do it, because he did not want "the sad antics of M. Perrin" to continue.

I had not served my apprenticeship in that particular land but I was without apprehension. From the Tuileries I went to read the necessary instructions in the office of the Maréchal Vaillant and gave him my commitment as I had given it to the Emperor.

The news of my appointment spread through Paris and I immediately got fifty letters of congratulations and of requests for favors. The next morning at dawn the ladies of Les Halles awoke me with their bouquets. I gave them twenty-five francs.

At ten, Cabinet meeting. M. Rouher, the Prime Minister, speaks first. He is a friend of the former director who has resigned and now wants to withdraw his resignation. He tells M. le Maréchal Vaillant that he does not have a lucky hand in choosing a director for the Opéra. "M. le Maréchal may do as he wishes, but I feel constrained to tell your Majesty that, if the appointment suffers the customary attack in the Legislative Chamber, I will not defend M. Houssaye; because with him we will have once more those lovely days of M. Roqueplan at the Opéra."

One of M. Rouher's colleagues recalls that Nestor Roqueplan's management had been brilliant and exciting.

"Yes," cries M. Rouher, "and the skirts were too short."

The Emperor, who, on occasion, wanted to be above reproach where moral principles were concerned, did not insist and asked Vaillant to request my resignation, adding, with a smile; "Let M.

---

* Presumably some of the major clubs of the rich, like the Jockey Club.

Rouher tell his candidate to lower the hemlines of the dancers, because they have horrible legs."

•

Virtue Rewarded

•

*Toward the end of his description of a day in a theater manager's
life (page 191) Houssaye briefly tells the story of a lady who had
muffed her chances with Napoleon III. In one of the two volumes
which he wrote as a sequel to the original set of the* Confessions,
*he returns to what is obviously the same story. He now tells it in
much greater detail. Perhaps he is merely embellishing it, but, more
likely, he feels that the added distance in time allows him to tell
it with all its savor.*

One day I was driving down the Champs Élysées in a small coupé
of novel design drawn by a horse from the Imperial Stables which
Colonel Fleury had given me, when Comte Gilbert de Voisins, accompanied by a very beautiful woman—as always not his own—
signaled to my coachman to stop. He came toward me, smiling
as usual. He opened the door of my coupé and said to the lady,
"Enter, you are at home here." She entered. As for him, he shook
hands with me and added, "Go on from here in any way you care."

He closed the door without any further ado and went on
his way. My coachman, not knowing what else to do, drove on.

"Madame, allow me to introduce myself."

But it was she who introduced herself, with all the charm of
the world. "I am the Marquise de ———."

"Oh, I know your name very well, madame. I have seen you
here and there, always adorably beautiful, but I did not recognize
you, undoubtedly because the only places I have seen you are at
the great balls. Your clothes cover you too much today."

"You are right. Nothing disfigures a woman so much as a
high-necked dress."

"And a veil," I added.

I raised the veil of the Marquise to see her more closely.

A moment or two more, and I kissed her. But I had a better opinion of her than she had herself.

"Where do we go, Marquise? To your house or to mine?"

"How do I know! That maniac who threw me into your carriage told me that you would get me an immediate audience with Napoleon."

"Oh, I am not that well-connected at Court. The longer the Empire lasts, the more the doors close. Moreover, I'd be worried, presenting a woman as beautiful as you."

"Don't talk nonsense! I absolutely must see the Emperor to-day or tomorrow."

"Would you like to come to my house? I'll write you a letter of introduction with my very best ink."

"No, I won't come to you until I have seen the Emperor."

"Very well then, let's go to the Tuileries."

No sooner said than done. Five minutes later I asked to see Comte Baciocchi, who was on duty and who, at that time, was the man at Court who presented the ambassadors. He much preferred to present ambassadresses because all his political activities were taking him away from the female sex. The Marquise had entered with me. He took a good look at her. He immediately launched a close inspection of that lovely living statue.

"My dear Baciocchi, that is the Marquise de ———, wife of the Prefect of ———, who would like to become Mme. Prefect of Versailles or Mme. Prefect of the Seine."

"We don't have a thing like that everyday. But we do have some first-class districts which are worthy of the Marquise."

She interrupted. "For me the question is not whether it is a first-class district. I'd rather have a subdistrict in Saint-Denis than a first-class appointment like Marseilles."

"I understand," said Baciocchi. "You need to be in Paris; you can't live anywhere else."

Without ado the Marquise took the hands of the future Lord

Chamberlain in hers: "For God's sake, get me an audience with the Chief this morning."

"That is impossible, Marquise, but I am going to prove to him that he agreed some time ago to give you an audience. Is Arsène Houssaye going to come with you?"

"Certainly not!" I cried. "I merely ran into the Marquise who asked me to bring her here. Moreover, I am already late for a rehearsal of *Pierre de touche*. Good bye! She will do best by pleading her own cause."

Having said this, I fled.

I was at the rehearsal when La Chaume came to tell me that a beautiful lady, who had just come from the Tuileries, wanted to speak to me right away. I found the Marquise in my office.

"Well—do you have a first-class district?"

"No, because I acted like a fool."

"I can't believe that!"

"Imagine that, after waiting for half an hour, Baciocchi introduced me. The Prince was standing at the fireplace. He moves toward me; I curtsy with my very best smile. He does not offer me a chair; he listens to me attentively and, without any change in his look, with his face a glacial mask, he first takes my hand, then my arm, then my shoulder, all in saying: "We shall see." I press him further. He remains silent but his hand continues the conversation. If he had changed his expression, if his face had assumed a more amorous look, if his eyes had broken the ice, perhaps I would have attuned myself to him; after all, though one ought to be chaste, one can't be too chaste with the masters of the world. But my native sense of dignity made me raise my head; I disengaged myself from Napoleon's hands with the kind of dignity that brought him back to himself. I saw my mistake at once—but now it was too late. His tone had changed quickly: 'Madame, I shall remember.'" And he concluded the audience with an imperial nod that seemed colder than all the ice of Holland, his real native land.

"And so," concluded the lady, "I have no choice but to ask

my husband to resign because he will never be anything but a third-class prefect."

I conveyed my condolences to Virtue. That evening the Comédie played *Jeux de l'amour et de hazard*. I offered her my box to let her study from up close the character of a high-style provincial who is starved for Paris.

What good is virtue to beautiful women!

Gérard de Nerval

•

Very early one morning I was at the Théâtre Français dictating a report to Verteuil which the Minister had asked for the preceding day. Suddenly, a man, completely out of breath, forced his way into my office.

"Monsieur," he cried from the doorstep, "come quickly, M. Gérard de Nerval has just been found hanged in the Rue de la Vieille-Lanterne."

Hanged! The word cut me to the quick. Hanged! I did not lose one second. The man had come in a hackney cab; the cab took us in ten minutes to the Rue de la Vieille-Lanterne going along the river in order to be as fast as possible.

Verteuil decided to come with me. "If he hanged himself," he said to me, "the reason could not be poverty because I sent him fifteen hundred francs not long ago."

That had been for a translation of *Misanthropie et Repentir* which I had asked of Gérard in the theater's interest and his own.

We finally arrived: we had discharged the cab on the quai because it was impracticable to drive the byways which lead to the Rue de la Vieille-Lanterne like a game of hide-and-seek. On one approach one needed to ascend a staircase. We came by that

κ*

route. Two or three hundred persons were crowded in there. What struck me most was the silence. People half-whispered as if they were afraid to wake the dead even though he had already been taken away.

Poor dear Gérard! He had not yet breathed his last when a milkmaid and a drunk found him at daybreak at that wretched iron grating. As one of his feet rested on a small step on the staircase and his hat was on his head, these two thought that he had stepped to the wall to let them pass. The drunk greeted him but the milkmaid exclaimed at the same moment, "Don't you see that he has hanged himself?"

The drunk mumbled, "Nonsense, nobody hangs himself with a hat on his head."

"In times like these, why not?" answered the milkmaid.

A few feet away was an inn of ill repute, a clip joint and police trap, where Gérard had passed a few hours that night, in the main dining room, pen in hand. We were told that "the hanged man was in there." Not without difficulty we parted the crowd; but no sooner had we reached the threshold than the ogre-like madam and one of her floozies, her breasts provocatively exposed to the glacial wind which blew the snow about, shouted to us that "the gentleman was at the Town Hall."

We noticed a police captain who was coming toward us to make his investigation. I gave him my calling card. He took us to the Town Hall, where I was able to embrace Gérard. They had tried to bleed him, but without reviving him. The doctor on duty told us, "They cut the rope one minute too late!"

I asked the police captain to take my friend to my house. He was not carried there, however: he was taken to the morgue. Why? Because I had no right to claim Gérard, any more than did Théophile Gautier or Roger de Beauvoir. He had family; we were merely friends. An emissary was sent to his legal father, M. Labrunie. He refused to receive his son's body, saying that the emotional strain would kill him. Oh! The selfishness of those who have lost their spirit in the battles of life! I returned at noon to ask once more for those dear remains, but the legal formalities had already got under way: it was necessary to go through the whole maze of Parisian legal procedure.

I met Théo at the morgue. He was deathly pale; he could hardly believe the horrible sight he saw: Gérard on the flagstone reserved for suicides, naked and cold like a statue, his eyes still open and staring at us without seeing. He had never been more handsome. The throttling had not changed his features, an almost radiant serenity enveloped his figure. We took his hand, we spoke to him, like an invocation, recalling his vitality and his golden heart: "Oh, Gérard, what have you done? Why didn't you come yesterday to throw yourself into our arms?" And Gérard, with his unalterable kindness, seemed to ask forgiveness for causing us so much sorrow.

All of Paris was shocked by that mysterious death. The Théâtre Français paid for Gérard's funeral. The funeral was worthy both of the theater and of the poet. Notre Dame de Paris was full of people, and more than three hundred friends followed the cortège to Père Lachaise Cemetery. We had decided with Théo that silence would be the only funeral oration of proper eloquence. One could not speak of his life without speaking of his death. And his death was inexplicable.

And how did it come about that the church opened itself up for the funeral services for a suicide? I had gone the evening before to seek out the Archbishop of Paris, who acceded to my request with perfect kindness. He only asked me for a letter from Dr. Blanche "to protect the Church." This was the letter:

Your Grace, Gérard de Nerval hanged himself because he saw his madness face to face.

Dr. Blanche

Gérard was a fatalist. He hanged himself on a Friday, the twenty-sixth of the month—twice thirteen—in the Rue de la Vieille-Lanterne (Old Lamp Post Street) at the bottom of the Rue de la Tuerie (Slaughter-House Street), near a ravine and under a symbolic sign of a key. Did he think of all that? Events can find their morality and their deep sense in their symbolic form.

Hurricane

·

Houssaye had resumed his usual life after more than a year of mourning for Fannie. He first had an affair with a lady he met in Rome and found again in Paris, the Marquise di Saddeï, a highly placed courtesan who becomes the protagonist of his novel Mlle. Cléopâtre. *Then fate intervenes.*

·

Fate

·

Fate in its malice led me to a dinner given by Ponsard at the Frères Provençaux, in honor of a young singer who wanted to become an actress. Ponsard was in love with her but had not become her lover. He loved beautiful girls for the love of art or the love of love.

One afternoon he brought Mlle. Marie Garcia, the future actress, to me at the Théâtre Français. She had just come back from London where she had sung grand opera at Covent Garden and had slightly hurt her voice. Ponsard, in love, wanted to go by way of the marriage office, but Mlle. Garcia was a free spirit who did not want to give herself except in love. She admired the author of *Charlotte Corday* but did not love him; she wanted to get a role in a play by him. Beauty is always such an effective letter of recommendation that Ponsard let himself be caught. He swore to Marie Garcia at first sight that he would write a role for her as long as she let him rehearse it with her. That evening they had not yet begun to rehearse with each other, but as it concerned a role in a play destined for the Théâtre Français, Ponsard wanted to introduce me to the actress before introducing me to the play.

We dined at the Frères Provençaux that evening: Ponsard, Roger de Beauvoir, the Marquise di Saddeï and Marie Garcia. It was a very entertaining dinner, the kind where one does not expect to find fierce and mortal passions lurking among the convivial guests. Maria Garcia captivated us with her air of distinction, as Roger de Beauvoir put it. At the end of the dinner she sat down at the piano to sing arias from *La Juive* and *La Favorite*. All four of us were enchanted—I should say, all five of us because she seemed happy to have conquered us, me above all.

After dinner the Marquise surpassed herself in hiding her jealousy. We all went for a walk in the Gardens of the Palais Royal. Ponsard, who had Marie Garcia on his arm, put that lovely arm into mine, telling us that he wanted to go and find some cigars.

"He does not know what he is doing," I said to the young singer. "What if I were to keep your arm?"

"Well—keep it."

We looked at each other, a flash of fire went through our hearts, we were in love without knowing it yet. I asked Beauvoir to tell Ponsard that we were leaving never to return.

We did not tarry in the Palais Royal. I said to Mlle. Garcia, "I really think that we just had our engagement dinner and that we'll have our wedding feast tonight."

"I think so, too," she replied.

She leaned on my arm and looked gently at me.

"Well then, shall we abandon our tragic author to his handsome lady tobacconist?"

"Excellent idea!"

We did not see Ponsard for three months. He forgave me the crime against friendship, with a bantering letter supposedly from Mme. di Saddeï, but he never forgave Marie Garcia.

I imagined that we were involved in one of those Parisian adventures that have no tomorrow, but not only did it have a tomorrow—it lasted six years. Without being head over heels in love with that beautiful creature, I was completely taken with her figure and her voice. She sang like a true Garcia. And why not confess it—she died, after all, of her love—she sacrificed everything to stay with me, both her fortunes: her beauty and her voice.

One evening she opened her heart to me. "Look, I have found all I ever want: I don't look for anything else, you can do with me what you want, I have resigned all my own will. I don't ask to live in your house; put me in a garret, if you want, but come to me every day. You need an illegitimate wife because you don't want to remarry—I'll be that for you, don't be afraid that I'll ever want to be called Mme. Arsène Houssaye. I'll be good to your son who will love me like a big sister. But don't leave me."

I answered her that anyone who knew Paris should know better than to expect that to work. She would be pursued by a crowd of admirers who could make her fortune; if she did not want love alone, the theater would be a gilded pedestal for her. On the other hand, if she formed an illicit attachment to a man, no matter who he was, who would not marry her, she would waste her youth. She replied by bursting into tears, which I kissed away. That was the ink of our marriage contract.

Marie and I attempted the impossible: to try and disarm the strictures of public opinion; but Paris itself does not permit those who have not been properly signed and sealed to be happy. It seems to challenge those who have not gone through the legal formalities. Poets, up in the clouds, disdain the laws of the real world, but since I had descended from Olympus to the precise world of Paris, I heard the imprecations. My family crossed themselves and consecrated me to hell. A cabinet minister, who had a pretty mistress at whose house I dined with him, was the first one to act disgusted on seeing me with mine. So goes the world!

Marie wanted only to continue that drifting existence, when a Neapolitan count appeared on the scene, presented to her by the Marquis de las Singadas, a Spaniard of our acquaintance. He was a musician who believed himself to be of royal blood. He sang duets with her, but if he was Romeo, she was not Juliet. When he despaired of making her come down from the balcony, he proposed to come up, not on a silken ladder but by the grand staircase of marriage.

That was the start of the drama. The idea of being an Italian countess and a member of society, something which many actresses dream of, began to affect Marie slightly. As she kept no secrets from me, she said to me suddenly one day, "Do you want to marry me?"

"No."

"Why?"

"Because I am not one of those who marry their mistresses."

She raised her head with dignity. "Well then, as for me, I am not one of those who become old mistresses. I love you with all my heart, but I'll break that love in order to marry."

I looked at her half-smiling, half-surprised. "And to whom?"

"To Count ———."

Though I felt a pang of jealousy, I told Marie with complete sincerity, "You ought to marry him. He is worth more than I. He is wealthier, he is younger and he is a better musician. You can sing duets when it rains."

"You can't be serious," said Marie, disturbed. "If you really meant it you would be more upset; or perhaps you don't have a heart."

"Listen, Marie, don't be dramatic. I am completely serious. If I were thinking only of myself I would not advise you to marry the count. Do you imagine that I won't suffer a great deal if we separate? To tear love from one's heart is like tearing the oak out of the forest."

Marie had expected a different turn; she would have wanted me to throw myself at her feet begging her to give up the count. But I was too conscious of the benefits of that marriage for her not to sacrifice myself.

·

The Ball

·

At a ball at the house of M. de la Torre, a wealthy banker from Lima, Houssaye meets the daughter of the house. They waltz to-gether—to Houssaye the waltz is always an instrument of passion—and feel drawn to each other. At the midnight supper she bites off half of a luscious strawberry and gives him the other half. She re-grets it and blushes at playing with fire, but the die is cast.

A window opened on the balcony and we went to get some air. When we were on the balcony I bent over Jane as if to prevent the wind from striking her too roughly.

"You are a hothouse flower," I said, "the cold will kill you."

Jane shivered.

"No," she said, suddenly turning serious. "The cold will not kill me; love will."

She had turned pale; her beauty seemed transfigured; sudden passion had transformed her.

"I love you," she said, "since the beginning of time; I have loved you without knowing it; now I know all too well that I love you."

I had taken both her hands. "You love me? It's not true, but I like to hear you say it."

"And you don't love me?" she murmured.

"I adore you."

Jane protested against that word, but I had spoken it with the eloquence of the heart.

"Adoration can be above love or below it," she said softly, "but in any case it's important."

"I love you, I love you, I love you," I answered.

Jane looked severely at me. "Listen carefully to what I am going to say: you must love me sincerely or not at all, so that you will not make a game of my life and my heart. You will come back here tomorrow. You will ask my father for my hand in marriage. If you do not want to come back tomorrow, then you do not love me. If you do not love me . . . I'll throw myself from this balcony."

After that balcony scene Houssaye is assailed by doubts. He does not believe in the lasting qualities of sudden passion. But he remains behind on the balcony, disturbed and half-convinced that he is dreaming. When he finally returns to the ballroom he sees Marie, as in a vision, but she is not there of course, and Jane begins to be more and more on his mind.

None of these events could remain secret, of course. Marie, who has rejected the Italian Count, challenges Houssaye about Jane a few days later; evidently he had not been to see Marie, for they meet at a party given by a mutual friend. She airily casts him off, telling him to marry and to hurt her no more. But the next day he receives a letter from her:

Yesterday toward midnight I sensed that you were about to betray me. Come at once or never come again.

I am like a poor dog who licks at your feet and then is chased away on the next best occasion.

But take care! I see the shadows falling on your marriage. The bells will ring somberly for it because they will ring for my funeral, too.

I am mortally wounded. I have not slept one hour in the last week. I rise with horror each morning. You have cut me to the heart and the blood floods my bed.

You are causing your own misfortune, as well as mine, and the misfortune of that woman who robs me of my happiness and who will awaken with the shreds of my winding sheet in her hand.

I have loved you so much! I have given you centuries of love while you gave me hours.

And I shall die, carrying my passion to the grave so as to love you for centuries to come.

Marie

Houssaye loses his head when he reads the letter and rushes to Marie's side. She, already ill, sways between self-reproach and burning jealousy. Jealousy wins and she attempts to break up the impending match, going so far as to make a highly placed friend go to Jane's father in order to talk him out of the marriage. He almost persuades M. de la Torre, but Jane wins the day. There is a tragi-comic scene when, after a dinner at Jane's house, Houssaye, driving home, notices a closed carriage following him. He sees Marie in its shadows—and then sees another carriage following hers, which hides Jane.

Houssaye visits Marie's friend and gives him a document establishing a life-annuity for Marie—with the sum of money left blank, for her to fill in. She returns it to him with a note:

You can do as you like, monsieur, you can crucify me as you please, but, I swear to you by my soul and by my God, you will never belong to that woman.

Yet he is still sure that this will blow over, and Marie's furious despair is no more than a cloud on a bright and shining horizon of new love. Her letters become more and more despairing until he finally talks to Jane about Marie, believing for the first time that the break with Marie may lead to a bad end. But Jane dismisses it, and so, ultimately, does he.

·

The Wedding

·

Marie's chambermaid had married my coachman; that man informed Marie every day of my comings and goings. One day he told her that the wedding would take place the day after next. For him, as for everyone else, the civil ceremony did not count.

We had decided that the church wedding would take place at midnight, on June 20, at the church of Saint-Louis-d'Antin. We intended to have the civil ceremony on the nineteenth. That fact saved us from the horrible drama Marie Garcia intended to play. She wanted to place herself at the door of the marriage office in the City Hall and say to me, lifting up a bottle filled with prussic acid, "Houssaye, if you pass that threshold it will be my end!"

And she would have done it without blenching. All her actions were too precipitious to stop once she had started them.

She did not come to the office in the Rue Drouot because she, after hearing the coachman's story, believed that the civil wedding would not take place until the twentieth, but accident led the coachman to that street where he saw us. He ran to his wife and told her, "It looks as if the wedding is already on."

His wife ran to Marie to tell her. The poor woman searched for her bottle but could not find it; she had forgotten that it was in her black dress, the dramatic dress.

In her frenzy she opened the window and threw herself out of it. But by the grace of heaven her dress got caught in the balcony and Marie remained suspended in space. The coachman and her maid saved her, not without great difficulty, but she was horribly mangled on her right side.

Dying, she was put on her bed.

We had wanted to be married at midnight thinking that we would have only members of the family present. Eugène Delacroix, Théophile Gautier, the United States Minister and M. de Corvaïa were the witnesses. But the fashionable world of Paris wanted to be present at the event, particularly because it was to be at midnight.

Marie's willpower was so great that she was the first person we saw on entering the church. Jane's father was furious and spoke vehemently to the prefect of police who had promised to prevent Mlle. Garcia from approaching the church, but she looked so distinguished that the police had not dared to eject her. She remained, leaning on a pillar, during the entire ceremony which took an hour. We saw her in all her pallor, looking at me with her huge blue eyes under her black eyebrows—a true daughter of Aeschylus, a terrible apparition, that pale woman in her black dress. I felt a violent blow as if my happiness were dying in front of me. Jane also recognized her; the two of them looked at each other with murder in their eyes. As Jane was walking in front of me on the arm of my father, she turned to see the expression of my face. I was so heartbroken that I did not attempt to hide my soul. I wished myself dead a thousand times; I felt that I was killing Marie, but how could I stop in my path now?

I went up to the altar, drawn more by fate than by my heart, though it was Jane whom I loved and not that poor afflicted woman who had come to witness the spectacle of her undoing.

A great supper awaited the guests. Fifty small tables had been set for it in the drawing rooms of the mansion belonging to my father-in-law, but there were two guests who did not eat, my wife and I.

"I can easily see," she said to me, "what is going on in your heart; you are shedding tears for the sorrows of your mistress but not for mine."

I offered her my arm and took her away in my carriage. Ten minutes later we were at my house where, in complete distraction at her feet, I swore to her that I married her because I loved her. She shed many tears, but in the end fell trustingly asleep at my heart. I was determined to do what I could so that both women would not be unhappy: because of love for Jane, because of friend-ship for Marie.

Though Jane was cheerful once more the next day, she made a mistake: from that day on she armed herself against her rival with all the blind rage of jealousy. Marie's mistake was to come all the way to my house to say good-by, supported on the arm of a fe-male friend because she was in such terrible condition.

Jane told her servants, "Throw that woman out of the house!"

When I saw a maid insulting Marie, I intervened. That was simply too much for Jane, who told me, "Take her home and don't come back."

I took Marie as far as the street, begging her to regain her composure. But one does not reason with passion. She broke into violent sobs and held out her hand. "Good-by!" she said. "You have condemned me to death. I am asking you for just one more thing—that you will come to my funeral."

It was actually a dying woman who spoke.

When I reentered my house, I saw Jane fleeing up the staircase. She had wanted to witness the farewell but she did not want to see me.

"Jane," I called, to make her turn, but she disappeared and the door of her room slammed shut.

Yet—how strange are the follies of passion—at dinner we acted like lovers, sat close to each other and drank from one glass in memory of our strawberry.

If her family had not come to console her, Jane would have consoled herself with me; but she took the tears of her mother and her sister too much to heart. She believed herself to be singularly unfortunate because everyone around her wept as if she were already dead.

God is my witness that I did not want to see Marie again and that I did not see her again except on her deathbed. I had no other purpose in mind than Jane's happiness.

A few days after the wedding we left for Dieppe where we spent the summer while Marie, showing some signs of life, spent the season in Eaux-Bonnes. Jane regained her natural gaiety without losing the fear that my thoughts were too often in Eaux-Bonnes. She believed that Marie play-acted her despair to draw me back. She obstinately refused to believe in Marie's illness. The doctor in Eaux-Bonnes wrote me that Marie would not live until winter and that it would be an act of kindness to send her a word of remembrance. I found it now as easy to write to her as I would to my sister. Unfortunately she replied to that letter, and her response burned Jane's hands who saw treason in it. Yet I had done no more than write to a dying woman.

On our return from Dieppe Jane's jealousy grew, though Marie's letter had been no love letter at all. I talked to her about going to Venice but she was afraid to leave her mother and sisters. She said that she liked only imaginary countries. Her jealousy was so great that she feared Mlle. Garcia would be a partner in the journey.

Autumn was rainy and proved fatal to Marie. Friends who saw her told me that she did not have long to live. Her agony drew me to her, but I feared to arouse all of Jane's sorrows, for she knew everything, not because people told her everything but because she sensed everything, being able to read foreheads and eyes.

Finally I went to say good-by to Marie, at the request of Abbé Caron, confessor to both my first and second wives, who by chance also assisted Marie in her final days. He wanted to reconcile all in forgiveness. In fact, Marie's first words to me were, "Tell your wife that I forgive her my death as I forgive you. Tell her that I die wishing her to be happy in your love. Abbé Caron has shown me God. I am no more than a spirit now."

But Jane kept the fires of her Latin jealousy burning until the last, until after Marie's death. Marie forgave, but Jane did not.

·

Marie's Death

·

On the evening before her death Marie told me, "You know that little novel I wrote at Eaux-Bonnes; tell Lévy to publish it. And give to the poor what little money it will bring."

Marie was right about the day of her death. On that December 12 she told me, "I'll die tomorrow, don't forget to come."

When I came to see her in the morning, I found her all in smiles. She had ordered that she be dressed as carefully as always. Someone brought her *Intermission*, the professional journal for actresses. She looked at it without wanting to read it.

"I no longer belong to this world," she murmured.

"Isn't madame doing well?" said her maid.

"Yes, I am doing well," said Marie, "because I feel that I shall die without pain."

I tried to comfort her.

"No," she said, "I won't have to postpone my journey again, I'll set out at four o'clock when dusk falls. Don't forget to come and see me at three."

I returned to see her at two o'clock. Abbé Caron and the curate of Saint-Philippe-du-Roule had just arrived to give her Extreme Unction. She was happy in her meditation. The two priests and the Sister of Charity congratulated her. Two friends of hers were there, praying, on their knees beside her aunt and her cousin: they were Mlle. Judith of the Comédie Française and Mme. Jeanne de Tourbey, today the Comtesse de Loynes.

Dr. Contour signaled to me and I followed him to the small salon.

"It does not seem possible," I said to him, "that she will die today as she said yesterday and this morning."

"Oh, good Lord, yes. The emotion of that great scene will do it. Look, my dear friend, for an actress, whether she believes in God or not, Extreme Unction is her last role; she gives up her soul in it and dies on stage."

The physician was wrong as far as Marie was concerned, or at least her role, for she acted for God alone and not for her audience.

When everyone had departed she entered her last hour. She had believed she would escape its agony; her last moments were not terrible, but they were hard.

I don't know how to record what she so eloquently said about her vision of another world, or her good-bys to those she loved. At her last moment I felt her hand, already ice-cold, tighten on mine.

"I can see you," she whispered.

But she could not see anything any more.

Her clock was close by. "I don't hear it any more," she murmured. "Soon it will be my heart that won't beat any more."

She prayed aloud so as not to cry out. I held her hands. She raised her head once more and then fell back.

The end! One of the best beings of this world no longer belonged to it.

Overwhelmed by my grief, I kissed her lovely hair and then went home to lock myself in my room. In a crisis of that kind, solitude is the only friend.

The dinner bell sounded. I collected myself and went down. I found myself, alone, face to face with my wife.

"Well, sir," she said banteringly, "did you just come back from that lady?"

"Yes, she called me to be present at her death.'

"Well really—more play-acting."

"Strange play-acting, madame, because Marie is dead."

"A stage-death no doubt. Especially as she expects you for a late supper tonight."

In vain I told Jane that her own confessor had been to see Marie with me. She refused to believe a single word I said.

"Well then, madame, if you desire to attend her funeral I shall send you a letter of invitation tomorrow."

Everything turned out tragically in that adventure. Life in death, death in life. At Père Lachaise Cemetery, only a few graves away from the funeral for Marie Garcia, people could see a handsome purple bonnet on the head of a veiled lady. It was Jane, who had been unable to subdue her feverish excitement and had come to see the event. Some friends of Marie recognized her and were indignant, but they could see that she seemed less alive than the one at whose bier they stood; they saw her collapse and dissolve in tears.

When Jane came home I knocked at her door. She did not open. I wanted to tell her that I was leaving for a few days because my duties as Inspector General of Provincial Museums called me south. It seemed impossible to me to live under the same roof with her until time, which soothes everything, would appease her resentment and my pain. One of her sisters appeared and told her that she must not see me because the whole of Paris was scandalized that her husband had gone to receive the last words of his mistress.

On the evening of Marie's funeral Arsène Houssaye departs for Venice, leaving a farewell letter for Jane: as she did not want to see him, he would never see her again. In Venice, on arrival, he found a short dignified reply: "I am Mme. Arsène Houssaye, I shall die Mme. Arsène Houssaye."

He buys a palazzo cheaply, intending to stay because he cannot face Paris and Jane. But in the end he takes his duties as Inspector General of Museums as his excuse to return. After six weeks he is back at his house in Paris. Jane is desperately unhappy and desperately proud. They divide the house between themselves, hardly see each other, and months pass before their relations gradually return to a normal state, by deft, cleverly observed stages. They begin to dine together, to meet at social occasions (though they do not attend them together).

The reconciliation, once it has finally come, and happiness are heightened by the birth of his second son, on May 4, 1864, whom he saved from death when the doctor, worried about the mother's state, abandoned him on a couch. However, Jane does not recover and dies within a few months.

Social Notes

·

Adelina Patti

·

When the Marquis de Caux married that lovely girl who not only sang like a bird but looked more like a bird than a woman—Mlle. Adelina Patti—he came to tell me that the lovely bluebird wanted as its cage the small mansion, in Moorish style, which then formed one unit with my own mansion. That Moorish building had taken her fancy at one of my entertainments. The matter was soon settled. I rented him the house as it was, complete with furnishings and pictures. I was delighted with my new neighbor because often in the morning the lovely Marquise opened the connecting door to let me witness her morning trills and flourishes. She was a true nightingale. Everything about her sang; her eyes, her smile, the curve of her throat and the shimmer of her hair. Fortunately for me, I was not in love with her no matter how much I was charmed by her; moreover, in addition to my well-known virtue—and hers —her husband was always at home.

At that time she had eyes only for her husband even though he proved himself more entrepreneur than marquis. In fact, he had to some extent become the Barnum of that still rising star and offended her each evening after her performance with the oft-repeated phrase, "Well, another show in the bag." And he counted the box-office receipts. Nevertheless he was an agreeable man of wit and good society.

Before long, he began to be sorry he had a wife and took a mistress who resembled Patti and who sang a little like her. Such is man and such is humanity!

I often had dinner with the Marquis de Caux, at the Moulin Rouge and at the Ambassadeurs. He told me a huge number of stories about strange events in the Tuileries, and he told stories well. People who make it their task to be clever are all too ready to believe that all the rest have no wit; that is where they often go wrong. The Marquis also did wrong not to write his memoirs once he had retired from the conjugal battlefield.

He could, for example, have told about that comedy of mistaken identity. Here it is, in a few words: One day I was invited to dinner at an elegant house where I had been given the lovely Adelina Patti as my partner. She was then in the possession of the tenor Nicolini. We knew each other from long ago, as she had been my neighbor during the first days of her marriage. Well, on that evening I reminded her of her days as a bride and asked her why she had replaced Caux with Nicolini.

"Because Caux always said the same one thing to me."

"And Nicolini does not say the same thing all the time?"

"Yes, he does; he says he loves me."

I tried to defend the Marquis: "I have seen him cry no matter how he tried to hide it."

"Don't be sorry, he consoled himself very fast. Would you believe that he paid court to Nicolini's wife because she looks like me?"

On the following evening, another dinner—this time with the Marquis de Caux in the garden of the Ambassadeurs. And what do I see—Adelina Patti with her arm in his! But it seemed to be her only from a distance because, when they came closer, I saw that it was an illusion, and moreover a particular illusion for Caux. He had caught in clear water, as one catches trout, a false Patti who made him believe in his luck. But that is not the end of the story.

On the next evening I dined at the house of Count Kowalsky, one of those half-professional, half-social pianists, the kind of man one hopes is in America when one is in Paris, even though he had the brilliance of Liszt. I was seated between the lady of the house and Adelina Patti.

"Well—are you still in love with Nicolini?"

"He is a monster—I am suing him for divorce."

I took a look at the lady—the lady was Mme. Nicolini, a true replica of Patti but a little more worn by time.

"Oh, how you resemble Patti!"

"I can well believe it—the Marquis de Caux is always at my heels."

·

Marie Taglioni

·

It was in 1847; we were returning from the Lido, three gondolas abreast, Meissonier and Ziem, those lovers of Venice, and I. We met two Venetian ladies who had been goddesses of the Opéra, Marie Taglioni and Rosine Stoltz. The three of us rose to salute them. They returned the greeting, one of them with a charming smile, the other with an almost glacial air. The singer did it with her heart, while the dancer bowed with choreographic dignity.

When we disembarked at the Riva degli Sciavoni we talked some about the two stars who had fallen from the firmament of the Opéra. The French consul in Venice, Léon Pillet, a former Director of the Royal Academy of Music *, happened to join us for a cigar. There we had the right man to talk about them. He was still enchanted with the great singer but appreciated the unappreciative dancer considerably less: she still pretended to be fault-

---

* and former Director of the Paris Opéra, where he had hired Lola Montez for an abortive debut as a dancer.

less, she still believed herself to float on air. When she was asked why she had come to Venice she invariably answered, "Because this is the only place which has two heavens: one above and one below."

I saw Taglioni again in 1852, at the Comte de Morny's, a few days after he had resigned as Minister of the Interior. He had invited his artist friends to dinner. Though it was a party for men, he had two women at his side: Mlle. Taglioni and Mlle. Rachel—two great ladies because they knew how to preserve the grand style of simplicity. I was seated between Delacroix and the Comte Gilbert de Voisins, who arrived when we were already at the table. His first question was: "Who is that schoolmistress next to Morny?"

I was not exactly worried that I would upset him by replying, "That's your wife."

He searched far back in his memory before answering: "Well, that is possible."

Mlle. Taglioni, pointing to her husband, asked Morny why he had had the curious idea to make her dine in such bad company.

After dinner Gilbert de Voisins, who was afraid of nothing, not even his wife, had the impertinence of having himself presented to her.

She took it well. "It seems to me, monsieur, that I had the honor of being presented to you around 1832."

That was the fatal year of their marriage. On the day after the wedding Gilbert de Voisins had forgotten that he was married.

In 1852 the goddess Taglioni was still agreeable to look at, though already rather decomposed. That woman who was a goddess on the stage did have something of the air of a schoolmistress when in public, even though she played her role as star very well. The good days went by fast; she had a fashionable admirer when she herself was in fashion. But when she danced no more she was loved no more, like Orpheus' friend whom the Corybants loved only for her music. She had brought a beautiful girl into the world who left some fine day with a prince, an intimate of the household. That marked the end of the joys of life and the joys of the heart for her.

Ruin came step by step. She had too much dignity to try to climb to the firmament of the dance once more, like Mme. Sagni remounting the tightrope.

Step by step, she went down until she became a dancing teacher for ladies and girls. It was a sad sight to see her, white-haired and dressed like a chambermaid, conduct an English school at Hyde Park in the winter and at Brighton in the summer. She gave lessons in deportment at Court where the Queen was always known to keep a collection of beauties. The Princess of Wales learned from Marie Taglioni how to curtsy like a queen, somewhat as Napoleon learned from Talma how to act imperially. One had to see her in the company of that tiny old Italian whose coattails swept the floor, playing diminutively at being dancing master: truly a character out of Hoffmann.

And so he and she taught the various dances: the pavane, the romanesca, the gavotte, the trenitz and all the figures of the cotillion. The quavering voice of that poor woman could be heard: "Bow, bow, Miss Helena! Glide, glide, Miss Arabella."

That was her last song; neither Miss Helena nor Miss Arabella managed to glide with French grace or bow in the airy manner of the Italians, and Marie Taglioni was distressed.

In the end, though, it was a consolation for her to see people dance, even English ladies!

Taglioni finally went to die in Marseilles, in the misery of her eighty years. May the earth rest lightly on her who never placed her foot on it!

•

Cora Pearl

•

Cora Pearl neither danced nor sang—not seriously, anyway—and should therefore not really be grouped with Patti and Taglioni. She was one of the great courtesans of the Second Empire, the girl to whom the Duc de Grammont-Caderousse gave a silver bathtub filled with champagne.

Houssaye shows her not in her glory but as a fallen woman also fallen from grace. He sees her not so much as a beauty but as an object of conspicuous consumption whose great appeal to a gentleman lay not so much in having her as in showing that he could afford her.

Cora Pearl passed like an unruly comet across the sky of the Bouffes-Parisiens, all starry with beautiful girls—not to mention all the beds to which she gave stardom. She did not have the nonchalant and dreamy grace which English girls usually have. At first sight she recalled, rather, something like a cross between a King Charles spaniel and a bulldog.

I met the lady at Ems walking gracefully like a doe and with a sullen air: coral and pearls, "tiny prints of coral on her lips and milk of pearls in her cheeks." She was soon enough undressed but, good Lord, what labor in the morning to put on her makeup! It was art hiding nature. She had the skill of being beautiful and inspired the idea of beauty through skill among the female sex.

She had her day as one of the greatest objects of adoration, completely taking in her stride the most beautiful letters from princes and the most hotly amorous notes from all sorts of men. They kissed the ground she walked on. In one word—an idol! And why? Because she had beautiful horses which she drove more smoothly than her lovers.

In those days one talked about the mines of California; at Cora Pearl's, after supper, one could meet up with them. She never kept accounts, until the day when she fell to the rank of the fifty franc girls. That's how things go. She came to me to confess her rage and despair: "There's nothing left, only fatheads and whores." She showed me her arms, she showed me her legs, she showed me her bosom: who, who among these whores, could strut her stuff with such great endowments? I advised her to return to England, but she was dreaming about a pyramid in France, to be her grave, like that of Semiramis.

I knew Miss Cora Pearl when she was in the ascent. I wanted

to see her again when she had fallen. I had been running into her here and there, in the bois, at the races, in the theater, and I was eager to study more closely that princess who had all the haughtiness of an English Countess enthroned in her castle and unhumiliated even in the act of love. But her fall had come before I could.

She lived at that time near the Païva Palace, two doors down, in some odds-and-ends sort of place, above a carriage maker. One afternoon I went and knocked at her door. "Good afternoon, Cora!"

She fell around my neck, overjoyed to see a friend from her better days. "Yes, Cora," she said to me, "but Cora without pearls."

"Still as beautiful as ever!" I said without conviction.

"Not at all; look, my cheeks are furrowed with tears; don't write that in the papers, because Parisians don't like women who cry."

Then she showed me that poor apartment, a veritable satire on her former luxuries: "Step by step, I have finally come down to this wretched place, but I have not said the last word yet." She raised her head with pride.

"What, my dear Cora, of all your friends not one has remained in your days of neglect?"

"Look, they don't come back because the Republic has hit them just like me, and because I have not changed my showy ways. I am like those curio merchants who go bankrupt because they won't lower their prices."

And with that she well characterized those supposed ladykillers who were less interested in the woman than in her publicity value. Not long ago they enjoyed, to use the term loosely, a Cora Pearl who received them in a palace, whom they bowed to in the bois in a carriage drawn by English thoroughbreds, who gave them an audience backstage.

She did not want to admit to herself, any more than to me, that the appeal of her form had greatly lost its spell. Where was the bedeviling cast of her eye, her insolent bosom, the promise of her firm, white arms, all that radiance of youth which is the glory of woman?

Good fellow that I am, I tried to comfort her, but without intending to make her feel that my consolations had a serious intent. "It's well for you to talk," she replied. "I have played my hand, I just did not expect to come to the end of the game so soon. It doesn't pay to be sorry that I threw myself so completely into this sort of existence, or rather that I didn't get well out of it." She held out her hand to me. "Imagine, my dear friend, that by the grace of God I could have pulled out of this in time. I am not only speaking of those idiots who offered me their hearts for life, I am speaking of some decent fellows who loved me to the point of sacrificing their good names for me. In addition to Bouillon Duval."

Cora Pearl sighed. "Well, well, more than once I wanted to come to you to give you the story for a real novel you could have written."

"I'm at your orders," I said banteringly. She told me a sweet little romance which could not have offended the chastest pen. "You write that," she said. The doorbell rang and saved me the need to reply. I picked up my hat to avoid being introduced to a tardy lover.

.

A Resplendent Soul

.

The Franco-Roman or Franco-Florentine prince who turned all the heads of the *demi-monde*—and, one might add, of the ladies of good society who were tired of their virtue—time and again threw himself at the famous Jeanne of the sea-green eyes, nicknamed the Incomparable in her circle of playmates.

He was her titular lover, or should I say her true lover, for the beautiful sinner always had need of some sleeping partnerships for adornment, though these sleeping partnerships remained unofficial. She used to say artlessly, "I live morganatically with the Prince who would marry me if marriage were one of his habits."

A Duke bearing a famous name of the First Empire presented himself one morning—after the Prince's dawn—at the beautiful creature's house.

L

"What brings you here, my dear Duke?"

"You, madame, my passion for your beautiful eyes."

"You know very well that I am unattainable, as the Prince's dazzling love has placed me on a fortified island without any landing place."

"Yes, but I have a rather good reason to pay court to you."

And saying these words the Duke opened his cigar case and took from it, with thumb and index finger, a lovely check for three hundred thousand francs, drawn on the Bank of France.

"That is very pretty," said the goddess.

"Don't you think I have here, just for a start, three hundred thousand good reasons to plead for me?"

"My dear Duke, I am overcome by your eloquence."

"Don't hesitate, your couch is right behind you."

"Oh, but I am not yet that overcome, I ask you for twenty-four hours to think about it."

"Twenty-four hours is too much; I give you until dinnertime. If you agree, send me word; if you don't, I have other adventures to go to."

Upon which the Duke planted a chaste kiss on the lady's forehead and returned the check to his cigar case. The lady, as if the check already belonged to her, enjoined him not to smoke it by mistake. As soon as he had left she ordered her horses, not to run after him but to seek the advice of two of her friends.

The first one was I. She was somewhat agitated when she came to me, at the same time acting the woman who is not troubled by anything.

She told me the story. "What would you do in my place, my dear?"

"My dear, I can't put myself in your place because I don't have the means, but if I were in your place, with time running out, crushed by luxury as you are, I'd take the three hundred thousand francs. Remember what the wife of Louis XV said: 'Who could resist that?' "

"That remark is not applicable to me because I do not share

the virtues of that queen. But I think you are right, I don't have the right to be so virtuous—oh, but if you knew how I love the Prince!"

"I don't doubt it, but the Prince loves you too much not to come back at the first call."

The lady dashed off to see her second friend, Émile de Girardin. He made the opposite recommendation: "When one has a lover like your Prince, one must never leave him. Your whole circle of friends would leave you if he does. What, after all, are three hundred thousand francs? I myself would give them to you, merely for letting me loosen your hair after supper."

The lady went back home and wrote to the Duke that he need not come. She had firmly adopted the great virtues of the great king's court. The Prince came to dine with her.

"If you knew how I love you!" she cried, throwing herself into his arms. The Prince, always ready to tease, denied the existence of female love. According to him it was nothing but straw fires and shooting stars. They sat down to dinner armed with La Rochefoucauld and Chamfort. During the dessert the lady threw her bouquet at the Prince, who threatened to spank her with its roses.

"And when I think," she exclaimed suddenly, "that I sacrificed three hundred thousand francs for you today!"

She recounted the story of the Duke's impertinent proposition and of her indignant refusal.

"You stupid bitch!" cried the Prince—he was even worse than I.

·

Parisian Nights

·

The Second Empire was in deep trouble both internally and externally in the later 1860's, but no one who observed the social scene in Paris would have had an inkling of it. The festivities rose to dizzying heights toward the end of the Empire, and Arsène

Houssaye, with his magnificent mansion in the Avenue Friedland and his several châteaux in the country, was a chief contributor. In 1868 he gave his first Venetian Masked Ball, and repeated it in 1869. These fêtes were among the most brilliant social events of their seasons, uniting courtesans, actresses and ladies of society and of the Imperial Court, all hidden behind their masks, and all the gentlemen who could wangle invitations. The secret of success of these balls was that they were unplanned: witty conversation, plenty of room to dance, an excellent buffet, but no organized amusement.

Houssaye's greatest entertainment, a "country-fair party," was held in September 1869, after the success of his book Les grandes dames. *It was a fête at his Château de la Folie—Riancourt-en-Breuil, not far from Bruyères. It provided whole oxen, sheep and pigs, partridges, hares and quail roasted on spits over open fires. The roasting pits stretched for a full quarter mile, fountains flowed with wine, one thousand bottles of champagne were consumed and the tombola had a thousand prizes. There were orchestras, clowns, tumblers, games, and special trains to carry the guests from Paris and back again. It was, almost to the day, one year before the battle of Sedan in which all that carefree glory vanished. Before that, however, there were many nights like the ones which follow.*

Prince Radziwill said to me one day, when we happened to meet on the Boulevard des Italiens, that he was happy to see me because he wanted to invite me to dine with him that evening at the Russian restaurant in the Rue Favart. But, he said, I needed to have a lady with me, like the other guests. A lady for dinner can be found. Just then a pretty actress, Mlle. de la Colombe *, not to give her name, was coming toward us. She knew how to dine, tooth and claw—she was really entitled to a degree in dining, often being the chief seductress at the best Paris dinners.

At eight o'clock sharp I made my entrance with her into the

* Miss Turtledove

company of Russian gentlemen and of ladies from all over: divorced women, separated women, women of the world, women of adventure, in a word the most amusing company in Paris. The host received us warmly and offered me the best place because he put me at the side of the mistress of an absent guest, a lovely creature nicknamed The Pearl of the New World, who had taken her *nom de guerre* from *Clarissa*, a famous English novel. The absent guest, Prince ——————, was not expected until dessert because he had to dine at the Italian Embassy.

My charming neighbor had read my novel *Mademoiselle Cléopâtre;* she believed that I knew women, that is, that I made a game of them. So, in order to defy me, she said when I was seated, "You came with that dove who is opposite you. I forbid you to look at her, otherwise you will never be my lover."

"Be your lover? That's my heart's desire. I swear to you that, if you will be my mistress for an hour, I shall spend a week without looking at that woman, whom I really like."

"Shake hands. The treaty is concluded."

I almost replied with the words of the Prince de Joinville: "Where? When? For how much?" But my table partner's diamonds were too brilliant to permit me to ask the last question. She answered the first two on her own. "All these people here have come to dine and to gamble; when they are at their dessert, we'll go and munch the apple at your house. I want to see your famous gallery by torchlight."

The dinner was brilliant even before the dessert. Suddenly my table partner asked for my arm. "Fantasio, take me outside for a few minutes to catch some fresh air. I have had too much champagne."

No one seemed disturbed by that slightly strange exodus. We jumped into one of the cabs on the Place de l'Opéra Comique. Ten minutes later we were at my door. Of course I did the honors of my gallery by torchlight; that gallery starts at the dining room, continues by the side of the drawing rooms and salons and ends at the bedroom. I am not so sure, in fact, that we did not start at the end. The loveliest picture, the loveliest sculpture was surely she. Raised as she was according to the principles of Princess Borghese, she did not act the prude but displayed herself in the full splendor of her nudity, wanting to rival all the painted and sculptured goddesses.

When we reappeared at the Russian restaurant, heads held high like people who had just done a good deed, Prince _____ had arrived but was undisturbed by his mistress's absence. He was already deeply involved in a game with Count Kazikoff. You'll see what a game. It was not simply to keep the cards busy.

Count Kazikoff had not wanted to start at less than two thousand francs. From that they had gone on to ten thousand francs. He was losing and always asked for a return match. Well, the lovely American, feeling that the evening would be advantageous for her, immediately turned her back on me and went to kiss her lover, saying, "Prince, as I share half your life, I want to share half your game."

When Kazikoff had lost all his ready money, plus one hundred thousand francs on his word of honor, he offered the victor to play for his mansion in the Parc des Princes for two hundred thousand francs.

"As you wish," said the Prince. Everyone was very excited. Even the most cynical felt their hearts beat.

Clarisse murmured, "The mansion will be for me."

I was furious with Kazikoff because I knew his wife, the kindest of creatures, who suffered greatly because of his passion for gambling.

Kazikoff scored three, then four. Everyone breathed a sigh because he would doubtlessly win his money back. But the cards refused. The Prince scored three, then four.

"You won't trump the king!" said the Count.

The Prince trumped the king.

To hide his chagrin, Katzikoff murmured, "I never liked kings!"

He had once been captured in a revolt at Wilna and sent to

Kazan, condemned to death. Alexander II had pardoned him, but he had never pardoned Alexander II.

"I'll beat my bad luck," he said decisively. "Prince, I shall play you for the furnishings of my mansion."

"I thought they went with the mansion," said the Prince. "But I don't insist. Let us play for them."

To help Kazikoff, the furnishings were estimated at seventy-five thousand francs.

It turned out the same, the Prince won.

"Very well," said Kazikoff, "as I have to stake my last penny, I'll play for the tapestries and pictures of the mansion. That's another seventy-five thousand francs at least: two Boucher, two Van Loo, two Delacroix, two Diaz, and four sixteenth-century tapestries."

The Prince, frightened by his luck, said that he would take the pictures and tapestries for one hundred thousand francs.

We hardly breathed. Only the lovely American laughed, knowing full well that the mansion, the furnishings, the pictures and the tapestries were for her. She was the kind of woman who was used to sudden profits and had no doubt that the Count would go down to complete ruin.

She was not mistaken. The last hand was played slowly. The Count went up to three. But at the fifth card, though the king was on his side this time, he lost.

One would have imagined that this frenzied gambler, who had nothing left except his mistress, would now propose to the Prince to wager her against everything he had lost, but the image of his mistress was eclipsed by that of his wife. He had been heroic thus far, but now he turned pale. He rose, bowed and departed murmuring, "My wife!"

In fact, what could he say to his wife who had just come from Wilna expressly to spend three months in that mansion?

"Clarisse," I said to the American, "as all of it will be yours, you can do no less than allow Mme. de Kazikoff to spend the season in her house—I mean, in your house."

"With the greatest pleasure," said the American, "but only to please you and to have my revenge on virtue."

"Every woman has her particular virtue."

"Just as an example, her husband offered me all he just lost here for my own virtue, and I refused without batting an eye."

A game of baccarat had been planned, but after that great show everyone said that one could not play a small game after a big one.

The lovely Clarisse took the arm of Prince ———— and whispered in my ear, "Tomorrow you take me to Rosalie Léon's ball."

I knew the lady well: an artistic dilettante, especially in collecting furniture. She did not give balls except now and then because she was afraid that someone would break her Dresden or Sèvres china. What a lovely nest it was for that great cocotte who was to die with an annual income of a million from her lover.

So the next day we went to excite ourselves for an hour in that little nest; I should have said for a night, for the ball did not end until broad daylight.

Tout-Paris was there, of course—that is to say, the non-Parisian *tout-Paris*, the pick of the basket of all nations. You can imagine that the lovely American was the apple of all eyes. Everyone wanted to court her; but, as she had told me the evening before, I now told her: "I forbid you to hear one golden or silver word, or to look at one white tie."

Like everyone else we took a turn at the waltz, but then, suddenly, one of the twenty lovers whom she kept at a distance with her disdainful looks came up to me and said in her presence, in lugubrious tones, "Monsieur, I assume that you are a gentleman."

"Not another word, Monsieur, until you have retracted that 'I assume.'"

"Very well, Monsieur, you are a gentleman. I am sure I can trust you. The lady present here is my fiancée. I am agreed to let her converse with you, but I do not permit her to waltz with you."

Clarisse and I broke into laughter.

"Monsieur," I said, "our majesties—that lady and I—say: 'We will dance.' "

"I assure you, Monsieur," he continued in a raised voice, "that I shall marry that lady before the end of the month."

"You might put it in commercial terms—by the thirtieth instant—Monsieur, because I imagine it's because a bill falls due."

He took out a calling card and handed it to me. "Monsieur, I do not joke. Madame here knows very well that I shall marry her in two weeks because I love her and because she wants to be a princess."

"What, yet another prince?" I said, looking at Clarisse.

"I never saw any other specimen in Russia."

"So it's a serious prince?"

I noticed a somewhat strange air in the lady, half-serious, half-mocking. It was true, actually, that she was inclined to marry him for his title. She therefore did not want to say yes or no.

The Prince turned more provocative. Noting it, I told him with becoming British gravity, "Monsieur, you intend to marry this lady one of these days; very well. But I have the right to waltz with her for one good reason: I married her yesterday."

Silence.

I knew very well what I was doing. In a lifetime one ought to experience everything.

After looking closely at Clarisse, who did not deny it, he said, "Monsieur, you will receive my witnesses."

"Monsieur, I shall expect them."

Right then and there the husband-to-be began to search for two witnesses through the salons. They were soon found.

"What if we were to dance?" said Clarisse.

"Yes, my lovely friend, on condition that one of your other bed-partners be one of my witnesses."

A Frenchwoman would have been in hysterics at the prospect of losing either a lover or a fiancé. But Americans are more practical minded and never expect the worst to happen. Clarisse began to dance gaily, showing her graces like a peacock showing his tail.

Moments later the Prince's witnesses approached the quadrille, but they respected our gaiety. After the last figure they lit upon me like one man. I indicated my witnesses to them. The Prince had said, "Duel to the death," believing that he would get the better of all the lady's admirers, especially Prince ———, by putting me in my grave. My witnesses refused pistols at five paces, then at ten paces. They proposed swords, but the Prince had once had a broken arm. They then offered to let him kill me at twenty-five paces, maintaining moreover that I was the offended party as the Prince had come "to importune me in the midst of a festivity where I had gone to enjoy myself."

The gentleman finally deigned to kill me at twenty-five paces.

I am not particularly fond of going to see dawn opening the portals of the sun and closing the portals of the grave at the same time. But in these affairs one must act at once and act gaily.

The same thing once happened to me at a ball at the City Hall with the Deputy Lherbette. We were not destined to leave the ball without trying to slaughter each other. Well, that end was not any more tragic than the one with the Prince. We were to meet at the Bagatelle. The witnesses had woken up Gastine Renette in the Champs Elysées to supply the dueling pistols.

We were all assembled.

When I say "all" I am wrong: one person was missing.

That person was the Prince, who had sent an ambassador. In the meantime he had found out my name and no longer wanted to kill me. Moreover, he vowed me eternal thanks for keeping him from the foolishness of marrying, by the thirtieth instant, a woman whom I had endorsed the night before.

We returned from the field of battle, chagrined of course to have gone there to no purpose. To console myself I continued to marry the lady for several days. She has since become a very proper lady, the wife of a handsome Spanish prince. You should consign her to heaven even after reading these Confessions.

Toward the End

·

The End of the Empire

·

In the summer of 1870 the Second Empire fought its fourth and last war. In July a sudden crisis, created by Bismarck in Berlin, erupted over the succession to the Spanish throne. By the end of the month Napoleon III, sick and dispirited, had been dragged into war, as much by the conservative faction of the Bonapartists as by the Prussians. Early in August the gigantic miscalculation of their own strength by the French military was apparent. Napoleon wanted to return to Paris to save the Empire, but the Empress Eugénie, left behind as his regent, dissuaded him. On September 2, the Emperor himself had to surrender his army at Sedan; two days later the Empire fell in Paris, and the Empress fled.

Many years earlier, when Houssaye and Musset were leaving the Tuileries after the reading of L'Âne et le ruisseau, their conversation concerned the Empress and expressed the widespread antipathy against her. To Houssaye, as to many Frenchmen of his time, she was "l'Espagnole"—that Spanish woman—a fitting successor to "l'Autrichienne," or rather, those two Austrian women whom popular belief blamed for many of the misfortunes of France: Marie Antoinette who married Louis XVI, and Marie Louise, the second wife of Napoleon I.

With the Empire swept away, a new provisional government attempted to improvise new armies. Within a few weeks the Prussians had reached Paris and laid siege to the city. Throughout the fall and into the winter fighting continued, and Paris resisted valiantly in spite of famine. The city surrendered on January 29, the same day that the preliminary peace between Prussia and France was concluded at Versailles.

We dined at Mme. de Païva's mansion on September 4, twenty guests from the world of letters and politics. Aubryet aroused controversy with his strident attack on the revolutionaries who were not content with the peaceful revolutions of the spirit of man. Girardin shouted to him across the table: "Forces beyond anyone's control have sent these revolutionaries into the street."

"Yes," added Mme. de Païva, "one day the whole structure finally cracks all over. It's like an earthquake. Those who are inside don't even try to defend themselves. All they can think of is escape."

"Let me answer you," said Théophile Gautier, "that those who are in the Tuileries now will defend themselves to the last bullet and the last dagger."

"We shall see," said Émile de Girardin. "As for me, I am sure that even the bravest there won't think of anything except hitching four horses to a carriage. It's bound to happen."

"Let me tell you," answered Gautier, "that the Emperor and the Empress will let themselves be slain on the grand staircase if they do not retain the upper hand."

Emile de Girardin shrugged his shoulders and forbore to reply to his former editorial writer, as if to say disdainfully: oh, you poets! Théo made every effort to prove that the Empress would rather die than give ground; he pronounced the paradox that she was brave because she was a woman.

"No," answered Mme. de Païva, "she is an empress and she won't know how to die."

On September 5, we again dined together, not at Mme. de Païva's, who had fled to Pontchartrain, but at a small restaurant which has since gone, the little Moulin Rouge.

We recalled Girardin's prediction. Aubryet tortured the French language the better to be able to abuse the revolutionaries. Théo, calm as ever, declared that the Empress had not been worthy of his predictions.

"Look," I said to him. "She wanted that war: every place ought to have been a battlefield for her. It would have been the Emperor's duty to die at Sedan, and the Empress' duty to die in the Tuileries."

We examined how the revolution could have overcome the Empire so quickly. It has always been a mistake in those countries that have the Salic law to have female regents, for nobody takes them seriously. One defers to them and passes them by. Women don't build anything, they only destroy, because they live in dreamland.

.

The Siege of Paris

.

At the charity fête I gave for the wounded during the siege of Paris, Auber, who was then ninety-one years old, was the center of that night of stars: always smiling, passing from group to group with inspiring conversation, being kind enough to accompany the singers at the piano, among them Marie Roze who sang "The First Day of Happiness."

It was Auber's last day of happiness, for he did not survive that improvised triumph by more than three months.

When several generals complimented the singers and the illustrious composer, Auber collected a whole crowd around him by the charm of his conversation. No one could tell as much as he, or could tell it better.

"I have seen so much," he sighed. And, addressing General Read, "Think of it, General, I was present at the tragedy of André Chénier going to the guillotine.* The poet Roucher was able to move his hands a little, the only one who could do that in that fatal tumbril. He constantly took snuff. They had been kind enough to leave him his snuffbox, as one gives criminals a glass of brandy at the supreme hour. He sat face to face with André Chénier; I could not hear them but I was told afterwards that they spoke of a better world where there would be no guillotine.

"Two noble heads about to fall! I was on the steps of St. Paul's Church, and I escaped the friend of my father, who had stopped there with me, in order to follow the tumbril, all of whose figures, men and women, wrung my heart. A horrifying spectacle! There was a rumor in the crowd that somehow they would be saved, but that was not what the spectators wanted who were used to seeing heads roll. And what heads! Chénier is much admired now, Roucher is not sufficiently remembered; his "Poëme des Mois" is a beautiful thing, an early romantic work, as Chateaubriand said. Well, General, they were not saved. I heard the frightful cries of the crowd, I almost breathed the smell of blood, as precious blood as there ever was."

After a painful silence, Auber continued: "Let us not talk too loud; who knows whether we won't witness that spectacle once again? But I am ninety-one; they can work their guillotine on the Place de la Bastille or the Place du Trône or the Place de la Concorde—I won't be one of the spectators."

No one dared to ask Auber what he meant by that. Did he have a presentiment of his death or did he rather want to say that he would not again be present at these bloody festivities of humanity? I had joined the group and knew well the history of the last moments of Roucher and Chénier. Auber added, turning to Marie Roze, dazzling in the bloom of youth: "Fouquier-Tinville

---

* In 1794, during the French Revolution, the great poet André Chénier was arrested on bogus charges of conspiracy by agents of the Committee of Public Safety, condemned, and summarily executed.

would have exclaimed if he had seen you: 'Isn't that a lovely rose to be cut off at the scaffold?' "

Only a short time before I had seen Auber at one of the Monday receptions of the Empress; he conducted the orchestra in a concert for which no one had thought to give him more than a simple list of works to be played. As he remained intrepidly on his feet while the rest of the assembly was seated, the Empress graciously went up to tell him:

"Monsieur Auber, if you still refuse to be seated, you are going to force us all to remain standing."

"I beg of your Majesty," answered Auber, "that you do not force me to recall my age. When I am before you, madame, I feel that I am always twenty years old."

And Auber, eyes bright as always, remained resolutely on his feet.

Some time ago I found a letter I had written to Aurélien Scholl:

Maurice d'Hérisson, as valiant with the pen as with the sword, wants to make me out a gourmand of the siege, but he cannot.

He accuses Ricord, you and me of having consumed all the parrots in the zoo. We don't need that sort of thing in order to live up to all the misdeeds of man, but the truth is that we have been good friends to those who have gone hungry: we bought the parrots and parakeets only to offer them up at meals that were veritable military occasions, when we deluded the hunger of all of us by sheer force of spirit. Ask General Schmidt, or General Monselet, survivors of the famine, how many of us died like poor Théophile Gautier.

Your friend

Arsène Houssaye

Though my table was not exactly princely, some friends came every day to ask me for a leg of hare or a wing of parakeet.

Oh—how the potato had replaced the truffle! Coligny said to me one evening, "Give me two potatoes for my mother," as if he were saying, "Give me two pearls for my mistress."

I came across letters from Charles Monselet, Olivier Métra and Arnold Mortier, who invited themselves to dinner at my house in the same way as I used to invite them:

Monsieur Charles Monselet requests the honor of M. Arsène Houssaye's company at the house of the Historian of the Forty-First Chair, Avenue Friedland 49.

Toward the very end of the siege, Métra and Monselet once more want to eat a bite with me—a simple lunch that will have to serve as their dinner. I go out of my way so that they will not have a chance to complain.

The English butcher has been my chief resource since the beginning of the siege. The master of that house, who calls himself my friend, and who merits that title, suggests four parakeets, a filet of elephant and some donkey sausage. Total: sixty-six francs. A bagatelle! I search up and down the whole district. The pie makers still have some pies, but I don't fall for them, I am too much afraid to find rats in them. A cat is offered to me for eight francs; I decline. A hunter of the rooftops offers me three sparrows for six francs, and I take them at once. I still have some eggs and potatoes at home. My son, who came to see me from Champigny the day before, brought me some officer's bread—"for you alone," he told me. I'll give some to Métra and Monselet, but I'll ration them. Heaven be praised! A woman just passes by hiding a hen under her apron.

"How much is your hen?"

"I don't have any hen!"

"Don't talk nonsense"—and I take the hen by the neck.

"Be careful, sir, someone might see us."

"Twenty francs, all right?"

"Oh! La la—you are joking. No less than fifty."

On January 10, just another bagatelle. I give her fifty francs and carry off the hen, intending to offer up no more than half for one lunch. So I march, hen and sparrows in hand, back to the English butcher from whose shop everything is sent to my house.

There I preside over the preparations for the feast; fortunately I still have some containers of salted butter. I sacrifice four eggs and four potatoes. At eleven-thirty my guests arrive and I outline the menu. Métra promises to play two waltzes for dessert. Monselet will write three stanzas of poetry if he is satisfied. The table is set in the great gallery as for a major occasion.

"Why four settings?" asks Monselet apprehensively.

"At my house we always set an additional place for the unexpected."

"That's nice, but for today we shall announce that you are out."

Monselet has no sooner spoken than the doorbell can be heard throughout the house. He rushes immediately to the stairs to instruct a young ambulance driver to say that I am out.

But it is not a gentleman who has rung the bell but a lady. Monselet is somewhat shaken. Métra now dashes out to meet the visitor. Her first remark is completely appropriate: "Has lunch been served yet?"

All seems well, but a cloud passes my brow: I am thinking about the two officers of my own hospital; I decide that their portion of the lunch is to be sent out to them. Oh! How everything seemed to dissolve in hunger that day!

"If we were to give them just a little bit?" I say to Monselet.

"No," he replies, slapping his fist on the table, "they ought to be killed."

We did not go quite that far, but we promised ourselves to leave them the head and the legs of the chicken. O Mischance! The bell rings once more. This time it is Ricord. He does not ask for permission: he sees us at the table and shouts, "What luck!"

Monselet pales. But Ricord, who is a prince of a man, says gaily, after first threatening to eat everything, "You are lucky; I have just had lunch."

My two guests breathe more easily. I seem to remember that Sarah Bernhardt and Marie Colombier, good friends at that time, appeared at dessert time. Métra promised to dedicate a waltz to them entitled "The Angels of the Siege."

No one slept during the last night of the siege. In the morning neither the dawn nor the sun were visible. A glacial mist cast its veil over everything; it seemed as if heaven wept for our sorrows. At eight o'clock one could still see the student's lamp or the morning candle.

Charles Coligny and I had spent the night going through the papers, trying to look into the future—downcast, but still not able to believe that the last word had been spoken. I had written to my two sons, one in the army, the other ill in Biarritz. Three or four times during the night we had gone to talk to the soldiers of my little hospital. The last time silence and sleep had fallen on the whole place, even the orderlies.

The Duke of Almaviva, one of my friends during the siege, surprised me when I opened the door.

"So early?" I asked, taking his hand.

"Do you know," said the Duke, "if the Prussians will enter Paris through the Avenue de L'Impératrice or the Avenue de la Grande Armée?"

"They wouldn't dare," said Coligny.

"You'll see if they won't!"

A minute later we were near the Arc de Triomphe lost in a crowd of spectators, National Guardsmen, and some urchins who shouted, "Down with the Prussians."

A captain of infantry told the bystanders, especially the urchins, that they should have dignity even in defeat.

"We are defeated," he said, "but we are not disarmed. The Prussians will be here. Let us not look at them."

But no one heard the captain. The citizens of Paris were streaming in through the Avenue des Champs-Élysées, the Avenue Friedland, the Avenue Wagram.

Some additional friends came: Eugène Giraud, Dr. Contour, Maddrazo, Hector de Callias.

"What are we doing here?" I said. "Come to my house. The Prussians are too proud to want us to be present at their triumph."

But wave followed human wave. We were pressed against the chains and stone of the Arc de Triomphe. Suddenly, the sounds of German martial music punctuated with the hoofbeats of galloping horses. The Prussians! The Uhlans! The Bavarians! They were coming up the Avenues de L'Impératrice and de la Grande Armée. Alas—where was the Grande Armée? All of us seemed enveloped in a nightmare. Suddenly, though the enemy's regiments were still at a distance, some horsemen emerged right next to the Arc de Triomphe. It seemed as if they had risen from the ground. Horror of horrors! They swept up against the citizens who had crossed the chains of that monument built to commemorate the heroism of those who had fought the Germans not long ago. They drew their sabers and beat about them at random. That was their way of presenting themselves to that capital that had laid down its arms. They were soon followed by King William, proud to let the hooves of his horse resound on the victories of Napoleon. The military band was still playing its victorious music. I wished I could be a hundred feet under the earth, but I had to confront the spectacle—a forced confrontation because we could neither move forward nor backward. We looked at each other, pale, disconsolate, out of breath as if trying to take counsel. Suddenly— hurrahs, and more hurrahs: that was for the King. Then violent hissing could be heard from everywhere, which William did not want to tolerate: full of anger he spurred on his horse in our direction. We held our ground, confronting that man on horseback to whom his mathematical victories gave no right to pass through our triumphal arch. Yet for all that we were not reduced to dust.

After that surge of anger the king reined in his horse in order to ride solemnly under that triumphal arch where even Napoleon had not trod!

He was still greeted by hisses but he went on, followed at a distance by von Moltke, von Bismarck and others. My eyes had closed; I could not see clearly if they also strutted through the Arc; I think they did not dare. When the king had reached the other side and had seen Paris ruined by his bombs and by famine, he was satisfied with himself and retraced his steps. It had been agreed that he would not enter Paris itself but he had wanted to defy Paris under the Arc de Triomphe.

"Well," said one of us, "to Paris belongs all the glory for having been killed by famine in this cowardly way."

Glory—alas, there was no glory for conqueror or conquered.

The German occupation of Paris was a symbolic act rather than a military fact. Though Houssaye merges surrender and occupation into one in the Confessions, *the Prussians did not make their entry into Paris until March 1, a month after the surrender, and remained only for two days. They contributed greatly, however, to a further unanticipated trial for the city. The withdrawal of the French government and army to Versailles gave scope to the radical left, already apprehensive about the disbanding of the National Guard and the rightist, monarchist tone of the National Assembly. The Commune was proclaimed on March 18, civil war and a second siege of Paris ensued, and Houssaye, always as much a journalist as anything else, came from Versailles to witness the final, brutal suppression of the revolution. He was on the side of law and order, of course, far from the days in which he had lightheartedly followed the funeral cortège of General Lamarque.*

In spite of total defeat, a bloody civil war, and two periods of siege, Paris—at least the Paris of which Houssaye was a part—regained its social and cultural equilibrium with ease and rapidity. To Houssaye, however, it was not the same. He still attended the salon of the Princess Mathilde, the Emperor's cousin; he is unlikely to have mourned the disappearance of such imperial figures as Persigny or Rouher; he shared the hatred of his compatriots for l'Espagnole, the Empress whom they held responsible for the war. But he did not care for the leaders of the Third Republic: Gambetta, another foreigner; Thiers, resurrected from the July Mon-

archy; Jules Grévy, a clever manipulator. The social life had no focus with the disappearance of the Imperial Court and was toned down by the humiliation of defeat.

Houssaye continued to write, to entertain and to be entertained. In 1873, he renewed the prewar custom of giving an annual Venetian masked ball. It was the first great social occasion since the disasters of 1870–71, and tout-Paris thronged to it. He continued these fêtes for two more years, but his heart was evidently not in them any more. Much more important to him, he watched with pride the rising fame of his son Henry, by now a historian of considerable reputation. Approaching seventy in 1885, he began to collect his confessions, making them the point of withdrawal from the social life he had so relentlessly pursued for more than fifty years. Now his thoughts turned increasingly to death, and to recollections of his friends who preceded him.

·

The Last Words of Delacroix

·

At last a statue to Delacroix has been put up. It is as Auguste Vacquérie said: "Time makes an apotheosis of the injustices of one's contemporaries."

Eugène Delacroix recalled the great figures of the world of art until his final hour.

"Oh," he told me, the day before his death, "if I had time yet to paint 'The Ceiling of Apollo,' without drawing my inspiration too much from 'The School of Athens' or 'The Apotheosis of Homer,' or the great effects of Delaroche, I would paint an Olympus of all the gods and demigods of the nineteenth century, with David, Prud'hon, Gros, Géricault, Chateaubriand, Lamartine, Hugo, Musset: at the summit would be Napoleon, the great poet in action."

"Why not Delacroix?" I asked.

"No, Ingres takes precedence over him. I'd redress justice, I'd avenge all the great landscape painters of our time who are not members of the Academy: Decamps, Rousseau, Dupré, Millet, Diaz."

A spasm interrupted him.

"My dear Delacroix, I can clearly see not only how right you are, but how loyal."

"And you," he said to me, "you who have written the *History of the Forty-First Chair*, haven't you done that out of a sense of justice?"

Delacroix had been the witness for my second marriage. Now he talked about my wife.

"A woman, that's what I have always lacked," he said. "I have always had such a high ideal of womanhood that I would undoubtedly have lost it. And then, the sorrow if she had died before me! Now that I make the final reckoning, I think all has been well after having been sure that all had been ill."

Delacroix' maidservant, who was almost a sister to him, told me that after my visit he had fallen into an almost deathlike sleep. He woke up only one more time to suffer the breathless agonies of death. I have thus set down his final words with the true faith of friendship.

·

The Death of Balzac

·

I cannot think of any event more dramatic than the last hours of Balzac. He was hard at work on the *Tragédie bourgeoise*, a new cycle of works like the *Comédie humaine*. He could never have thought out a more desolate or terrifying final act than that of his own life.

He wanted to enjoy himself once more on his last voyage to Russia where he went to marry that lady of twenty-five whom he found more beautiful than the women of thirty he himself had created. Death was his companion on his honeymoon. Mme. Hanska was waiting for him, bedecked with vine leaves because the

time for orange blossoms was past. Alas! That searcher for the absolute arrived too late to gather the fruit.

> Done is the harvest,
> Put your baskets by!

When Balzac returned to Paris proud of his new bride he
imagined that he had gathered up a new spring garlanded with
roses. An illusion! Russia had cast its snow on both of them.

Two steps from his tomb Balzac still lived in his dreams. He
imagined himself to be rich and in love. He would overwhelm Paris
at last—as well as his old creditors. His lovely dream lasted no
longer than dreams usually do.

In the afternoon of August 20, 1850, when I was about to
ring the doorbell at Balzac's little house, I saw Eugène Giraud
descending its steps.

"Balzac?" he said. "I have just come from him. He is no more;
it is all over."

I felt myself growing pale. "Already?" I exclaimed.

Giraud opened his portfolio to show me a magnificent crayon
drawing in three colors: life in death. It was Balzac on his deathbed. Mme. de Balzac herself, as a close neighbor, had gone to ask
him to preserve that view for history.

I looked with emotion upon the picture of the great man in
death.

"I was well aware that he did not have much more time," I
said, "but I did not imagine that he was so close to death."

"Nor did he."

I asked Giraud to go upstairs once more, on the pretext of
touching up the picture, so that he would come with me. A nun
received us with that stately smile of resignation which speaks of
heaven and earth.

Death had cast the grandeur and dignity of eternal life on the
somewhat rabelaisian face of Balzac. I saluted the great novelist
with respect by touching his hand. The greatness and misfortune
of man! That forehead behind which a whole living world had been

created no longer radiated its thought. We passed through his study, where we found Mme. de Balzac who said to us, "Death undoes all, but it does not change the things in here. This table still reflects Balzac's genius; no one must touch it. Time will drain this inkwell, but I will not touch this pen."

On the table were many letters and cards; some yellowing galley proof, much corrected; several manuscript pages, fragments of a play whose title I did not see; and the last word of life and death: the doctor's prescription, dated the day before.

History is a statue of gold, copper and bronze, slowly built with the small change of one's contemporaries. Eugène Giraud was aware of many personal details and could give me much intimate information. His studio was next door to Balzac's house. When we had bid farewell to the desolate widow I went to his place with him.

"You don't know how Balzac died," he said. "Listen!"

And he described a scene to me that was more terrible than any the master had conceived in his novels.

The invalid, not very disquieted because he had the expert ministrations of Mme. de Balzac, nevertheless wanted to question his doctor.

"My dear doctor," he told him, "I am not a man like any other; I don't want death to take me unawares. I still have much to do to finish my work."

"Yes, you have built one of the great edifices of the nineteenth century."

"How many windows are still missing in that edifice! How many ornaments, how many statues!"

Balzac slapped his forehead. "The pediment is still here. People don't understand that: that light is the key to genius."

He became feverishly animated. "Doctor, I want the whole truth from you. You are a prince of science. Listen: I see that I am more ill than I thought. I feel that I am losing ground. No matter how I excite my hunger for life with my imagination, I see nothing but horror before me. How much time do you think I still have to live?"

The doctor did not answer.

"Look, doctor, do you take me for a child? I have already told you once before that I don't want to die like any ordinary man. A man like me owes the world a testament."

The word testament opened the doctor's mouth. If Balzac owed the world a testament, he perhaps owed one to his family and his wife as well:

"My dear sir, how much time do you need for what you want to do?"

"Six months," answered Balzac, like a man who had calculated carefully. And he looked fixedly at his physician.

"Six months! Six months," replied the doctor shaking his head.

"Ah," cried Balzac mournfully, "I can see that you won't give me six months . . . Do you give me six weeks, at least? . . . Six weeks with this fever, that's almost an eternity. Hours seem like days . . . And the nights need not be wasted."

The physician shook his head as before. Balzac raised himself, almost indignant. Did he really believe that the doctor could lengthen or shorten his existence at will, like another *Peau de chagrin?* *

The doctor had decided to take his patient's demand literally and to tell him the truth. Balzac in his anxiety heightened his own moral strength to be worthy of the truth: "Really, doctor, am I then a dead man? Thank God, I feel in me the strength to fight. But I also feel the courage to submit: I am ready for the sacrifice. If your conscience does not deceive you, then do not deceive me. What can I hope for? You will at least give me six days!"

The doctor could not speak any more; he turned away to hide his tears.

"Six days!" repeated Balzac. "Well then, I'll sketch out in rough form what remains to be accomplished; my friends will be

---

* Balzac's novel *La Peau de chagrin* is the story of a magic piece of leather that has the power to grant its owner's wishes.

able to dot the i's. I'll have time to cast a rapid glance at my fifty volumes. I'll tear out the poor pages, I'll strengthen the good ones. Human will power can achieve miracles. God created the world in six days: I can give eternal life to the world I created. I'll rest on the seventh."

Then, a mournful look and an even more mournful sigh. Since he had posed these terrible questions, Balzac had aged ten years. He no longer found his voice to ask the physician who in turn no longer found his voice to reply.

"My dear patient," the doctor said at last, trying to smile—a professional smile—"who can answer for one hour here on earth? He who seems well will die before you. But you have asked for the truth; you have spoken about a testament for your public—"

"Well?"

"Well—that testament you need to make today. Besides, you perhaps have to make another testament as well; you must not wait until tomorrow."

Balzac raised his head: "Then I don't have any more than six hours," he cried in terror. His head fell back on the pillow. The doctor's last word had been his death blow.

He who had been called Balzac entered his last agony. That forehead of genius took on its final pallor, the luminous spirit was fading into the shadows. He had asked for the truth, and the truth had killed him before his time.

It had been the error of that great physician—whose name I will not reveal—to unveil death which was already present when he could have masked it. We would not have had one page more, but Balzac might have lived a few days longer and would not have heard his death sentence. He would have left for the other world with the illusions of a man going to sleep who expects to awaken once more.

But such a spirit awakens always, no matter what the horrors of the night may be. The creator of the *Comédie humaine* has now been dead for more than a third of a century. His devotees—I should say his readers—are indignant that no monument has yet risen for him. No statue of him exists in a public place or at his grave; no bust in the Academy. But what good would a monument be other than his work! In this age of statue-mania marble is not pure enough nor bronze sufficiently lofty to represent a man of genius. Molière also does not have a statue.

·

Last Dinner with Victor Hugo

·

Victor Hugo had returned in triumph from exile after the fall of the Empire and resumed his role as the central literary figure of Paris. Houssaye dates this dinner April 1885.

Victor Hugo refused all invitations; he wanted only to dine at home.

"I much prefer," he told me, "to drink from the beautiful Bohemian glass you gave me, which recalls my days in the Place Royale, than from the most fashionable crystal."

Nevertheless he promised once to come to dine at my house with two of his fervent admirers, the Spanish ambassador and the former Italian ambassador. A few days earlier he had come to the Lion d'Or to celebrate with the Committee of the Literary Society my election as its president. As he was silent, sitting opposite me, people thought that he was dozing; they were quite wrong. He was meditating eloquently in silence. He had not known that I was going to give a toast to him, but he collected himself to give one to me. I was the first to speak and I attempted to talk about him in his own style. I heard some of those around me say, "Hugo doesn't understand a word Houssaye is saying," but no sooner had I finished than Victor Hugo rose, radiantly inspired; it was truly a god who spoke. He had understood me so well that he responded to each stanza of my Hugo-esque prose.

We embraced. I had spoken a sonnet to his glory and was astounded by his prodigious memory when he repeated the last six lines of that poem. Until his last hour Hugo remained the valiant Hugo.

At that banquet Hugo was enchanted to hear the Spanish ambassador, who spoke a more exquisite French than most of the French men of letters who were present. He invited him to dinner for the next day, and for the rest of the week, except Wednesday when Silvela was to dine with him at my house. In order to remind him of my own invitation I sent to his house that day a young lady of my acquaintance who did not let herself be asked twice, so great was her desire to see Victor Hugo in his own home. That turned out not to be that simple, because Victor Hugo was more or less held captive on the second floor of his house, so afraid was his household that he might lose one of his precious final hours of life. But the lady was one of those who simply don't recognize closed doors. She spoke in a loud voice, taking care to mention the ambassador's name as well as mine. Hugo heard her even though he was quite at the other end of the staircase. He came down a few steps to take a look at the messenger. She ran up. When they met on the landing, Hugo—seeing that the lady was pretty—did not confine himself to kissing her hand. He put his arm around her and carried her off to his room. There were few chairs in his room. Nimbly the master seated the ambassadress on his couch, telling her, "You'll be more comfortable there." It turned out that he was going to be more comfortable there himself because he seated himself by her side, holding her energetically in her place. I would not say that they went very far, but the conversation was lively. In that way Hugo left the lady with an unforgettable memory.

A few days later another lady came to see me bathed in tears, her beauty faded but touching in its sadness. She told me that Victor Hugo was dying.

"Alas," she said, "all my dreams die with him."

I knew that the lady felt a friendship for Victor Hugo which bordered on love. To her he seemed beautiful in spite of his white hairs; he obliterated all her other admirers.

I was curious to know if she had crossed the Rubicon with the poet.

When a woman is in tears, she tells the truth: "What do I know," she replied. "For me, if not for him, this was a sacred love. I always hoped to have children. God denied them to me. But I wanted to force God, in the intoxication of my idolatry, to give me a son by Victor Hugo."

.

The Twentieth Century

.

The Third Republic had little meaning for Houssaye. The world he loved came to an end at Sedan and he was too old for la belle époque *when it eventually followed after the dislocations and frustrations caused by the war. He had his doubts about the idea of progress and saw no point in the spreading colonial adventures. "What good is the steamship if it is only to travel to Viet-Nam? Why have the Eiffel Tower, if it is only to show us man getting smaller and heaven farther away?"*

These are sentences from a section called "The Twentieth Century" with which he concludes the sixth and final volume of the Confessions. *It is an affirmation of his belief in man and God, but most clearly it emerges as an affirmation of his belief in Paris. Apart from his little daughter Edmée, perhaps, Paris was his great love, if one can compare the two. To Paris he remained devoted as to no other woman in his life, even though he had too cool an intelligence not to mock his own devotion.*

At a dinner of the Spartan Society one day, when we were talking about the future, Théophile Gautier denied the idea of progress because the Egypt of the Pharaohs was his real native land. Between two glasses of champagne I threw out this prophecy: "We are in the year 2000. Because of the fantastic rapidity of our move into the age of electricity, the twentieth century has been a period of unexcelled progress. The test of strength which the inhabitants of the planet looked for has been passed victoriously. Paris was yesterday and will be for another thousand years the host of all that lives, the central home of all the arts. On this seventh day of our genesis, we have the right to stop face to face with the creation of those six days and to judge if it be good. The hosts coming to us from Saturn and Mars forget, when they debark here, the horizons of their paternal planet. Paris remains the center of creation . . . And now, as the heavens bathe with their eternal rays the city where the great work lies accomplished; now that man, reconciled to God through his infinite effort, may seek repose by his fertile fields and ever raise his voice in happy song; now that within these walls of marble and gold all the scourges of man—illness, misery, death even—are conquered by science; now that one hardly recalls the era shrouded in the distant past when man lived by hate; now that discord among men is tamed like the waves of the ocean; now that woman, mistress of her own destiny, has forgotten the lie that she was fit only for slavery; now that for Paris, capital of the universe, all is serene, luminous, joyful—who would now dare to deny God? Who would not pity our ancestors in the nineteenth century who were so devoid of sense, so far removed from the wealth which we enjoy by right of conquest, we, the Parisians of the year 2000?"

I had concluded. Around the table everyone was scoffing and laughing.

Théophile Gautier exclaimed, "Gentlemen, what remains of Golconda, of Babylon, of Athens, of Carthage, of Thebes with its hundred gates, of Rome with its hundred ruins? Six grains of dust. Paris will be the seventh."

List of Original Passages

•

The original passages are listed by volumes and page numbers and refer to the second edition (July, 1885) of the first four volumes. Their content is identical with the first edition, but the pagination differs at times. Volumes V and VI had only one edition.

Glossary

•

The brief sketches of persons, palaces and places of entertainment below do not include every name and place mentioned in *Man About Paris*, only those that occur with some frequency, or are given some prominence, or need an explanation beyond the one given by Houssaye.

ALTON-SHEE, EDMOND, COMTE D' (1810–1875), began his political career as a conservative but moved gradually to the left. He fought for the Republic on the barricades in 1848.

ANAÏS, MLLE. (Anaïs Pauline Albert, 1802–1871), made her debut at the Comédie Française at the age of fourteen. In the 1840's Anaïs competed with Rachel—for a man, not a role—and lost, but she was still sufficiently charming in 1849 to obtain from Musset the title role in *Louison*.

AUBER, DANIEL FRANÇOIS (1782–1871), composer of ballets and operas, served as director of the Conservatoire. His opera *La Muette de Portici* was an enormous success in 1828 and sparked the revolution that separated Belgium from the Netherlands in 1830.

AUBRYET, XAVIER (1827–1880), playwright and essayist, whom Houssaye began to publish in *L'Artiste* in 1849. Like Houssaye, he modified the spelling of his name to make it more aristocratic.

AUGIER, ÉMILE (1820–1889), dramatist who wrote plays which seemed very realistic to his time. Several were in the repertoire of the Comédie, and Houssaye clearly approved of them.

BACIOCCHI, FÉLIX MARNÈS, COMTE DE (1803–1866), whose father married Napoleon's sister Elisa Bonaparte and became a count, was himself born in Ajaccio, the Bonaparte home town. Napoleon III made him Superintendent of Court Entertainment and later General Superintendent of Theaters. He was often accused of pandering for his master, but according to Houssaye the Emperor had little need of such services.

BALLANCHE, PIERRE SIMON (1776–1847), a Christian antirationalist philosopher whose work has considerable affinities to that of Chateaubriand.

BALZAC, HONORÉ DE (1799–1850), came from Tours to Paris to study law, but like so many of his contemporaries turned to writing. He had a number of very unrealistic ambitions—he wanted to be a businessman, a politician, an elegant man about town—but these did not interfere with his writing. Apart from his novels, from which his lasting fame derives, he wrote for journals and tried his hand, mostly unsuccessfully, at playwriting. His writing plans, like his other plans, always exceeded the realm of possibility. In 1832 he began to correspond with Mme. de Hanska in the Ukraine whom he finally married in 1850, only five months before his death.

BAROCHE, PIERRE-JULES (1802–1870), politician, served in the Chamber of Deputies in 1847 and participated in the antigovernment banquets of that year. After the election of Prince Louis Napoleon he joined his side. In 1850 he replaced Ferdinand Barrot as Minister of the Interior and served in several imperial governments.

BARRÈRE, BERTRAND (1755–1851), politician and powerful orator, served in the National Assembly from 1789 on, turned more and more radical and became a ferocious advocate of the Terror. A timeserver, he deserted Robespierre just in time to save his own neck. He also served Napoleon and even managed to avoid the wrath of the restored Bourbons.

BARROT, FERDINAND (1806–1883), lawyer and politician, served Louis Philippe and the Second Republic where he was a conservative member of the Chamber, and was Minister of the Interior in 1849.

BEAUVALLET, LÉON (1828–1874), acted at the Odéon and later the Comédie Française. In 1855 he was Rachel's leading man on her American tour, and wrote a book about it, translated as *Rachel and the New World* (1856).

BEAUVOIR, ROGER DE (Auguste Roger de Bully, 1806–1866), wrote romantic novels like *L'Écolier de Cluny*. In 1847 he married Eléonore Doze but obtained a separation from her soon after, with a public trial that scandalized Paris. He was briefly imprisoned and fined for a satirical poem called "Mon Procès" ("My Trial").

BELGIOJOSO. Princess Cristina Trivulcia Belgiojoso and her husband now figure only in memoirs and the biographies of Alfred de Musset. They were Italians, exiles from Austrian-ruled Milan, and had parted company in Paris to lead separate, gay existences. He was a typical rake and she, a very beautiful woman, was for a time Musset's mistress.

BÉRANGER, PIERRE JEAN DE (1780–1857), a writer of songs and poems whose romantic and liberal sentiments endeared him to Houssaye's generation. In his old age he was Houssaye's neighbor at Beaujon.

BLANC, CHARLES (1813–1882), art critic and artist, became Director of Fine Arts after the Revolution in 1848. After the Coup d'État of 1851 he withdrew from public life. He was the younger brother of Louis Blanc, who played a prominent role in the February Revolution as a labor leader and was exiled in May, 1848.

BOCAGE, PIERRE FRANÇOIS (1799–1862), a great romantic star in the 1830's and 1840's, became director of the Odéon in 1849, a position in which he was a signal failure at the time when Houssaye was just beginning his rule at the Comédie Française.

BOIGNE, LOUISE ELÉONORE, COMTESSE DE (1781–1866), born in Versailles of noble parents, had her own salon in Paris after 1809 and was part of the cultural establishment of the July Monarchy.

BONAPARTE, MATHILDE PRINCESS (1820–1904), a daughter of King Jerome of Westphalia, Napoleon's youngest brother; a major social figure in the Second Empire and the Third Republic.

BOREL, PÉTRUS (1809–1859), one of the more extravagantly melodramatic writers in the Romantic circle, befriended by Gautier and Mme. de Girardin.

BRESSANT, JEAN BAPTISTE (1815–1886), a great popular favorite, was at the Théâtre du Gymnase in the late 1840's and early 1850's, acting Des Grieux in *Manon Lescaut* and Faust in *Faust et Marguérite*. Earlier he had spent six years in St. Petersburg, where he broke many hearts and acted in one hundred and forty-two roles.

BRINDEAU, LOUIS PAUL (1814–1882), made his debut at the Comédie Française in 1842 after acting on the Boulevards. On February 27, 1848, when the Comédie reopened after the Revolution, he was the first to declaim the *Marseillaise* from the stage—text in hand, because he, like everyone else at the theater, did not know the words of the song.

BROHAN, JOSEPHINE AUGUSTINE (1824–1893) and ÉMILIE MADELEINE (1833–1900), were, like their mother Suzanne, graduates of the Conservatoire and *sociétaires* of the Comédie Française. Augustine made her debut in 1841, Madeleine in 1850; both became members of the company before the age of twenty.

CARMAGNOLE, a song of the French Revolution, like the *Marseillaise* brought from the south of France; unlike it, not a marching song but a dance.

CASSAGNAC, BERNARD DE (1806–1880), a journalist who wrote for some of the same publications as Houssaye, like the *Revue de Paris*, the *Journal des Débats*, and the *Constitutionnel*. He opposed liberalism and democracy during the Second Empire.

CAVAIGNAC, GODEFROY (1801–1845), son of a republican general and an ardent republican himself, but a gentle and generous man. He was acquitted after the revolution of 1832, where he met Houssaye, and remained active in opposition to Louis Philippe. He served as president of the Society for the Rights of Man. His funeral in 1845 resembled that of General Lamarque and almost precipitated a revolution.

CHATEAUBRIAND, FRANÇOIS RENÉ, VICOMTE DE (1768–1848), a brilliant exponent of the intellectual reaction to the French Revolution, spent some years in exile. He fell out with Napoleon, who vetoed Chateaubriand's speech upon his election to the French Academy in 1811. After the Restoration he served Louis XVIII with distinction, but would not be reconciled to King Louis Philippe. His most ambitious work was *Génie du Christianisme* (1800). By the time Houssaye knew him he was a discouraged man writing his memoirs.

CHAUMIÈRE. The *Bal de la Chaumière* was a dance establishment for students and young bachelors on the Boulevard Montparnasse. It had a large garden with trees, bushes, secluded walks and grottoes.

CLÉMENT DE RIS, COMTE DE, the scion of a prominent noble family, moved on the fringes of Bohemian life and does not seem to have had any other accomplishment in his record.

CLÉSINGER, STELLO (1814–1883), a sculptor who studied in Italy and became fashionable after 1847. He married George Sand's daughter Solange in 1847.

COMÉDIE FRANÇAISE, the first state theater of France, had its origin in the company of actors which Molière established in 1658. Its occupancy of the theater in the Rue Richelieu dates from 1799.

COURTILLE. The Jardin de la Courtille in the Faubourg du Temple was fashionable toward the middle of the nineteenth century as a place to go late at night to drink and dance as a conclusion to an evening on the town. On the eve of Ash-Wednesday, the last day of the Carnival, the festivities reached a riotous climax.

DECAMPS, ALEXANDRE (1803–1860), a painter who traveled in the East and painted pictures of Oriental life, realistic in the eyes of his time, over-dramatic and romantic for twentieth-century taste.

DELACROIX, EUGÈNE (1798–1863), a painter of large-scale historical subjects and leader of the Romantic movement, an enduring friend of Houssaye's in spite of their difference in age.

DÉSAUGIERS, MARC ANTOINE (1772–1827), a popular writer of operettas, satirical and romantic songs.

DIAZ, NARCISSE (1808–1876), a member of the Barbizon school of painting, friend of Théodore Rousseau, who taught him to paint forest scenes.

DORVAL, MARIE (1798–1855), was the greatest star of the Boulevard theaters in the 1840's and 1850's. She acted the major romantic roles with tremendous power and reflected them in her romantic, tempestuous and unhappy life. Her relations to the Comédie Française were unhappy, too. She became a *pensionnaire* in 1834, left soon after, returned at the request of George Sand in 1840, left again after failing in Sand's play *Cosima*. She was never happy with her repertoire and tried, unsuccessfully, to become a classical actress like Rachel. In May, 1848, she wanted to return once more to the Théâtre Français, as a simple pensionnaire and—crowning humiliation—was refused.

DOZE, ELÉONORE (1823–1859), actress, was a great success at sixteen, much praised by Gautier. She married Houssaye's friend Roger de Beauvoir.

DUMAS, ALEXANDRE (*père*) (Alexandre Marquis Davy de la Pailleterie, 1802–1870), was born in Houssaye's home Department, the Aisne, the son of a French revolutionary general and grandson of a black woman. His father adopted her name—Dumas—in place of his own father's title of nobility.

Alexandre grew up poor, as General Dumas had fallen out with Napoleon. Like many ambitious young men he made his way to Paris, where he spent most of his life, except for extensive travels. A writer of stupendous industry and facility, he is mainly remembered for his historical novels (*The Three Musketeers*, *The Count of Monte Cristo*), but in his own day he was as well known for his romantic plays.

DUMAS, ALEXANDRE (*fils*) (1825–1895), was the illegitimate son of Dumas *père*, who did not exactly look after him in the best manner. The son became a brilliant writer in his own right eventually, the most highly regarded French dramatist of his age. His most famous novel and play, *La Dame aux Camélias*, is based on his own affair with the courtesan Marie Duplessis. He and many of his contemporaries thought that his plays were realistic treatments of subjects of great moral significance, but later generations have not seen his work in that light.

DUPLESSIS, MARIE (ALPHONSINE PLESSIS, 1824–1847), daughter of an alcoholic and a prostitute, abandoned by her mother at the age of eight, sold to a septuagenarian at fourteen by her father, became one of the great courtesans of Paris in the early 1840's. Alexandre Dumas *fils* loved her (see above). Marie Duplessis died of tuberculosis at the age of twenty-three.

ELYSÉE PALACE. Built in 1728 and owned later by the Marquise de Pompadour, it is the traditional residence of French presidents to this day.

EMPIS, ADOLPHE DOMINIQUE FLORENT (1795–1868), playwright, was elected to the French Academy in 1847, and headed the Comédie Française from 1856–1859. Many of his plays were written in collaboration with Mazères, another enemy of Houssaye.

ESQUIROS, ALPHONSE (1812–1876), wrote *L'Évangile du peuple* (1840) which was considered offensive to religion and decency and led to his imprisonment. He served in the Legislative Assembly after the 1848 Revolution and was exiled by Prince Louis Napoleon in 1851. From then until his return to France in 1869 he lived in England.

EUGÉNIE, EMPRESS OF THE FRENCH (Marie Eugénie de Montijo, 1826–1920), the daughter of a Spanish nobleman, lived in Paris with her mother after 1834, where she was educated at the Convent of Sacré Coeur. The Prince-President Louis Napoleon met her at balls at the Elysée Palace and invited her to Fontainebleau and other residences for house parties. Very clearly he did not obtain what he wanted, and so proposed to her a few weeks after becoming Emperor. They were married at Notre Dame Cathedral on January 30, 1853. The Empress gave birth to a son in 1856. During the Emperor's absences in war she acted as regent, the last time in August-September of 1870. She was brave but very conservative and may to some extent have had the kind of baleful influence on French politics which Houssaye and his contemporaries attributed to her.

FAUBOURG SAINT-GERMAIN. A fashionable district in Paris inhabited by many members of the aristocracy.

FAUCHER, LÉON (1803–1854), a journalist who became a politician particularly conversant with economic matters. He was anti-republican and served

Louis Napoleon as Minister of the Interior in 1849 and 1851, but broke with him over the Coup d'État in 1851.

FECHTER, CHARLES ALBERT (1823–1879), son of a German father and English mother, acted at the Comédie Française in 1845 and had an extensive career that took him to many countries. He was the original Armand Duval in *La Dame aux Carmélias* by Dumas in 1852.

FIORENTINO, PIER ANGELO (1806–1864), a Neapolitan who made Paris his home and wrote dramatic criticism for Girardin's *La Presse* and later Véron's *Constitutionnel*.

FIX, DELPHINE ELÉONORE (1831–1864), a pupil of Provost, made her debut at the Comédie in 1849.

FLEURY, ÉMILE FÉLIX, COMTE DE (1815–1884), a dashing general of cavalry who served Napoleon III at court and in the field.

FOULD, ACHILLE (1800–1867), a French financier and politician, son of a Jewish banker. A strong conservative, he was Napoleon III's Minister of Finance and Interior.

FRÈRES PROVENÇAUX, a fashionable restaurant in the Palais Royal.

GAUTIER, THÉOPHILE (1811–1872), poet, novelist, painter and dramatic critic, was one of Houssaye's best friends. A Romantic of the circle of Victor Hugo, he dressed and behaved flamboyantly—red vest, long flowing· hair— and wrote a charming account of his friends. *Mademoiselle de Maupin*, his first important novel and one of his best, appeared in 1835.

GAVARNI (Sulpice Guillaume Chevalier, 1801–1866), caricaturist and illustrator, worked, like Daumier, for *Charivari*. In later years he turned his satire on social abuses and, still later, became interested in science, especially aerial flight.

GAY, SOPHIE (1776–1852), author and hostess of a famous salon. Her major work, as Houssaye put it, was her daughter Delphine, who became Mme. de Girardin.

GEORGE, MLLE. (Marguerite Josephine Weimer, 1787–1867), made her debut at the Comédie in 1803 and shortly after became the mistress of Napoleon. In her early years she was the chief rival of the great actress Mlle. Duchesnois, who was supported, not unnaturally, by the Empress Josephine. Mlle. George was a trial to the Comédie, taking many unauthorized leaves of absence, including one for a tour of Russia. After 1815, with Napoleon gone, the Comédie was able to avenge itself, but her beauty served to protect her almost as well. In 1849 she began to give farewell performances and continued this practice for ten years.

GÉRARD, FRANÇOIS BARON (1770–1837), painter, a pupil of David, whose portrait of Mme. Recamier vividly records the beauty and elegance of her youth.

GILBERT DE VOISINS, COMTE DE, was a member of a distinguished and wealthy noble family, the son of a high judiciary official of the First Empire. His own prominence was merely social; he was married to the dancer Marie Taglioni.

GIRARDIN, DELPHINE DE (1804–1855), daughter of the novelist Sophie Gay, had a fashionable salon and wrote essays, stories and plays. Her social influence was greater than her talent, and though Rachel acted in several of her plays, they were not too well received.

GIRARDIN, ÉMILE DE (1802–1881), Delphine's husband (in name only, as Houssaye and others aver), an extremely successful publisher from the 1830's on (*La Presse*). He killed a fellow publisher, Armand Carrel, in a duel. He was politically influential under the Orléans Monarchy and the Republic, but opposed the Empire.

GIRAUD, EUGÈNE (1806–1881), a painter and engraver, a friend of Balzac and Alexandre Dumas père.

GLEYRE, MARC CHARLES GABRIEL (1806–1874), a painter of romantic inclinations who traveled extensively in the Near East and painted eastern, classical and religious subjects.

GOT, EDMOND FRANÇOIS (1822–1901), a great actor of comic roles, especially Molière, at the Comédie, which he joined as a *pensionnaire* in 1845. He became a *sociétaire* in 1850 and remained active until 1895.

GRISI, CARLOTTA (1821–1899), a dancer who performed with immense success all over Europe. She was an admirable Giselle at the Paris Opéra.

GRISI, JULIA (1811–1869), an Italian opera star, cousin of Carlotta, who appeared in Paris in 1832 in operas by Rossini and Bellini.

GUIMOND, ESTHER (died 1879), came of obscure origin and probably started as a *grisette*. Guizot, Louis Philippe's Prime Minister, was her first important lover, followed by Émile de Girardin among many others.

GUIZOT, FRANÇOIS PIERRE (1787–1874), of Protestant origin, came to Paris from Nimes and served in the governments of the Bourbon Restoration. He headed or controlled several governments under the July Monarchy and was Prime Minister at the outbreak of the Revolution in February, 1848.

HÉDOUIN, EDMOND (1819–1889), a painter mainly distinguished for freshness of tone and simplicity. He mostly painted rustic scenes and Paris street scenes, but also did some pictures for the main lobby of the Théâtre Français.

HUGO, VICTOR MARIE (1802–1885), the greatest literary figure of nineteenth-century France, was, like Dumas, a general's son. His play *Hernani* was the signal in 1830 for the overthrow of the old classical tradition at the Comédie Française, a tradition brilliantly revived by Rachel after 1838: one reason why Rachel and Hugo were not on very friendly terms. Houssaye attempted to reconcile them in 1849 because the Prince-President Napoleon wanted Hugo to be one of the cultural adornments of his impending Empire. Rachel acted in *Angelo* but Hugo refused to be an adornment. He broke with Napoleon after the Coup d'État of 1851 and spent the years of the Second Empire looking at its distant shore from the island of Jersey. Though Houssaye supported the Empire, he and Hugo remained on friendly terms.

INGRES, JEAN AUGUSTE DOMINIQUE (1780–1867), received less recognition than several of his fellow painters of romantic–classical subjects in the First

Empire. He was not sufficiently classical for the classicists and he himself abhorred the romantic school. Recognition came late and remained more official than popular for a long time.

JANIN, JULES (1804–1874), a French critic (*Journal des Débats*) whose influence was greatest under the July Monarchy; the earliest advocate of Rachel, for whose career he was partly responsible.

JOINVILLE, FRANÇOIS FERDINAND, PRINCE DE (1818–1900), was the third son of King Louis Philippe, and is remembered for his response to Rachel's offer to go to bed with him: *"Où? Quand? Combien?"* An unlikely story.

JUDITH, MLLE. (Julie Bernat, 1827–1907), a beautiful woman rather than great actress, played dramatic roles at the Comédie from 1846 on, and had a son by Prince Napoleon in 1853.

JULLIEN DE PARIS, MARC ANTOINE (1775–1848), may have seemed ancient to Houssaye in 1832, not because he was so old, but because his prominence in public life dated back forty years. Jullien de Paris had an amazing career in military administration during the early years of the French Revolution, which carried him to positions of considerable power before he was nineteen years old. He was accused—falsely, it seems—of complicity in the Terror under Robespierre.

KARR, ALPHONSE (1808–1890), critic, novelist, and above all journalist, editor of *Le Figaro* and later *Le Journal*.

LAMARQUE, JEAN MAXIMIN DE (1770–1832), one of many of Napoleon's able generals, opposed the Bourbon Restoration, joined the liberal side and supported the Revolution of July 1830. Mainly remembered for his funeral.

LAMARTINE, ALPHONSE DE (1790–1869), second only to Hugo as chief poet of the Romantic movement, drifted more and more into politics under the July Monarchy. From 1833 he served as Deputy in the National Assembly. His *Histoire des Girondins* was published in 1847 and had great influence on the rising revolutionary spirit. In February 1848 his voice was decisive in establishing the Second Republic rather than continuing the monarchy. However, he lost control of the situation and was no longer a force when Louis Napoleon became President a few months later.

LECOMTE. JULES (1814–1864), a prolific author, critic and popular historian. He spent some time in Parma, at the court of the former Empress Marie Louise, and is reputed to have been one of her lovers.

LE HON, LOUIS XAVIER LEOPOLD, COMTE (1822–1897), served the Emperor Napoleon III in politics. His wife was one of the Duc de Morny's mistresses, and the small château of Napoleon's half-brother adjoined the large Le Hon mansion on the Rond Point des Champs Élysées.

LEMAÎTRE, FRÉDÉRICK (1800–1876), the greatest of the French actors in the Romantic tradition, never entered the Comédie Française but spent his long career in the Boulevard theaters.

LESLIE, CHARLES ROBERT (1794–1859), an English painter of American origin who mainly produced imaginative impressions of scenes from great novels and plays.

LISZT, FRANZ (1811–1886), the Hungarian composer, was the most famous concert pianist of his time. He belonged to George Sand's circle in the 1830's and 40's.

LUTHER, AMÉDINE (1834–1861), an ingenue at the Théâtre Français in Houssaye's day.

MALITOURNE, ARMAND (1797–1866), journalist and author. He is supposed to have ghost-written a major portion of Dr. Véron's *Mémoires d'un bourgeois de Paris*.

MARILHAT, PROSPER (1814–1847), with Decamps the originator of the vogue for oriental subjects in art. He went mad in 1846.

MARS, MLLE. (Anne Françoise Hippolyte Boutet, 1779–1847), was the great star of comedy at the Théâtre Français from the 1790's until 1841.

MAZÈRES, ÉDOUARD (1796–1866), a dramatist who often collaborated with Scribe and had several plays performed at the Comédie Française before Houssaye's arrival. He had a considerable reputation as a writer of comedies.

MEISSONIER, JEAN LOUIS ERNEST (1815–1891), a painter of somewhat romanticized scenes from life, particularly of battles and other military events.

MÉLINGUE, ÉTIENNE MARIN (1807–1875), a great interpreter of Alexandre Dumas on the stage, was at the height of his career in the late 1840's in the Boulevard theaters.

MÉRIMÉE, PROSPER (1803–1870), novelist (*Colomba, Carmen*), civil servant (including Inspector General of Historical Monuments); generally, though perhaps wrongly, considered a cold cynic by his contemporaries. He had a very brief affair with George Sand.

MÉTRA, OLIVIER (1830–1900), popular composer, especially of waltzes. He was conductor at the Folies Bergères after 1872, and composed many divertissements for that theater.

MICHELET, JULES (1798–1874), historian and Professor at the Collège de France, an ardent democrat who lost his position when he refused to swear allegiance to the Empire.

MONSELET, CHARLES (1825–1888), drama critic of *Le Figaro*, wrote witty, interesting accounts of his contemporaries.

MONTEZ, LOLA (DOLORES ELIZA ROSANNA GILBERT, 1818–1861), daughter of a British officer in Ireland; she grew up in India, eloped into a bad marriage in 1837 and became a dancer. As a stage artist she failed spectacularly in London and Paris, but that hardly mattered. Liszt left the Comtesse d'Argoult for Lola, and King Louis of Bavaria became so infatuated with her that he made her a countess and let her influence his reign in the best eighteenth-century manner. However, the time was the mid-nineteenth century and Lola eventually had to flee his kingdom. She traveled to America and performed in California and the gold-mining towns of Nevada. She died in New York—deeply religious and in reasonably good circumstances, not in the manner Houssaye describes.

M*

MONTIGNY, AUGUSTE (Auguste Lemoine, 1807–1880), for twenty years Director of the Théâtre du Gymnase.

MORNY, CHARLES AUGUSTE, COMTE, later DUC, DE (1811–1865), was the illegitimate son of Hortense Beauharnais (wife of Louis Bonaparte) and the Comte de Flahaut, and therefore a half-brother of Napoleon III. He was a brilliant man who distinguished himself as a statesman and financial speculator. He was one of the chief planners of the Coup d'État of December 2, 1851, and became Minister of the Interior that day. He was made a duke in 1862. Like Houssaye he was a great womanizer and art collector.

MURAT, NAPOLEON LUCIEN, PRINCE (1803–1878), was the second son of Joachim Murat, whom Napoleon I made King of Naples. He followed his older brother to America but returned to France in 1848 and became a courtier of Napoleon III.

MUSSET, ALFRED DE (1810–1857), a native Parisian, was one of the most talented writers of the generation of Hugo and Gautier. A poet and delightful storyteller, he must have been a delightful man to know as well when he was in a good mood. Very much affected by the success and failure of his work, he could, when moved, produce a little masterpiece like the play *Les Caprices de Marianne* in six weeks. But after 1845 he wrote virtually nothing and devoted himself to chess and absinthe.

NAPOLEON III (Charles Louis Napoleon Bonaparte, 1808–1873) was the son of Hortense Beauharnais (the daughter of the Empress Josephine by her first marriage) and of Louis Bonaparte, who briefly served his brother Napoleon as King of Holland. He was Hortense's third son—the others died young—and spent a wandering childhood in exile with her. He made two unsuccessful coups to gain control of France before being elected President of the Second Republic. As Emperor he fought four major wars, including one in Mexico, and yet seems to have been inclined to peaceful solutions and the avoidance of bloodshed. The influence exerted by his advisers, and of course his name, were against him. He wanted a brilliant rather than glorious reign and achieved neither, except at moments. In 1870, at Sedan, he surrendered to the Prussians to avoid a suicidal battle.

NERVAL, GÉRARD DE (Gérard Labrunie, 1808–1855), learned at an early age some Arabic and Persian, in addition to Greek, Latin and several modern languages, and read extensively; old books on mysticism and the occult seem to have been his favorites. He traveled with Alexandre Dumas *père* and once nearly married a sheik's daughter in Syria. He wrote some plays and novels, and books and articles about his travels.

OFFENBACH, JACQUES (1818–1880), the great operetta composer of his day in France, had his first successes while serving at Houssaye's behest as conductor of the diminutive orchestra of the Théâtre Français, where he composed incidental music for Musset's play *Le Chandelier*.

ORSAY, ALFRED GUILLAUME, COMTE D' (1801–1852), a famous dandy and witty man who made friends with Byron in Genoa in 1823 and spent much of his time in England. In 1839 he returned to France and, in financial straits, painted portraits to support himself. He was appointed Director of Fine Arts by Napoleon III shortly before his death.

OURLIAC, ÉDOUARD (1813–1848), a prolific writer, came to Paris from Carcassonne shortly before Houssaye. He belonged to the same bohemian circle and was a wit and spirited amateur actor. A bad marriage made him lose his humor. He died of tuberculosis.

PAÏVA, MARQUISE DE (THÉRÈSE LACHMANN, 1819–1888), was born in the Jewish ghetto in Moscow. She was without doubt the most successful courtesan in the Empire. She obtained the Portuguese Marquis de Païva in marriage in 1851 and maintained a great house in which she collected not only the elegant but the intellectual elite of Paris. In the 1860's she built the most luxurious private mansion in Paris for herself, next to the mansions of the Duc de Morny and the Comte Le Hon on the Champs Élysées. She had a country château at Pontchartrain.

PALAIS-ROYAL, the Paris residence of the Dukes of Orléans. Louis Philippe lived there until he became king. The Palais Royal had an arcade of elegant shops which paid rent to the Duke, and which included the restaurant of the Frères Provençaux.

PATTI, ADELINA (1843–1919), the great soprano, was born in Madrid; her singing career began at the age of seven. She married Henri Marquis de Caux in 1868. After her divorce from the Marquis in 1885 she married the tenor Nicolini, and eventually became the Baroness Cederstrom.

PEARL, CORA (Eliza Emma Crouch, c. 1835–1886), born in Plymouth and convent-educated, turned to high-level prostitution in London and later in Paris. The Duc de Morny and Prince Napoleon were among her lovers. In her heyday in the 1860's she had a town mansion, a country château, liveried grooms and a great stable of horses. The end of the Empire and a particularly unsavory affair made an end of her glory.

PERRIN, ÉMILE (1814–1885), began his career as a painter with historical leanings, a student of Gros. In 1848, after the Revolution, he was appointed director of the Opéra Comique which he managed so well that the Théâtre Lyrique was also entrusted to him. Roqueplan was his successor at the Opéra Comique in 1857.

PERSIGNY, JEAN GILBERT VICTOR, DUC DE (1808–1872), whose real name was, more prosaically, Fialin, became a devotee of Prince Louis Napoleon when he was still in his twenties. He did the groundwork for both Napoleonic coups d'état (1836 and 1840), and unkind souls attribute their ineffectiveness to his planning. Much more imperial than the future Emperor, Persigny urged him on toward autocratic rule and staged, as Minister of the Interior in 1852, the devotions of loyalty and enthusiasm that Napoleon needed to be able to assume the imperial title. Persigny, being neither very tactful nor very bright, failed spectacularly as ambassador to London and in several other roles that the loyal Emperor provided for him.

PLESSY, MME. (Jeanne Sylvanie Sophie Arnould-Plessis, 1819–1897), started her stage career as a child, made her debut at the Comédie in 1834, and became sociétaire two years later. She broke with the Comédie in 1845 in order to accept a fabulous long-term engagement in St. Petersburg.

PIOT, EUGÈNE (1812–1890), participated in the Romantic Movement with Hugo and Gautier in the 1830's but turned to the collection of ancient artefacts later on.

PONSARD, FRANÇOIS (1814–1867), dramatist and leader of the School of Good Sense, a movement of reaction against the excesses of Romanticism. His play *Lucrèce* was presented at the Théâtre Français in 1843 and considered a great defeat for the Romantics. Rachel acted in some of his plays and had an affair with him.

PRADIER, JAMES (1792–1862), a sculptor of the classical School of Canova.

PROVOST, JEAN BAPTISTE (1798–1865), became, after an inauspicious start at the Français, a professor at the Conversatoire (where he rejected Rachel as a pupil) and *sociétaire* (1839). He played dramatic leading men.

RACHEL (Elizabeth Félix, 1821–1858), the daughter of itinerant Jewish pedlars who spoke German as their native language, rose meteorically in the fall of 1838, when she was not yet eighteen, to become the star of the Comédie Française. Single-handedly she revived the classical drama of Racine, which had been thoroughly eclipsed by the romantic plays of Hugo and Dumas. She became the first great international star in the history of the theater, toured all over Europe and dominated the Théâtre Français, where she was generally hated for her dominance and her long absences. In 1855, when she toured America—the first non-English actress to do so— her long incipient tuberculosis led to her collapse and ended her career.

RADZIWILL, PRINCE. The Radziwills are a noble family of Lithuanian and Polish descent who owned immense estates in Imperial Russia. Members of the family served the Czars as well as the Kings of Prussia (and participated in the various Polish revolutions) in the nineteenth century. Houssaye may be referring to Prince Louis-Nicholas, called Léon (1808–1882).

REBECCA (Rebecca Félix, 1829–1854), Rachel's youngest and probably most talented sister, acted like her at the Théâtre Français and, like her, died of tuberculosis.

RECAMIER, JEANNE FRANÇOISE (1777–1849), married a banker and had one of the most brilliant salons in Paris in the 1790's and through much of the Napoleonic era. Napoleon's brother Lucien was in love with Mme. Recamier, in whom beauty and wit formed a deadly combination. In 1819, no longer rich, she withdrew to the Abbaye-aux-Bois, a kind of retreat for noble ladies, where she kept a modest apartment and maintained a salon, mostly as a background for Chateaubriand. Casanova had called her "la belissima Zulietta," but by the time Houssaye knew her, her beauty had vanished and her wit had been submerged by the disappointments of her life.

REGNIER, FRANÇOIS JOSEPH PHILOCLES (1807–1885), a great actor of comic roles, who performed at the Comédie from 1831 to 1872.

RÉMUSAT, CHARLES FRANÇOIS, COMTE DE (1797–1875), the son of Napoleon's Chamberlain, became a conservative politician in the July Monarchy and the Second Republic, in opposition to Napoleon III. He left France after the Coup d'État of 1851.

RHÉA, MLLE. (Hortense Lauret, died in 1902), taught school before becoming an actress in St. Petersburg and New York, as well as in some of the Boulevard theaters in Paris.

ROGIER, CAMILLE (born in 1811), painter, engraver and very successful illustrator of novels, stories and volumes of poetry.

ROMIEU, AUGUSTE (1800–1855), a son of one of Napoleon's generals, was famous as a wit and dandy of the Boulevards in the Restoration. Under Louis Philippe he became a civil servant and attached himself in 1848 to Prince Louis Napoleon, whom he served, among other duties, as Director of Fine Arts in 1852.

ROQUEPLAN, NESTOR (1804–1870), a great boulevardier and dandy, a journalist, co-founder of *Le Figaro* and for some time Director of the Opéra.

ROTHSCHILD, JAMES DE (1792–1868), the youngest son of Mayer Anselm, the founder of the family establishments, he was sent to start the Paris branch after the Bourbon Restoration in 1815.

ROUHER, EUGÈNE (1814–1884), was elected to the Chamber of Deputies in 1848 and served as Minister of Justice. An opponent of the Second Republic, he supported the Coup d'État (1851) and the autocratic measures of the Emperor, and served with considerable ability in several imperial governments.

ROUSSEAU, THÉODORE (1812–1867), one of the foremost painters of the Barbizon school, shared the difficulties of the romantic painters whom the dominant classicists rejected. His fame began to spread only after 1848. Millet and Diaz were his friends and colleagues.

ROUVIÈRE, PHILBERT ALPHONSE (1809–1865), began a promising career as a painter but turned to acting. His strength lay in romantic roles, including Shakespeare. He was too mercurial and untraditional for the Théâtre Français, where he performed briefly in 1856.

SAINTE-BEUVE, CHARLES AUGUSTIN (1804–1869), perhaps the most influential critic in his generation, wrote copiously for the *Revue des Deux Mondes*. In 1844 he became a member of the French Academy. After 1848 he wrote regularly for Dr. Véron's *Constitutionnel*. He was a friend of George Sand, among others.

SAINT-VICTOR, PAUL DE (Comte de Saint-Victor, 1827–1881), did not use his title of nobility. He was an influential critic and succeeded Théophile Gautier at *La Presse*.

SALVANDY, NARCISSE ACHILLE (1795–1856), was a conservative member of the Chamber of Deputies under the July Monarchy. He also served as a member of the government and as an ambassador.

SAMSON, JOSEPH ISIDORE (1793–1871), a great actor and great power at the Comédie, the former teacher of Rachel with whom she was on terms of bitter enmity by the time Houssaye became Director. His repertoire was wide and included comic and dramatic roles.

SAND, GEORGE (Aurore Dupin, 1804–1876), came from a most remarkable family full of brilliant illegitimate offspring of high nobility. She grew up on her grandmother's estate, Nohant, which she inherited and which meant much more to her than a piece of property. In 1822 she married a country squire, the Baron Casimir Dudevant, whom she bore two children. In 1830 she met Jules Sandeau and moved to Paris the next year. Her literary work, first in collaboration with Sandeau (pseudonym: Jules Sand), came about largely because she needed money after her separation from Dudevant and found the more genteel pursuits like needlework or embroidery not to her liking. She assumed the name George Sand, wore men's clothing, and was the center of an intellectual and literary circle which also included several lovers. After Sandeau came Musset, then Michel de Bourges, a radical politician, Charles Dider and, most famous, the composer Frédéric Chopin.

SANDEAU, JULES (1811–1883), was sent to Paris to study law but became a writer. He collaborated not only with Houssaye but also with the dramatist Émile Augier. Their comedy *Le Gendre de M. Poirier* still holds the stage. Sandeau had affairs with, among others, Marie Dorval and George Sand.

SCHOLL, AURÉLIEN (1833–1902), a wit and journalist of the Second Empire.

SECOND, ALBÉRIC (1817–1887), the son of a civil servant, came to Paris to make his way as a writer. He wrote much—stories, memoirs, essays and a few plays, one of which was given at the Comédie Française in 1857.

SOBRIER, MARIE JOSEPH (1825–1854), a revolutionary of the far left who wanted to establish a socialist France in 1848.

SUE, EUGÈNE (1804–1875), a ship's surgeon in his youth, became famous as the author of novels set in the Paris underworld, like *Les Mystères de Paris* and *Le Juif errant* (10 volumes each).

TAGLIONI, MARIE (1804–1884), the great Italian ballerina, a star since 1822, made her debut in Paris in 1827. In 1832 she married Comte Gilbert de Voisins, by whom she had two children. Balzac and Thackeray were among her admirers.

TALLEYRAND-PÉRIGORD, CHARLES MAURICE DE (1754–1838), one of the outstanding diplomats of France, whose skill made him a figure of importance in virtually all governments from the Revolution of 1789 to the July Monarchy. He was Foreign Minister in the Directoire, the First Empire and the Bourbon Restoration, and Ambassador to London under Louis Philippe. Like many others, Houssaye saw the adroit Machiavellian twists and turns behind all that brilliance.

THÉÂTRE FRANÇAIS (see COMÉDIE FRANÇAISE)

THORÉ, THÉOPHILE (1807–1869), associated with socialist causes during the July Monarchy, he was active in the Revolution of 1848 and was exiled when the reaction set in.

TRIANON. Le Grand Trianon and le Petit Trianon are part of the palaces of Versailles; they were built under Louis XIV and Louis XV respectively.

TUILERIES PALACE. The residence of the kings and emperors of France, from 1790 to 1870.

VAILLANT, JEAN BAPTISTE (1790–1872), Marshal of France, who served in the army since 1811, as Minister of War 1854–59 and, more pertinently for Houssaye, as Minister of Fine Arts from 1863–1870.

VÉRON, DR. LOUIS-DÉSIRÉ (1798–1867), made his fortune with patent medicines, founded the *Revue de Paris* (1829) and served as Director of the Opéra. In 1844 he took over the almost defunct *Constitutionnel* and made it into a journal of considerable influence.

VIGÉE-LEBRUN, MARIE-ANNE (1755–1842), one of the most fashionable portrait painters of the late eighteenth century, sought after not only in Paris but in Vienna, Dublin and St. Petersburg.

VIGNY, ALFRED DE (1797–1863), major poet and playwright of the Romantics, whose plays, together with those of Hugo and Dumas, established the romantic vogue in the 1830's. For a time he was the lover of the actress Marie Dorval.

WAILLY, ARMAND DE (1804–1863), wrote his first play at twenty-one. He wrote many more and translated novels, such as Sir Walter Scott's, from the English.

WALEWSKI, ALEXANDRE FLORIAN JOSEPH COLONNA, COMTE (1810–1868), a son of Napoleon by the Countess Walewska, served Louis Philippe and wrote some plays. He was Rachel's lover for several years and built her a mansion. In the Empire of his cousin Napoleon III he served as Foreign Minister and was made a duke in 1866.

ZIEM, FÉLIX FRANÇOIS (1821–1911), a painter whose eastern travels inspired such orientalist paintings as "Sunrise at Stamboul."

Bibliographical Note

•

The General Catalogue of Books in the Bibliothèque Nationale in Paris contains twenty-four columns of listings of books by Houssaye. As relatively few items repeat themselves, this is a formidible array of written work. No attempt is made here to provide a complete bibliography. This note is merely intended to point to his more prominent work, and to indicate the kinds of things he wrote.

His keen appreciation for art, which is also evident in the *Confessions*, is reflected in his works of art history, perhaps the best books he wrote: *Le Dix-huitième siècle: poètes, peintres, musiciens* (1843), which was often reprinted, with the title *Galérie du dix-huitième siècle* and translated as *Men and Women of the Eighteenth Century* (2 vols. New York, 1852), *Histoire de la peinture flamande et hollandaise* (1846), *Histoire de l'art français au dix-huitième siècle* (1860), *Van Ostrade, sa vie et son oeuvre* (1874), *Jacques Callot, sa vie et son oeuvre* (1875).

As a general historian and biographer Houssaye confined himself largely to the eighteenth century: *Le Roi Voltaire* (1856), *Mlle. de la Vallière et Mme. de Montespan* (1860), *Rousseau et Mme. de Warens* (1864), *Molière, sa femme et sa fille* (1880).

Fictional history was a field Houssaye seemed to enjoy particularly, perhaps as a transition from history to the *romans à clef*. The best received was *Histoire du quarante et unième fauteuil de l'Académie française* (1845), which was reprinted many times for forty years.

Houssaye's fiction is mostly forgotten today, but there is a prodigious amount of it—about seventy-five volumes of novels, novellas and stories, a number of them in collaboration with Jules Sandeau. They cover a span of sixty years, from *De Profundis* (pseudonym "Alfred Mousse," 1833) to *Les Larmes de Mathilde* (1894).

La Pécheresse (1833) was a modest critical success, but a commercial failure; *La Couronne de bluets* (1834) was a reasonable success in both respects. *Les Onze maîtresses délaissées* (2 vols., 1840), like *La Vertu de Rosine* (1844), *Les Filles d'Ève* (1852), *Le Repentir de Marion* (1854), *L'Amour comme il est* (1858) indicate by their titles the preoccupation of most of Houssaye's fiction.

His collaboration with Jules Sandeau dated from 1840 and lasted for many years: *Madame de Kerouare* (1842), *Mme. de Vandeuil* (1842), *Milla* (1842), *Marie* (1843) were among the earliest.

Some of Houssaye's greatest successes as a novelist came in the 1860's. *Mlle. Cléopâtre* (1864), a novel about one of his own mistresses, had seven printings in its first year. *Les Aventures galantes de Margot* (1866) nearly equaled it. His three collections *Les Grandes dames*, *Les Parisiennes*, and *Les Courtisanes du monde*, twelve volumes in all, produced between 1868 and 1870, earned their author nearly three hundred thousand francs, at two francs royalties per volume. *Lucie, histoire d'une fille perdue* (1873) also had great appeal.

Throughout the 1870's and 1880's they kept coming, volumes entitled *Les Mille et une nuits parisiennes* (1875, 4 vols.); *Les Amours de ce temps-là* (1875); *Histoire étrange d'une fille du monde* (1876); *Histoire d'une fille perdue* (1880); *La Comédienne* (1884, with four printings); *Contes pour les femmes* (1885–86, 2 vols.); *La Confession de Caroline* (1890); and many more.

In contrast to his fiction, Houssaye was neither a prolific nor a successful playwright: some one-acts, like *Les Caprices de la marquise* (1844) and *La Comédie à la fenêtre* (1852) and a few full length plays: *Les Comédiennes* (1857), not performed, *Mademoiselle de trente-six vertus*, which failed at the Ambigu in 1873, and *Roméo and Juliette*, evidently not performed (1873).

Houssaye's poetry, quite voluminous by 1850, was issued as *Poésies Complètes* (1850, 1852); other volumes appeared in 1857 and 1877. His last volume of poetry, *Les Onze mille vierges*, appeared in 1884.

Houssaye's articles, prefaces and occasional pieces number in the hundreds. Throughout his life he wrote for journals and was also involved in the publication of several. In 1844 friends of his who had bought *L'Artiste* made him editor of it; in it he published some of Beaudelaire's earliest work. In 1851 he, together with Gautier and two others, took on the *Revue de Paris*. In 1857 the *Revue de Paris* published, in serial form, *Madame Bovary* by the virtually unknown Flaubert (whom Houssaye respected as a writer but found too provincial otherwise). In 1860, at Émile de Girardin's request, he became the editor of *La Presse* for three years. In 1871 he founded the *Gazette de Paris*, a political journal, which failed quickly. In the later 1880's, he founded the *Revue de Paris et de Saint-Pétersbourg*, also a failure. All this, besides his articles for the *Revue des Deux Mondes, La Presse,* Véron's *Constitutionnel,* the *Revue de Paris, Figaro,* etc. In the 1870's he wrote a series of articles for the New York *Herald,* of course translated into English. They were collected as *Life in Paris* (New York, 1881).

Some of Houssaye's essays on travel, on women and other subjects were also collected in volumes. At least one of them, *Philosophes et comédiennes* (1851), was translated as *Philosophers and Actresses* (New York, 1852).

INDEX